A BORNEO JOURNEY INTO DEATH

SYMBOL AND CULTURE

A series edited by

J. David Sapir, J. Christopher Crocker, Peter Metcalf,
Hildred Geertz, †Michelle Zimbalist Rosaldo, and Renato
Rosaldo

† *She sings as the moon sings:*
'I am I, am I;
The greater grows my light
The further that I fly.'
All creation shivers
With that sweet cry.
                    (W. B. YEATS)

We are as water spilled upon the
ground, which cannot be gathered
up again.
            (2 SAMUEL 14:14)

A
Borneo
Journey
into
Death

BERAWAN ESCHATOLOGY
FROM ITS RITUALS

PETER METCALF

UNIVERSITY OF PENNSYLVANIA PRESS
Philadelphia
1982

Library of Congress Cataloging in Publication Data

Metcalf, Peter.
    A Borneo journey into death.

    (Symbol and culture)
    Bibliography: p.
    Includes index.
    1. Funeral rites and ceremonies Berawan (Malaysian
people) 2. Berawan (Malaysian people)—Religion.
I. Title. II. Series.
DS597.367.B47M47   1982   299'.92   82-8460
ISBN 0-8122-7849-6   AACR2

Printed in the United States of America

TO MY FATHER

Contents

PART III
THE SEASON OF THE SOUL'S MENACE

PART V
COSMOLOGY OF THE ANCESTRAL SPIRITS

xi

Preface

Since I have already written about Berawan ritual, and plan to do so again, I should at the outset explain how the present study fits in with that other work, completed and projected. In 1979, Richard Huntington and I published a book entitled *Celebrations of Death: the Anthropology of Mortuary Ritual*. It arose out of conversations at Harvard, where we discovered that we had both worked in societies that gave a central position to funerals. Moreover, each of us had been drawn to the same early theorists, Robert Hertz and Arnold Van Gennep, to interpret our data. Building on their insights we attempted to put together a new anthropological synthesis on death. Following where the issues led us, we ranged over various continents and epochs, drawing widely on pertinent comparative material. The purpose of this study is entirely different; it is ethnographic. While I continue to lean on the same theorists, Hertz in particular, I deal comprehensively with Berawan death rites, letting them dictate what analysis is required.

But although Berawan death rituals are the entire concern of this book, there are some aspects of the rites that are not dealt with here. They are those having to do with leadership and social rank. These aspects are not neglected because they are unimportant. On the contrary, mortuary festivals provide a major arena in Berawan society for status competition, and the construction of elaborate mausoleums is crucial in the validation of political authority. In fact, the political implications are so important as to demand separate treatment, and in the context of the whole range of ritual activity. Death rites have a privileged place in this, but there are others: calendrical festivals, martial ceremonies related to warfare and headhunting, other rites of passage, such as weddings, and

xiii

celebrations that deal explicitly with achieved rank. Consequently, I plan a second volume that focuses on the perenially problematical relationship between ritual and power in Berawan society. It will, of necessity, involve itself with historical processes over the last century or so, and it will take as axiomatic that ritual is not a compartment of Berawan life, but an active agent in those processes.

Meanwhile, the present volume focuses upon eschatology, that doctrine of final things that underlies the complex mortuary rituals and gives them their characteristic form. I choose this dual format to describe Berawan belief and ritual in order to avoid the tedious laundry list approach so often seen in descriptions of primitive religion. Better two studies, each motivated by a question of general interest in the study of idea systems, than one unwieldy compendium of exotica. I do not intend by this division of subject matter to imply that Berawan religion in general, or the death rites in particular, fall into two parts, one concerned with meaning and the other with power. Nor will it be possible entirely to ignore political aspects in the present volume. These viewpoints are analytic; the reality is seamless. Meaning and power, and the meaning of power, are involved in every phase of the rituals.

Fieldwork was conducted between December 1971 and January 1974, supported by the Foreign Area Fellowship Program, with subsidiary grants from the National Science Foundation and the Wenner-Gren Foundation and under the sponsorship of the Sarawak Museum. During May 1975, a grant from the National Geographic Society enabled me to make a return visit in order to attend an important mortuary ritual. I thank all these organizations for their support. I would also like to acknowledge my debt to David Maybury-Lewis for his instruction, encouragement, and friendship over many years, and especially during the period of fieldwork.

The circumstances of fieldwork were pleasant. The longhouse mode of residence of the Berawan, involving hundreds of people living under one roof, made it easy, indeed unavoidable, to participate in the intense sociability of their lives. I spent much of my time at the village of Long Teru, and initially I lived in the apartment of the headman, Kajan Sigeh. To him, and his family, I am indebted for their warm hospitality. It is usual for visitors to stay with the headman if they have no relatives in the house, and the kindness extended to me is entirely typical of interior folk. But most travelers do not stay as long as I did. After a couple of months I feared that I was too much of a drain on the household despite frequent contributions of rice. I also wanted more privacy, and a place to work with my notes—a kind of academic nest-building instinct. No empty rooms were available in the longhouse, so I built a small house under the palm trees between the longhouse and the river. It was raised on stilts level with the main structure, about twenty feet in front of the veranda that provides the main gathering place of the village. Consequently it was not much more private or quiet than the longhouse had been, but neither did it remove me from the life of the community.

For the first year of fieldwork, I spent most of my time at Long Teru. Having gained some linguistic competence and grasp of Berawan culture during this period, I began in my second year to travel more frequently to the other Berawan longhouses, especially Long Jegan. I also visited the longhouses of communities ethnically or historically connected to the Berawan. Apart from a six-week vacation in West Malaysia, and occasional trips to the coast for medical treatment, the entire period of fieldwork was spent in Baram District.

There were at Long Teru a handful of young men and women who had had enough secondary schooling to speak good English. Initially I employed one of these, a young man named Michael Melai Usang, to be my linguistic informant. I soon found that Berawan would not tolerate being interviewed through an interpreter. They are people who value conversation, and one that had to be mediated through a third party struck them as too tedious, so that they would simply walk away. Consequently I was obliged to operate on my own from the outset. However, Melai remained with me as a companion and coresident of my little house throughout my stay, and his help was invaluable. Although not himself knowledgeable about tradition, at least at the beginning of our work, he was adept at securing the cooperation of those who did know about it. He was a popular young man. Without him, many things would have been much harder for me to accomplish, and I owe him a special debt of gratitude.

Relationships with the people of Long Teru and Long Jegan were at all times good. There were, of course, periods of strain when village gossip accused me of prying or of stinginess, and there were some individuals who never liked my presence among them. But these sources of friction never emerged into open dispute. This was partly because of my status as a Westerner, and partly because of the small services that I performed for the community, such as simple medical aid and occasional cash donations to people in need. But principally it was due to the tolerance and goodnaturedness of most Berawan, for whom I came to feel a very real warmth and respect.

During the two years that I was there, I struggled frequently to make clear to them what I was trying to achieve by my presence. I had to insist firmly that I was in no way connected with the Christian missionaries, nor directly with any government agency. It was difficult for them to grasp the nature of the remote academic world from which I came to intrude upon their lives. But they heard me out, and interpreted it in their own way. I was, it seems, to be their public relations man in the world outside the rivers that they knew, a world whose extent only the younger folk could grasp. Some of the older people who provided me with much of my information figure in the narrative below, such as Biló Kasi, Tama Usang Weng, and Sadi″ Pejong. Others, equally willing to help, do not, and I must mention Tama Avit, Tama Kallang, Sadi″ Miri, Tama Lanying, Tama Balleng, and Tina Lawai. These people made this book possible. They wanted me to know about Berawan ritual; they wanted me to get it straight. I hope I have not failed them.

Though my principal debt of gratitude is to the Berawan people, there were also others who helped me with hospitality and advice: Francis Knappen and Guido Gockel, priests at the Catholic mission at Long Loyang; Rev. Southwell and Mr. and Mrs. Bray of the Borneo Evangelical Mission; and, most of all, Henry Saunders and Roger Brooks, Peace Corpsmen in Marudi township, who so often shared their little house with my friends and me.

I am indebted to several people for reading and criticizing earlier drafts of this book. Professor Rodney Needham's many valuable suggestions were especially relevant because of his work among the Penan, who are close neighbors of the Berawan. My colleagues in this series, Professors Christopher Crocker, Michelle Rosaldo, and David Sapir, gave me a great deal of help. I especially thank David Sapir for his encouragement and editorial assistance over several months. Pamela Frese not only did a professional job of typing the manuscript, she also contributed several insights of her own. For support during part of the time that I was writing the book, I thank the Wilson Gee Fellowship Program, University of Virginia.

To conform with current usage in Malay and Indonesian, the vowel represented phonetically as [ə] is written e, [e] is written é, and [č] is written c.

/a/ is pronounced long as in Malay and Indonesian, but there is also a short low-front vowel as in English. So, for example, the Berawan pakăt is pronounced "pah-cat." /è/ is a mid-front vowel with the value [ɛ], as in English betting. /i/ is pronounced approximately as in English beating, /é/ as in baiting, /u/ as in booting, and /o/ as in boating. /i̱/ is a tense high-front vowel not similar to any English phoneme.

With the exception of the phoneme /é/, the acute accent indicates stress. /a/ and /o/ both occur stressed, and /i/ occurs lightly stressed: /í/, and heavily stressed: /í̋/. /e/ does not occur stressed.

A glottal stop is indicated by an inverted comma.

Throughout I have used the Bitokala isolect as spoken at Long Teru and Batu Belah to render Berawan words. At Long Jegan, diphthongs replace several of the vowels found in the Bitokala isolect, including the conspicuous /i̋/.

	front	central	back
high	i̇ i̱		u
mid	é è	e	o
low	a ă		

When Berawan words or phrases are *italicized*, the two high front vowels *remain unchanged*.

xix

It is sown in corruption; it is raised in incorruption:
It is sown in dishonor; it is raised in glory:
It is sown in weakness; it is raised in power:
It is sown a natural body; it is raised a spiritual body.
Howbeit that was not first which is spiritual,
but that which is natural;
and afterward that which is spiritual.

1 Corinthians 15:42–4, 6

Our father Alang is dead now,
he follows you, he returns to you,
he is together with all of you,
his mothers, his fathers,
you his grandparents.
These your grandchildren, your children,
left behind,
to look after the longhouse of Long Teru.
You spirits of our grandfathers,
protect this community,
look after this community.

Fragment of a Berawan prayer

I

Approaches

to

Berawan Eschatology

CHAPTER ONE

The Character of Berawan Religion

"Human souls and pure spirits are different kinds of things."
St. Thomas Aquinas, *Summa Theologica* Ia.lxxv.7

Aquinas the philosopher, confident of the universal human faculty to perceive truth, would no doubt have been gratified to learn that the distinction he drew between soul and spirit is fundamental to Berawan eschatology. Aquinas the Christian apologist would have been unmoved: No last trump, no judgement day, and certainly no raising of the dead. Moreover, there is a difference in the use of terms. For Aquinas souls and spirits are separate realities; for the Berawan there is a traffic between the two, and that indeed is the crux of their view of it.

To make clear what that traffic involves, it is necessary to translate abstract ideas from a language and culture far removed from our own. Just how different these ideas may be is illustrated in Reo Fortune's (1935) study of the religion of the Manus of the Admiralty Islands. He begins his account incisively: "Each Manus man worships his Father, not in Heaven, but in his own house front rafters, not one Father for all, but each man his own" (Fortune 1935:1). The spiritual guardian of each family is usually the deceased father of the current head of the household, and his name is honored. But every guardian is sooner or later replaced by the son who now keeps his memory. Then his ghost joins all the other recently dead, a nameless ghost of the middle sea spaces. From this condition the dead gradually fade away, turning at last into sea slugs, hundreds of which litter the lagoon. For the theologian the beliefs of the Manus are striking comparative data. So materialistic an account, one so much at variance with our own, takes us by surprise. It is hard to accept that the Manus believe it, but how shall we gainsay them?

In the Berawan case, the difficulty of comprehension is less extreme. They at least have a recognizable afterlife, and a unitary supreme deity as well. But, as with the distinction of soul and spirit, the superficial similarity of doctrine masks a world of difference. The problem in grasping Berawan conceptions is not in identifying with what we are told about them, but in making sense of what we are told. Manus eschatology is at least clear, in fact baldly so. But what is to be made of accounts that are elliptical, or inconsistent, or incomplete? Shall we conclude that Berawan belief is vague and individually variable, or shall we construct models that incorporate the fragments of explanation that we are offered into a systematic whole? If we do the latter, what reality will this construct have? In what sense can it be said to be "true"? These are the difficulties in the study of Berawan eschatology.

To solve them I draw upon a century-old tradition of ritual analysis in anthropology that extends from W. Robertson Smith to Emile Durkheim, E. E. Evans-Pritchard, and Victor Turner. All of them have sought to characterize primitive religion, and in many ways the religion of the Berawan exemplifies those characterizations.

Discussions About Religion Are Usually Discussions About Ritual

The Berawan language contains no word that could be translated as "religion." The general category of things under which the usages of religion are subsumed is called *adèd*, but *adèd* involves much more than religion. Table manners, or the Borneo equivalent, are *adèd;* so are rules concerning who may fish where, and who may wear what kinds of beads, and how fruit trees are inherited, and a thousand other things besides. *Adèd* is everything from etiquette to law, everything, in short, that is governed by explicit rules or prescriptions, including ritual. *Adèd* is variable from one community to another, but as a concept, it is something that is widely shared by the societies of the whole Indonesian area. The word is a cognate of the Malay *adat*, itself a borrowing from Arabic, and in this form is familiar throughout the archipelago. Cooley (1962) offers a comprehensive account of the *adat* of Ambon in Eastern Indonesia, and the range of items covered is closely paralleled in Berawan society. For the Dutch scholars of Indonesia, studies of *adat* were a standard and well-developed concern (Koentjaraningrat 1975:86–113).

Nowadays, the Berawan speak of their religion as *adèd luna* (*luna* = old), or in Malay *adat lama*. But this is a new term designed to distinguish traditional religious practices from Christianity, which has secured many converts in the last twenty years. The concept of *adèd* is wide but precise, and I can find no exact English equivalent. It is simply "the way of doing things," and the *adat lama*, the traditional religion, is the old way of doing things.

This conception of religion, or rather this incorporation of religion into a wider conception, preconditions Berawan ways of talking about religion. To be wise in the traditional religion is to know how things should be done, and since this varies from one longhouse to another, each must have its corps of sages. It is not difficult to draw these men and women into a discussion of the proper manner of execution of a ritual, perhaps sitting around a lamp in the evening with a glass of rice wine at their elbows. While rituals are in progress, there will be from time to time an interruption while someone raises an objection to some procedural detail, and the matter may be thoroughly aired before continuing. On suitable occasions, the discussion can be moved to another level; the reasons why particular rituals are done the way they are, and the charter myths that back them up. But it is not always possible to extract exegeses. With frustrating regularity, people will respond to questions about the meaning of rituals with some variant of the formula: it is *adèd*, it is the way. Were one to stop there, and be satisfied with that answer, then one could only conceive of them as mechanically carrying out the "customs" of their ancestors, unreasoning ritual automatons like those portrayed in much of nineteenth century literature on ritual. Consequently, I recruited a coterie of informants who were willing to respond to my questions, or tolerate them at least, and on occasion I pressed them hard for explanations of aspects that troubled me. Since this is obviously a kind of activity that would not have been going on had I not been there, the danger exists that I manipulated my teachers. That is why it is sometimes necessary in what follows to describe in some detail the circumstances under which I gained information, especially indigenous analyses of major features—whole rituals or sequences of rituals—that were produced only after considerable persistence on my part. I do not believe that I led my informants, but I am obligated to note when pressure was necessary and what response it elicited.

As for questions on a yet more abstract plane, questions about ideology phrased in terms of ideology (what is a soul?), they almost always produced blank looks. The Berawan reaction is similar to that which Evans-Pritchard describes among the Nuer of Sudan. Nuer philosophy is dominated by the idea of Spirit, but:

> . . . if we seek for . . . a statement of what Spirit is thought to be like in itself, we seek of course in vain. Nuer do not claim to know. They say that they are merely *doar,* simple people, and how can simple people know about such matters? What happens in the world is determined by Spirit and Spirit can be influenced by prayer and sacrifice. This much they know, but no more; and they say very sensibly, that since the European is so clever perhaps he can tell them the answer to the question he asks. (Evans-Pritchard 1956:315–16)

In much the same way, Berawan would respond to abstract questions by saying: How should we know? We are merely humans. Sometimes they would ask disarmingly what the answer was, as if I somehow knew, and was setting them a test. Yet, as Evans-Pritchard shows, the Nuer claim to being just simple folk does not prevent them from having a highly refined conception of the godhead, and, as I shall argue, it does not prevent the Berawan from having an elaborate doctrine of souls.

Ritual Is Embedded in a Social Matrix

If Berawan religion must be located through ritual, then ritual is equally located in the whole range of social action.

For most participants, and certainly for a visitor, the most conspicuous feature of major public rituals, the aspect that thrusts itself upon the perception, is of an extended party, noisy and nonstop. Amid the exuberance of horseplay and drinking, the religious observances seem lost, almost an afterthought. So much is this the case, and so unfamiliar is this to a Westerner, that it is possible to overlook the whole point of the proceedings. I was once frustrated to find that an Englishman, ex-Sarawak civil service, could tell me nothing of a mortuary festival that he had attended some years before. He had arrived on the final climactic day of what he knew only to be a great celebration. As is the custom, his hosts pressed food and drink upon him, but especially the latter, making a game of it to see how much rice wine and distilled liquor they could cajole him into drinking. They began early; the afternoon and evening he passed in a haze. He left next morning with a sore head, oblivious of having participated in the final rites of a great leader of the community.

At all major festivals the rhythm is the same. Preparations to conduct the next phase of the ritual are made in a dilatory manner, with the participants ambling off to fetch something, or summon someone. Always one is told that the rite will begin as soon as food has been served, or so-and-so returns from his bath. Meanwhile, of course, there is time for a drink. When the rite finally does begin, it is conducted with a manic intensity, as if everything depended upon the speed with which it is completed. It is difficult to take in everything that is happening. Then, as suddenly as it began, the rite is over, and the crowd turns to languid socializing.

At the weddings of important people, the hosts, aided and abetted by the young men and women of the house, devise elaborate entertainments designed to make it next to impossible to remain sober. For distinguished visitors from other communities, an appropriate approach is a praise song. These songs are a verbal art form, containing expressions of delight at the visit, and elaborate compliments, couched in poetic language. While the song is in progress, a full glass of rice wine sits between singer and guest. Occasionally the former will pick it up, raising it toward the latter. At the end of the song, the visitor must quaff it down at one go, or as near as can be managed. For a good attempt, the audience will let out a roar of approval. He may now respond in kind, but the guest is always outnumbered by his hosts, so that he will be hard put to retain his equilibrium.

Other devices are legion: Straightforward drinking races for the hardy or foolhardy; little games of manual or verbal dexterity, for which the prize is a glass of wine (the penalty for failure is often the same); or invitations to make everyone laugh by impersonating someone or recounting some well-remembered gaffe, with the same prize at the end. For the very coy, more forceful methods are sometimes employed. No one could take offense at the attentions of the young girls of the village. Flirtatiously they press a glass to the lips of the too sober guest. Meeting resistance, two or three will pin him squarely to the floor, hold his nose until he is forced to open his mouth, and gaily pour in the wine. While the imbiber splutters, the crowd cackles in good-natured delight.

The annual festival held after the harvest is another ritual occasion dominated by exhuberant socializing. The festival, called simply "prayers of the house" *(papĭ lamèng)*, involves the preparation of shrines and the making of sacrifices for the welfare of the community. But it is primarily a rite of commensality. One wanders from room to room in the longhouse, sampling each family's new rice, and the wine that is prepared from it. There are other grand rituals, such as ones celebrating the status of great personages, or the warrior values of young men, that are held irregularly, and there are smaller rites such as the naming of a child, and on all these occasions there is drinking and merrymaking.

It would be easy to draw the wrong conclusion from all this levity in the midst of major rituals. It might be supposed that the Berawan do not take their religion seriously, or that old ritual forms have become empty under the pressures of contemporary acculturation. But this is not so. The more that one observes the rites the more meanings appear in them, meanings that are deeply felt by individual Berawan. Nor is there any reason to suppose that ritual was ever carried out in a more solemn vein. I was often amazed at the apparently inexhaustable Berawan appetite for sociality. But this must be set against the annual round of their lives, much of which is spent in relative isolation. The farms are remote from the longhouse, and life there is hard. The workday begins early, and lighting is too expensive to allow people to stay up much after sundown. The magnetic appeal of the longhouse and the festivals that occur there, funerals included, is the chance to escape this drudgery. The person that does not wish to participate appears strange to them, and is suspected of antisocial tendencies. For the Berawan it would be impossible to have a serious ritual without noise, confusion, and jocularity.

The sociality of ritual is an aspect of its sacredness, and not a byproduct or distraction. It also achieves an important psychosocial function, in that it promotes the integration and solidarity of the community. The agglutinative feature of ritual was so heavily emphasized by the structural-functionalists of the 1940s and 1950s, to the exclusion of all else, that it may seem redundant to point it out here. But, for the record, ritual is felt by the Berawan to constrain quarrels, and so it seems to be.

In the close social environment of the farms, tensions and jealousies inevitably build. Back at the longhouse, they are released into a wider group. Drink loosens tongues, and petty irritations are aired. When a group of men have been drinking for some hours there is sometimes a kind of brittleness to their hilarity. Tempers may suddenly flare, and hot words fly. But these scenes are tightly controlled: The majority looks on, clucking disapprovingly at this breach of decorum, and any attempt at an assault, especially if there are weapons anywhere at hand, is immediately prevented. Never, in my experience, did any serious consequence follow upon such a quarrel, and the purgative effect was noticeable. I have seen arch-rivals, after a night of drinking, sitting together in the thin morning light, too tired to pursue old grudges, and instead quietly smoking the stubs of the previous night's cigars.

Because they gather many people together, festivals provide a forum for all manner of unrelated business. It is a convenient time to arrange marriages, so that in the slack season of the agricultural cycle, after the harvest, rituals spawn rituals. Formal litigation, of which the Berawan are not unduly fond, usually occurs either directly before or directly after them, so that as many people as possible can hear the complainants and take part in the consensual decision that comprises the verdict.

In all these ways, and others besides, ritual appears entirely of a piece with the social world that nurtures it. As regards the death rites, we shall have occasion to observe their special communal significance in what follows.

The Priority of Ritual

The emphasis upon the social nature of religion, which we now associate with Durkheim and his students, is prefigured in the work of W. Robertson Smith: "Smith's view was firmly anchored in his conviction that the fundamental source of all symbolic behavior was the social group and that its modes of expression gained their validity from their relation to the readily apprehended world of persons and things" (Beidelman 1974:65). For a nineteenth century theologian, these attitudes were radical, and they were made worse in the eyes of his fellow churchmen by his assertion of the precedence of ritual over ideology. In primitive religions, Smith argued, theology takes the form of myth. But people were first of all moved to act together in rituals, and only later, slowly and hesitantly, to construct systematic mythologies that rationalized them. In contemporary religion there existed formalized dogma in place of mythology, but the precedence remained the same, and Smith pointed to the similarity of Christian ritual across a spectrum of doctrinal variation as proof of his assertion.

There are two senses in which we may take Smith's assertion of the priority of ritual. The first is literal; that rites preceeded dogma in the origins of religious institutions. In an era obsessed with evolution, Smith often casts his discussion in these terms. But his deductive historical reconstructions can no longer be taken seriously because their methodology is faulty and their conclusions untestable.

The second sense is that ritual is somehow more fundamental: "It must, however, be remembered that in ancient religion there was no authoritative interpretation of ritual. It was imperative that certain things should be done, but every man was free to put his own meaning on what was done" (1889:399). In the first sentence, there is perhaps an echo of theological condescension. Nevertheless, the characterization fits Berawan religion nicely, where the category of *adèd* indeed comprises accepted ways of doing and not of thinking. By emphasizing the individual's freedom from doctrinal constraint, Smith did not intend to deny that rituals have meanings. He merely meant that we cannot accept at face value what participants tell us is the meaning of rituals. Smith himself always located the significance of rites in sociological circumstances, usually set in an evolutionary framework, and some of this is still arguable, some not. For the present what is important is that these attitudes frame a transcendental view of ritual: Its true meaning is hidden, and it is up to us, the analysts, to find it.

The opposite view, and the one that Smith was struggling against, is intellectualist. In the writings of E. B. Tylor (1871, 1878) ritual is treated as the natural outgrowth of ideas. For example, he argued that rituals related to the recovery of souls have their origin in the experience of dreaming. It so happens that some of the key data on which he bases this argument came from central northern Borneo (Tylor 1878:5). Tylor proposed, by a kind of empathetic anthropology, to recover the mental processes of ancient man, and thereby to discover the ultimate origins of widely distributed ritual complexes (Burrow 1966:248). Shorn of the historical dimension, it would still be possible to argue from an intellectualist position. But such arguments will have to take account of Smith's observation concerning the scarcity of authoritative interpretation.

Tylor's speculations about the ultimate origins of religion are as untenable as Smith's, but their legacy was less useful. Tylor's approach culminated in Frazer's massive but sterile collection of bizarre beliefs and practices, *The Golden Bough*. Smith's gave birth to a tradition of ritual analysis that is the distinctive contribution of anthropology to the comparative study of religion.

CHAPTER TWO

Sketch of the Rites and Their Setting

The interior of northern Borneo is a region of broken, hilly country densely covered with tall rain forests, and intersected by streams that gather into mighty rivers. Population densities are very low, and the scattered communities exhibit great linguistic and ethnic diversity. The Berawan are a case in point.[1] They number approximately 1,600 people, divided between four main communities: Long Teru and Long Jegan on the Tinjar River, and Long Terawan and Batu Belah on the Tutoh (see map 1). But even between these four longhouses there are differences of dialect and custom.

Between the Berawan villages and dotted along the rivers toward the interior are other folk who share with them the generic name *orang ulu*, or "people of the upriver." The *orang ulu* have in common a way of life that includes residence in substantial wooden longhouses and a reliance on slash and burn agriculture of rice. Because of ancient cultural connections and borrowings, they also share many basic items of religious practice, or perhaps it would be better to say that their cultures interlock in a pattern of ritual similarities. The most numerous neighbors of the Berawan are the Kayan and Kenyah. The Kayan are culturally homogeneous, and spread out over a large area. There are over thirteen thousand Kayan in Sarawak, mostly in the Baram River watershed, and another three thousand or more in Kalimantan (Indonesian Borneo) in the Kajan River system, and also the Mahakam to the south (Rousseau 1978:78; see map 2). The Kenyah are even more numerous and widely distributed, with areas of relatively dense Kayan population lying interspersed among Kenyah areas (Whittier 1978:92). But the Kenyah are not homogeneous. For this reason, the Berawan are often classified as a kind of Kenyah, as a matter of convenience, since even within Borneo the name Berawan is not widely known. This despite the fact that there are important cultural differences between the Kenyah and the Berawan, notably with regard to death rituals.

In modern times, the *orang ulu* have come to feel a sense of identity in opposition to the greatly more numerous people of the coast, the Chinese and Malays. In the interior, small groups of Chinese are found in trading centers or bazaars. A few Malay villages are found in the lower reaches of the rivers, often adjacent to the bazaars. Finally, in the last century there has been a slow trickle of migration into the lower Baram by Iban people. The Iban live in longhouses and practice swidden agriculture, but are not otherwise culturally similar to, or ethnologically related to, the *orang ulu*. The main centers of Iban population are far to the south, and in the Baram watershed they are mostly found in the subcoastal belt.

Berawan Economy and Society

The Berawan economy is based upon the shifting cultivation of dry rice. Compared to other folk of central northern Borneo, however, they do not have the reputation of conscientious or skillful farmers. Many families run low on rice in the months before the harvest, and then they have recourse to less popular staples, in particular sago. All Berawan own sago trees which are deliberately planted in groves near the longhouse. It is a low prestige food, and people are embarrassed to be found eating it. Nevertheless, Berawan dependence on sago is considerable, and there is evidence to suggest that the Berawan have not been rice farmers as long as some of their neighbors. The Berawan have little ritual associated with the rice year. Another substitute staple is cassava, which has the advantage of a short growing time. If floods or droughts or the depredations of wild animals seriously threaten the crop, cassava gardens are planted.

Hunting is an important activity, and a major source of protein. All types of game are eaten: wild pigs, deer, monkeys, lizards, porcupines, and birds. The jungle also provides edible wild grasses, nuts, and fruits. All in all, the contribution of food

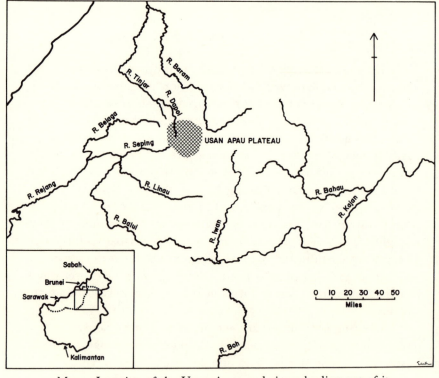

MAP 1. Location of the Usun Apau and rivers leading out of it.

14

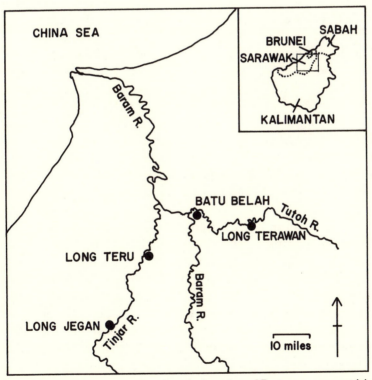

CHINA SEA

SABAH

BRUNEI

SARAWAK

KALIMANTAN

Baram R.

BATU BELAH

Tutoh R.

LONG TERAWAN

LONG TERU

Baram R.

LONG JEGAN

Tinjar R.

10 miles

MAP 2. Lower Baram area, showing the location of Berawan communities.

foraged from the jungle is considerable. In addition, domestic pigs are kept, but they are killed and eaten only on important occasions. Some individuals have large groves of fruit trees, especially langsat and durian.

Fishing is another important source of protein. Long Teru folk are fortunate in having abundant resources of fish in a large lake near the longhouse. At certain seasons there are large surpluses, and they are stored in various ways. Nowadays an ingenious technology has grown up that enables the fish to be brought alive to coastal towns by drifting them downriver in huge cages. In the bazaars they can be sold for large profits. This source of income has made Long Teru a relatively wealthy house, and contributed to its material acculturation.

Other cash earners include rubber, pepper, timber, and rattan. All the Berawan houses have large holdings of rubber trees, mostly planted in the boom years just before and after the Second World War. But rubber prices are now low, and it is usually cut by women, to ensure a small cash income when more productive activity is not available. Pepper is a recent cash crop, and the plantations are as yet small and inefficient. Good returns can be made by handlogging bilian, an extremely heavy and durable hardwood, in great demand on the coast for building. Rattan is sold to the lumber companies operating upriver, for use in tying log rafts together. Cash can also be earned by labor in the camps, but wages are so low that most Berawan prefer to avoid it. The great majority of Berawan are still subsistence farmers, but there is a significant demand for money to buy cloth and sugar and fuel for the lamp, and a thousand other things.

The Berawan lack descent groups, the only corporate groups being the apartment coresidents, and the longhouse community itself. The longhouse is an impressive structure, housing under one roof hundreds of people. Each of the four main Berawan communities comprises a single longhouse, although at the time of fieldwork the people of Batu Belah were still in the process of building a new one. They are solidly constructed, raised on massive hardwood piles ten or more feet above the ground. In plan they are long and narrow, as the name implies, with the main axis running parallel to a major watercourse, but set a hundred yards or so back from it.

Along one side runs an open, public area, the main street of the village, and this veranda looks out over the open space in front of the house, and, through groves of palm trees, to the river beyond. On the veranda people work and chat at all hours of the day. Men are sitting there repairing fishnets, and women gather to work together pounding rice in a heavy mortar with pestles as tall as themselves. At different seasons of the year, depending upon the agricultural cycle or the availability of good fishing, the house is sometimes full and sometimes relatively empty. But it always maintains an air of being the center of things. The longhouse is a veritable jungle metropolis.

Down the main axis of the longhouse runs a partition, behind which lie the individual family apartments, each with its own door opening onto the veranda. The size of a longhouse is often specified in terms of the number of such "doors." Long Teru, for instance, has thirty-two, yielding an average of a little less than ten people per apartment. Coresidents of a family apartment *(ukuk)* share one hearth and pool the produce of their labor. They jointly own such property as land, trees, and household goods. Title in these goods is lost by moving out of the *ukuk*, most frequently in marriage. Residence is structured by a rule of uxorilocality. At Long Teru, over 90 percent of married men moved into their wives' rooms on marriage. The exceptions mostly involved cases where the departure of the husband would have left his natal group without an able-bodied male to do the heavy work of preparing the farm, and thus without a means of livelihood. Alternatively a man of high rank may choose to keep his sons in an expanded family unit. In either case a specially elaborate marriage is required, and bride-wealth must be paid to the wife's natal group. To fail to fulfill these obligations is to be a "stealer of daughters," and the butt of gossip. Because of this residence rule, successive heads of household in any given room are often not closely related, being simply the imported spouses of the women of the group. When a large group splits into two or more *ukuk*, which can of course only happen when a new longhouse is built, then groups of sisters will be found in adjacent rooms. Adjacent clusters of such rooms related by female siblings are in turn related by female ancestors who were siblings.

If a man living in his wife's natal group decides to divorce his wife and go elsewhere, he abandons his rights in the property of the group, including trees that he planted and farms that he cut while he was living within it. He also abandons his children, but provided he remains within the longhouse this breach is not severe, since children are allowed to wander about and stay wherever they please. If the divorce is by mutual consent, or at the wife's instigation, some partition of property may result. Such divorces are common, but marriages made with bridewealth seldom end in divorce. If a man's wife dies, he may choose to remain in her natal group and this is common with old people who are well accustomed to their in-laws after years of marriage.

Heirloom property, such as brassware and beads, is not owned by the residential group, but by individuals. When an important old person dies, his or her heirloom property is divided among all of the children. The deceased may have indicated how this was to be done before death. If not, the sharing is approximately equal, save that the child who looked after the deceased in old age deserves a larger share. Distributions can lead to quarreling, but displays of avarice would be judged undignified and might anger the dead person. Ownership of heirloom property is one mark of high social rank. Others are a genealogy studded with famous leaders, and unadulterated by unrespectable connections.

Under the stress of increasing material acculturation, the social hierarchy is beginning to change. Ideological acculturation is also in evidence. Christianity began to make inroads among the upriver folk after the Second World War, and a revivalist movement sprang up that sought to oppose Christianity by jettisoning many of the burdensome demands of the old observances. By the early 1970s two of the four Berawan communities were almost entirely Christian, at least nominally. Batu Belah was Roman Catholic, and Long Terawan was split between Catholics and followers of Sidang Injil Borneo, a fundamentalist Protestant church founded by missionaries of the Borneo Evangelical Mission, who mainly come from Australia. Long Jegan still followed the revivalist cult, but there was a large Catholic minority. Only at Long Teru was the traditional religion preserved: There, the revivalist cult had never gained a hold, and the Christians were still few. It was for this reason that I chose Long Teru as my major fieldwork site, and why the rituals of that particular house figure prominently in my account of the death rites.

General Nature of the Death Rites

One reason for making the mortuary rites a focus of research was that they are strikingly different to anything familiar to most Westerners, involving a sequence of public festivals and private observances spread out over months or years. As with other phases of the traditional religion, there are considerable differences in the details of mortuary ritual from one longhouse to another, but at the same time there is an overall similarity of form. What I describe here by way of introduction to the rites is the schedule of events that is common to all Berawan communities. It is illustrated in figure 1.

Immediately after death, rituals begin that involve the entire community. These may last anywhere up to ten days, and are called *pata*i. I shall refer to them simply as the funeral. During this time the corpse is put into either a wooden coffin or a large jar. At the end of the funeral, the jar or coffin is removed to the graveyard, where it may be inserted in an individual tomb *(kubor)* or together with other remains in a group mausoleum *(salong)*. If, however, it is planned to continue with the secondary processing of the corpse, then the coffin or jar is stored in a temporary shelter *(salong)*. Exceptionally, the remains may be stored within the longhouse awaiting

Death

∇

Funeral	Period of	Rites of	Permanent
	temporary	secondary	storage
*(pata*i)	storage	treatment	
		(nulang)	
4–10 days	one or more	4–10 days	
	years		

Figure 1. The basic features of the mortuary ritual sequence.

secondary disposal. For the majority, there is no secondary treatment, and they are disposed of finally at the conclusion of the funeral. The only public observances that remain to be carried out are a series of rites relating to headhunting that release the community from mourning. Close kin observe another series of mourning usages.

For a select minority, a kind of second funeral is performed after the lapse of not less than one year and sometimes several years. It involves another extended public festival, again lasting up to ten days. There is drinking and feasting, with guests invited from other longhouses, and the expense involved is considerable. But the most significant feature of this festival in ritual terms is that it involves what is generally referred to as "secondary burial," that is, the mortal remains of the deceased are removed from their place of temporary storage and brought back to the longhouse, where they form the centerpiece of the celebration. Sometimes the container used for primary storage of the corpse is opened, and the bones are cleaned. They are then re-stored in a smaller container, usually a jar. When the festival is over, the bones are removed from the longhouse for the last time, and placed in a mausoleum, often of splendid construction.

Since both the place of temporary storage and the final mausoleum are typically wooden chambers raised above the ground, it is hardly appropriate to refer to the Berawan rites as secondary *burial*. The more general terms are secondary treatment, or secondary disposal, of the dead. But these formulae are cumbrous, and to avoid their repeated use below I frequently employ the Berawan term for their rites, namely *nulang*. I shall not burden the reader with remembering other words in foreign languages.

The derivation of the term suggests the most essential feature of the rites: It comes from *tulang*, a word found in the same or closely similar form in many Austronesian languages, meaning a bone, or bones. The substitution of *n* or *ng* for an initial consonant regularly converts a noun into a verb in Berawan, so that *nulang* could be glossed in some such way as "to do that which is associated with the bones." Though the most conspicuous feature of the festival is eating, drinking, and socializing, the characteristic feature hinted at in the name is the manipulation of the mortal remains.

When Berawan translate *nulang* into Malay, they render it as *ambil tulang*, to take, or acquire, the bones.

This schedule, with provision for two major public rituals, comprises the basic format, the details of which are described below.

The Importance of the Death Rites

Berawan mortuary rites are of interest not only because they are exotic, but also because they stand near the center of Berawan life. It would be difficult to study any major aspect of Berawan culture or society without being drawn into them.

Grand funerals and *nulang* are the largest events in the life of the longhouse: the most prolonged, the most costly, and the most crowded. Consequently all the psychosocial functions that are characteristic of ritual in general are most marked in connection with them. But beyond these functions, it is also the case that the death rites are the most ritually complex and symbolically dense of all communal celebrations. Their significance reaches into every domain of Berawan life, so that they comprise an example of what Mauss (1925) described as a "total social phenomenon." These are institutions that are, in Evans-Pritchard's phrase, "at the same time economic, juridical, aesthetic, religious, mythological and socio-morphological" (Evans-Pritchard 1967:vii). There is no other institution in Berawan society that has this total character.

The death rites are the most compelling of communal rituals: To consistently fail to attend them is to renounce membership in the community. Even when a person of little social standing dies, everyone should contribute something to the funeral. In theory, the wake should be attended every night that it is in progress by all adults present in the longhouse. In fact, it is sufficient if there is one representative from each family apartment, even the most prestigious, for *noblesse oblige*. Similarly, every family will make at least a token contribution of money or rice to enable the family that has suffered the loss to carry out the funeral properly. When the deceased is a person of high status, these obligations are felt more keenly. Then the activities of the whole house will revolve for days around the successful production of the ritual, and people will return from the farms, or from travels further afield, in order to play their part in them. The wake that occurs every night, and especially on the last night before the corpse goes to the graveyard, will be attended by all but the sick or very young. For a *nulang*, the community effort will be greater again.

From this it is clear that major mortuary rituals have a considerable economic impact. A *nulang* that occurred in 1973 cost in excess of 2,600 Malaysian dollars. At the rates of exchange then current, this amounted to more than a thousand U.S. dollars. But the true magnitude of the sum can best be gauged from local wage rates, which then ran at about five or six dollars per day for casual labor in the lumber camps. So this *nulang* cost the equivalent of about five hundred man-days of cash labor. But even this does not represent the total cost of the event, because it does not include gifts in kind, and labor donated to hunt for game, prepare food, work on the mausoleum, and so on. If these are included, the number of man-days of effort expended is probably doubled. In a community of approximately 150 economically active adults, this represents a substantial commitment.

Given the costs entailed in the largest of these rites, it is not surprising that they are closely connected with the formulae of social status and rank. They are related both as cause and effect. Only those people of superior social standing are capable of amassing the resources necessary for a grand funeral or *nulang*. But Berawan society lacks defined social classes, and there is room for mobility both upward and downward. In regard to chiefly roles in the community, the situation is even more marked. Leading positions are not inherited in any simple fashion, and are instead the result of considerable maneuvering. In this fluid situation, the death rituals provide a major arena in which influence may be reaffirmed or renegotiated. This is because, although they are public events, yet they are focused upon individuals and families. For the respectable, a certain elaboration is *de rigueur*. But the grandest events are often staged by leaders attempting to consolidate their positions. Particularly in the construction of impressive mausoleums, the leader demonstrates, for all the world to see, his ability to weld the community together in a corporate undertaking. This is the importance of the death rite in the traditional politics of the Berawan.

Berawan like to point out the death edifices, and name the great man associated with them. In this guise, *nulang* appears as a kind of ancestor factory. Current leaders are controversial; those of the former generation less so. As one proceeds further back in time, they become by degrees larger than life, heros who dealt with spirits as easily as with common mortals, and finally those who themselves became important spirit agencies. In this way the chain of magnates leads not only back in time, but up to the heavens. These men and heros are mentioned frequently in prayer, by which I mean formalized speech addressed to supernatural agencies in ritual situations.

The language used in prayer is called *piat*.[2] It is characterized by structured parallelism: Dyadic sets within one phrase, paired phrases, and patterned repetition of the name of the spirit addressed. Typically, the first word of a dyadic set is one that occurs in everyday Berawan speech, and it is often paired with a word not heard in normal conversation, but only in the context of *piat*. Such *piat* words are drawn from other languages, usually dialects of Kenyah, if they happen to rhyme or alliterate, or they may be peculiar to Berawan *piat*. Many of these *piat* words occur in formulae familiar to the audience, and their meaning is immediately recognized. Others are less familiar, and their meaning is deduced by the unskilled listener from the pair word in ordinary Berawan. Dyadic sets are not entirely fixed and there is some room for idiosyncratic variation and invention. *Piat* is spoken loudly and at great speed, producing a pleasing, melodic sound. Because of the speed of the delivery, however, even adepts make slips from time to time, omitting to provide the pair to some word or phrase.

Piat is an example of parallel ritual language that is found widely in Indonesia (Fox 1971a). Here, by way of illustration, is a typical section containing references to great men of the past:

Ooooou . . .	(noise to attract attention of spirits)
a pí kam	where are you all,
bilǐ vǐ bilǐ sadǐ	spirits of the ancestors, spirits of the grandfathers,
bilǐ ukun bilǐ dupun	spirits of old ones, spirits of the forefathers,

ka sadĩ ajan tama langet	great grandfather Tama Langet
ka sadĩ tama julan tinggang	grandfather Tama Julan Tinggang,
ka sadĩ lawai	grandfather Lawai,
lo migang atong luvak tu	that hold the region around this lake,
lo migang likó bunok tu	that hold this river Bunok,
bilĩ ka sadĩ orang kaya luwak	spirit of grandfather Orang Kaya Luwak,
lo adang suken atong likó tu	that actually prop up the region of this river,
suken tana tu	prop up this land,
suken dita tu . . .	prop up this plain . . .

Particular leaders of the past, Tama Langet, Tama Julan Tinggang, Lawai, are mentioned by name. Orang Kaya Luwak is singled out for specially honorific mention; he is the most removed in time, having been the principal man at Long Teru (where the prayer was recorded) before the turn of the century. All of these men are associated with geographical features of the area, and the powers attributed to them hint at the important place that they occupy in the Berawan spirit world. They are said to "hold" *(migang)* the region, an expression usually employed about governments, and implying rule, or control. But it is an overstatement to say that Berawan leaders "rule" over a domain, so that in death they are accorded, at least poetically, more power than they possessed in life. Even more graphically, they are said to "prop up" *(suken)* the land, implying an almost geological support, as if the land would sink away without them. Both these phrases serve to emphasize the close identity between the corps of named ancestral magnates and the particular environs of the longhouse and farms.

But the ancestors, all of the ancestors, are also mentioned collectively and anonymously in the prayers, and with less emphasis on their purely local connections. The formula used to refer to them is constructed in the manner of *piat.* The word *vĩ* means old people, ancestors. *Sadĩ* means grandfather or grandmother, while *ukun* has the same meaning but is borrowed from a Kenyah dialect. *Dupun* is a variant of another word found in several isolects of Kenyah, *tepun*, meaning grandfather, ancestor, or first inhabitants of the land. The crucial word in the couples is *bili̇́*. It has wide application, and is heard frequently both in prayer and everyday speech, in ritual contexts and otherwise. It is the term that I gloss as spirit, and I do so consistently. When the word "spirit" is used below, then there exists a corresponding Berawan phrase in which *bili̇́* appears.

The cosmological significance of *nulang* also has a mythic dimension. Significantly, Berawan stories of their ancient origins, from which they draw much of their sense of identity, begin with a rite of secondary treatment of the dead.

Originally, the stories say, the Berawan lived as one undifferentiated people, called the *Ma Semuka*, in the Usun Apau. The Usun Apau is a hilly, mountain-girt plateau, at a moderately high elevation, and intersected by numerous small streams. These streams drain into several major rivers: into the Batang Kayan to the east, via the Iwan; into the Rejang to the west, via the Plieran and Seping; into the Tinjar to the northwest, via the Dapoi; and into the Baram to the north, via the Silat (see map 2). Because of this central location, and because rivers are such important routes of travel, the Usun Apau has been the hub of central northern Borneo, mentioned again and again in the migration stories of all the peoples of this culture area. In each village they tell of the particular route that their forefathers took out of the Usun Apau to their present location, together with the wars, alliances, and wondrous events that occurred along the way. In common with other ethnic groups in central northern Borneo, the Berawan take the period when they lived in the Usun Apau as their historical datum.

The Berawan have no myths of the creation, or of their ancestors falling from the sky, or any such. Without preliminaries, their history commences in the middle of a *nulang*. The rites are for the mother of two brothers, usually called Kusai and Layong, who were the leaders of the Berawan at that time. The brothers go hunting to obtain meat for the feast that accompanies secondary disposal rites. Kusai is soon successful, and returns home. Layong, ashamed of his failure, pushes on ever deeper into the forest. Finally he sees a squirrel, and shoots it with his blowpipe. He rushes forward to catch it, and both man and squirrel fall together into a deep hole in the ground. Layong finds himself lying beside a stream, which borders a whole new world, very quiet and beautiful. He decides to skin and cook the squirrel, but when he puts it in the water to wash it, it immediately comes back to life and scampers off. Then Layong knows that this is the river of the dead *(likó bulu letá)*. He walks on for several days, until he hears the noises of a longhouse. He hears a voice calling two pigs, one black, one white, which he recognizes as the ones sacrificed at the funeral of his sister some years before. He reveals himself to the caller, who is indeed his sister. She tells him that he must go back at once or he will have no more descendents in the world. But he insists that he must first see his mother, who also urges him to return. Reluctantly, he leaves on the long journey home. Meanwhile, Kusai has collected a lot of game at the longhouse, and he taunts Layong for returning empty-handed. Layong tells his story and tries to convince everyone to abandon the *nulang* and move directly to the land of the dead. A quarrel ensues; some people agree with Layong, others doubt his story, or are unwilling to go. Finally, they split into two groups. One, led by Layong, goes off directly to join the dead, and disappears from Berawan history. The other, led by Kusai, completes the *nulang* rites, and then sets out to explore the rich lands discovered down-river in his hunting trips.

As they and their descendents split up to settle in different rivers, so the different communities came into existence. The account of their wanderings and adventures makes up the distinctive oral history of each village. But the opening episode concerning Kusai and Layong is common to all, with only minor variations. It has several aspects that suggest avenues of analysis, such as transitions by water, and the ambiguous relationship between the living and the dead. These themes are echoed in ritual, and they will be taken up below. The point that concerns us here is the statement about the meaning of the death rites that is implicit in the lack of any explanation, rationale, or origin myth offered for the rite of *nulang*. It is simply there, unquestioned, at the outset. This becomes more remarkable when compared with other segments of Berawan religion. For instance, a long cycle of myths explain the origin of the use of omen animals. The hero who initiated their use is placed in time after the Usun Apau exodus. Other items are explained as borrowings from neighboring peoples. The Berawan claim, for example, that they knew nothing of the taking of heads until they learned it from other peoples migrating in from the east. *Nulang* is by contrast asserted to be an original element in the heritage of the Berawan, and hence of cultural identity. It is an element shared with almost none of their neighbors. Perhaps the course of development in modern-day Borneo will eventually make such identities irrelevant. But while being Berawan continues to have meaning, the old practices will retain their significance. People will continue to tell of the *nulang* that Kusai performed for his mother in the Usun Apau long ago.

Outline of the Book

My account of the death rites follows for the most part a chronological sequence, dealing with the rituals as they unfold from death to final disposal perhaps years later. Chapter three describes a death that I witnessed during fieldwork. In the twenty minutes or so after a death is pronounced, there is frantic activity around the corpse, both utilitarian and ritual. The latter has a striking quality about it; it says, in the most direct manner, that somehow the dead person is still there, still present in the immediate vicinity. Consequently, in chapter four, we are immediately thrust into one of those problems of translation around which Evans-Pritchard built his approach. The question here is how the Berawan conceive of the continuing nonmaterial component of the individual. Their term is *telanak*, and I can hardly avoid glossing it as "soul," although there are differences between the Berawan concept of soul and the one that we generally share, stemming from a Christian tradition. The issue of translation is a delicate one; the concept of *telanak* is abstract, and not one that Berawan are given to discussing in any philosophical way. We must be careful not to assume that there is a consensus of ideas where none in fact exists. Chapter four outlines the contexts in which the notion of *telanak* is spontaneously mobilized, and draws what deductions seem safely to follow from that.

The account of the rituals following death, broken off after only a matter of minutes in chapter three, is taken up again in chapter five, and carried through to the completion of the funeral. The funeral involves all-night vigils kept over the body, but the crowd that keeps the vigil is not solemn. Everybody in the longhouse is enjoined to attend, and only the close kin must maintain a restrained demeanor. For the rest there is drinking and socializing. As in the rapid rites following immediately on death, there are several aspects of the funeral that call for explanation, of which the jovial mood of the occasion is only one. In chapter six the significance of the wake is examined, and here I draw upon the classic essay on death by Robert Hertz. This section is the linchpin of the account of Berawan eschatology.

After the corpse has been removed from the longhouse, there remains only one set of rites to perform in order to complete the public part of the mortuary sequence, unless and until it is decided to conduct the rituals of secondary treatment of the remains. These remaining rites, now tagged onto the end of the funeral like an appendix to the main events of the wake, have to do with headhunting. Previously, in more martial times when real heads were obtained, the rites had a more prominent and autonomous place. Until fresh heads were obtained, the entire longhouse remained under onerous mourning restrictions. No other ceremonies could occur, no weddings, no parties. Chapter seven explores the association of heads with the souls of the dead. Chapter eight examines the special mourning rites that are prescribed for close kin of the deceased, especially the widow or widower. Nowadays the community as a whole is released from restrictions soon after the conclusion of the wake, but the bereaved spouse continues to be hedged about by prohibitions for many months, and the symbolism of those prohibitions requires comment.

In chapter nine we come to the rites that are the most distinctive feature of Berawan mortuary ritual, those of secondary treatment of the dead. *Nulang* brings to an end the prolonged period of temporary storage of the corpse. That is, if the rites are performed. In the majority of cases corpses are removed to their final resting place at the end of the initial funeral, and not disturbed after that. *Nulang* is important in many ways to the Berawan, but it is, and always has been, a rarity. So much is this the case that chapter nine provides an account of the circumstances surrounding the two *nulang* that I witnessed. Chapter ten gives a description of the *nulang*, which in many respects resembles a second wake, only even noisier and more festive than the first. However, there are differences, in connection with prescribed and prohibited activities during the *nulang*, and also, of course, the manipulation of the skeletal remains. There are also variations between the rites as performed at different Berawan villages.

An important part of the *nulang* is the singing of a long cycle of death songs that are regarded with considerable awe. Their narratives of the journey of the soul provide a direct view of one aspect of Berawan eschatology, and they are the subject of chapters eleven and twelve.

The last two chapters examine the Berawan afterlife, as it can be deduced from explicit statements about the land of the dead and the mobilization of the ancestors in prayer. There are a number of anomalies about the location of the land of the dead, and the relationship between the spirits of the ancestors and other spirit agencies, which are resolved. Finally, in the conclusion, I draw together what has been learned about Berawan eschatology and its expression in ritual.

Notes

1. The true autonym is Melawan. But the Malay version of the name (i.e., Berawan) is the one normally used by other people in the Baram watershed to refer to them. It has also appeared many times in print, in sources dating back into the nineteenth century, and for that reason I will continue to employ it here.

2. Rodney Needham (personal communication) points out to me that in Western Penan the word *pia'* means speech, talk, discourse, harangue, ... in short a wide range of vocal activity. The same is not true of Berawan *piat*, which refers only to the production of this kind of ritual language. The normal word for speech or conversation is *paté*.

II

Notions
of
Soul

CHAPTER THREE

A Death at Long Teru

At the end of December 1973, not long before I left the village, a middle-aged woman died at Long Teru. Her name was Utan Nin.[1] She had been sick for many years with a degenerative disease that was readily recognizable as tuberculosis. The disease is common among upriver people, and the administration has in recent years had considerable success in making *orang ulu* folk aware of the symptoms and reducing the incidence of mortality. But Utan Nin's case was long established, and by the time that her husband, Tama Aweng, took her to the coast for treatment, it was too late. He was told that she had only a short time to live, and so hurried back with her, for it is considered a very unfortunate thing to die away from home. He redoubled his efforts to find a traditional cure, but to no avail.

It was a slow death. Day after day she sat in her room coughing in violent spasms, propped up against a pile of pillows in order to make breathing easier. To say that she sat in "her room" implies more privacy that was really the case. The inside of a family apartment *(ukuk)* within the longhouse consists in effect of one large room in which children play and adults go about their chores or doze in corners. In the rear is the kitchen, sometimes separated by a short walkway so as to reduce the risk of fire in the main structure. Often there are sleeping cubicles for married couples, but these are small and airless during the day. So Utan Nin was placed in a corner of the main room, and everyday life went on about her. Not only did the *ukuk* residents come and go, but also many other people came to sit there, to express concern, to talk, and to gossip. As Utan Nin grew weaker, the density of this traffic increased. These attentions are typical of Berawan reactions to illness or accident. If

33

someone is injured, or falls suddenly ill, then everyone within the house will rush to the scene. There is a strong sentiment that to fail to do so is callous and antisocial. There is also a vague suggestion that, simply by being there, the friends and relatives shield the afflicted from further harm or a worsening of the condition. Other motives are present, of course, simple curiosity being the most obvious. In any event, and whatever the feelings of the afflicted person, the close family usually seem relieved to have other people with them. The mood of the gathering will initially be one of clucking concern, but if the patient appears stable or not in great pain, the tension soon relaxes into sociality. A family member will then be dispatched to prepare coffee, or even to serve rice wine, and attention drifts away from its original object, who is left on the edge of things, attended only by a parent, sibling, or other close relative. Only if there is a sudden alarm will the company fall silent, and attention become riveted on the sufferer.

So it was with Utan Nin. Towards the end there were people about her all day long, but especially in the evenings. A kerosene lantern was kept burning, and people sat playing cards under its glare. Neither Utan Nin nor Tama Aweng, who was constantly at his wife's side, showed any sign of impatience, even when the players became noisy. There were non-Berawan there, people from the lumber camps who happened by the house on that particular evening. In these circumstances, the death itself is as open an event as the funeral that follows it.

I was also there much of the time. I had by then attended many funerals, some simple, others elaborate. But I had never witnessed the battery of small rites that occur immediately after death is pronounced. Always I had been somewhere else when a death had occurred. That was why I was sitting in Utan Nin's room; in order to see those rites and complete my observations. I did not feel comfortable with these motives, but they were not questioned by my hosts. I was in fact doing what a good Berawan would do. Meanwhile, everyone there knew of my interests, and what sort of things I had asked about in the past. I must have been transparent to them, but they only commented disarmingly that they had not known that I was so fond of Utan Nin. On no other occasion did I feel more sharply the contradiction between genuine friendship and detached observation that is inherent in fieldwork. At other times there had been conflicts between the two drives, and I had resolved them by dropping a line of inquiry, or quietly removing myself, when I saw that I was making my informants uncomfortable. But on this occasion, it was *my* sensibilities that were at stake. I had never before watched anyone die, and I was deeply disturbed by it. Beyond that, I felt like an intruder, a voyeur. But my hosts, I believe, felt little or no embarrassment; it was a public event.

Utan Nin died at three in the afternoon. She had been breathing only with the greatest of difficulty for several hours, and it was readily apparent when she finally stopped struggling to draw breath. There was no need to apply the test that is usually made at this time: a small feather or piece of down is balanced on the lips. If no movement of air can be detected from the mouth or nose, the person is pronounced dead. This is, for Berawan, the moment literally of "losing breath" (*ilang natachin*).

The death was immediately made known to the community by the beating of the largest type of gong found in the longhouse, the variety called *padung*. This gong has a diameter of over thirty inches, and thick walls ten or more inches deep. It lets out a boom so deep that it can be heard at the farms several miles away, if the wind is in the right quarter. The pattern of striking that is used to announce a death *(tucho)* consists of repeated clusters of four to eight blows, persons of high status receiving more than humbler folk. The rate of striking accelerates during each cluster and it is this that characterizes a death knell. By contrast, the alarm signal, as for instance if the longhouse caught fire, is a constant even beating. To use either summons fraudulently is a fineable offense.

Sitting in a neighboring apartment, I did not need the gong to learn of the death. As soon as it was detected that Utan Nin was no longer breathing, a wail arose from the women sitting nearby. The *ukuk* where I was at that moment contained a newborn child and a sickly older man. Everyone within it was nervous about the proximity of the impending death, because it represented a threat to the child and the frail man. As the wail rang out, they hastened to light a stick of *kamayan*, an incense-bearing wood whose smoke is supposed to repel evil influences. No one there made a move towards Utan Nin's room; they needed no closer contact with death.

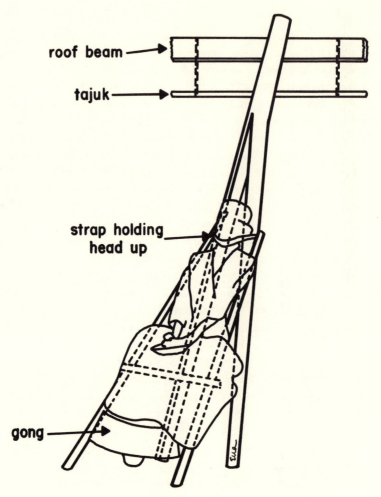

Figure 2. Details of construction of the death seat (*tèlorèn*).

Plate 1. Utan Nin's corpse seated on the *tèlorèn*. It is clothed in rich fabrics and a skirt of traditional design is draped across its knees. Its hands rest in a plate containing sweetmeats and coins, and hold a cigarette and paper money. Cloths of all kinds hang from a rack above, and valuables are stacked around the body: brassware, heirloom strongboxes, a shotgun, and a transistor radio. Precious old beads and jewelry hang behind its head, and its feet sit in a large old gong. A plate for food offerings is suspended in front of it.

37

I joined the other longhouse members rushing to the deathbed. There I found a scene of apparent chaos, with people running around aimlessly, or keening uncontrollably. The emotional outpouring was intense, and I found myself fighting back tears. But after a few minutes, I began to observe that a pattern was emerging in the activity in the room, and that there was a division of labor between the men and the women, the immediate kin and others. The expression of grief also varied. Most of the women were wailing in a formalized way, beginning on a high note and descending the scale in a jerky staccato fashion until they ran out of breath. Then they drew in air in a great sob, and began the ululation over again. Some knelt with their long hair thrown forward to cover their faces, and seemed lost in grief. Others were more restrained, and wove a kind of recitative into their wailing, which took the form of a rebuke addressed to the dead woman. "Why have you left those that love you?" they asked, "Why die at this moment, when we are not ready to part with you?" These dirges are a verbal art form, and proficiency at them is admired. Women known to be adept are desired at the wake. Meanwhile, a few women, perhaps shocked or stunned by the event, showed almost no reaction at all, and this was not later the subject of adverse comment. Tama Aweng sat by the corpse motionless, looking drawn and haggard, and the adult men looked on, solemn but dry-eyed. Children ran back and forth between the kneeling women and the standing men, looking for reassurance.

Gradually, as the first outpouring of emotion ebbed, the men began to slip away to do their work on the veranda. The senior woman of the house, Biló Kasi, who was experienced in these things and not closely related to the deceased, came forward to take charge of preparing the corpse. A child was sent to fetch a bowl of hot water. Then a piece of cheap fabric was torn up to make wash cloths, and the body was carefully mopped, turning it over to reach the back. During this operation, the clothes that Utan Nin was wearing when she died were removed and put to one side for disposal later, but modesty was preserved, even in death, by keeping the body covered with another cloth. This completed, the corpse was dressed again in a fresh bodice and sarong, the finest that Utan Nin had owned. Her hair was combed and oiled.

Meanwhile the menfolk were working feverishly to prepare the seat *(tèlorèn)*, the death throne, on which the corpse was to be displayed for a day or two until it was put into a sealed jar or coffin. The construction of this seat is shown in figure 2. Its form is fixed by custom, and each man could see what needed doing next without direction. The main structural member is a pole about six inches in diameter, which is split along about two-thirds of its length and pried open. The splayed end is set on the floor, and the other is lashed to a roof beam in such a way that the pole has an inclination of about 60 degrees. A cross bar supports a bucket seat made by forcing a folded mat into the triangle so produced. The chair is provided with arms made from sticks decorated by lifting shavings from their surfaces to form rows of curls *(pegerok)*. The seat faces downriver, in the direction that the soul must eventually travel. Above the seat a framework of bamboos is suspended *(tajuk)*. At Long Jegan the style of *tèlorèn* was simpler, a wooden plank only. The corpse sat on a gong with its back resting against the plank and its feet extended in front.[2] The poles required for making the *tèlorèn* had, in Utan Nin's case, been collected from a nearby patch of jungle some hours previously, because it was obvious that death was imminent, so work could begin on erecting the seat immediately. But the collecting of these timbers is positively the only preparation that may be made before the death occurs. No one will do anything else to acknowledge the proximity of death, even to mention the word, for to do so is to bring it about. This contrasts with Kenyah practice, which allows even the preparation of the coffin in advance (Stöhr 1959:95).

Back inside the apartment of the bereaved family, the principal activity, aside from keening, was rummaging through the family's valuables for items with which to decorate the body and *tèlorèn*. Every family has a substantial wooden chest tucked away somewhere, in a sleeping cubicle or high up under the rafters, which contains all the fine things that are only rarely brought out. The box is not for security against theft. Anyone so deranged as to try to steal heirloom property from his own people could easily carry off the whole box. Rather it is to keep them away from the prying fingers of little boys, against whom nothing else is proof, and to preserve modesty about these possessions. When I first arrived at Long Teru,

I assumed that the people there were poor in heirloom property because one so seldom saw it, by comparison with, say, a Kenyah house. This was particularly true of the polychrome glass beads that are worn around the neck. Some are several centuries old, and traded from as far away as Venice, and there is a vast lore and technical terminology regarding them. Among all the peoples of central northern Borneo a good necklace of beads is the premier mark of high status. But the Berawan only rarely wear them in public, reflecting a special tension in their society about the whole concept of rank. On the rare occasions when I could coax someone into pulling out their chest for me to see, it was invariably a treasure trove of heirlooms and browning old photographs, each to be wonderingly examined, each with its own story. Now in Utan Nin's room, I was surrounded by an *embarras de richesses*. It is propitious for the welfare of the entire house to surround the corpse with all manner of valuables when it is displayed on the veranda. The implication is that the dead person will somehow multiply them. So several families, particularly those closely related to the dead woman or her husband, had brought out their strongboxes. Each one would have provided an evening of entertainment and instruction, but now items were being held up and considered, and then rejected and put back into their place of storage with frustrating rapidity. Biló Kasi showed me a pair of cylindrical ornaments for the forearms, each made out of dozens of connected ivory rings. It had been given to her many years ago when her first husband was a *penghulu*, or government-appointed chief. They can be seen in the upper right-hand corner of plate 1, with other valuables. Another woman was sorting through several fine cloths of the variety called *kain songkèt*, which has a gold thread woven into the design. These valuable fabrics are associated with Brunei, the ancient trading center to the north. Others again were polishing silver and gold objects.

Another activity in the room at this time was the removal of all ritual apparatus that had collected around Utan Nin in the several attempts to avert her death. One shaman had caused to be constructed a large structure of wooden poles decorated with feathers. Others had required trays of offerings for their familiars to be prepared. A small spirit house, resembling a doll's house, had also been placed near Utan Nin. Now all this had to be completely removed. I was told that they were simply no use any more, but the motivation was stronger than that. It was as if they demeaned the arts of the shaman by being there near the corpse. Normally the small food offerings would be hung up in a little basket near the back of the room, but these ones were thrown away unceremoniously under the longhouse where other kitchen waste goes. The spirit house *(beran)* was removed to the other end of the longhouse, whence it had been brought for Utan Nin. It was old and had been elaborately dedicated, and could not be destroyed. But the structure that had been built especially for Utan Nin was completely torn down. Seeing a chance to lend a hand, I helped carry it out of the house, and several people laughed to see me joining in in this way. At the front of the house I was warned not to stand up any part of the structure, but merely to throw it in a rough pile, which would be augmented later by other waste associated with the death. Some time after the funeral was completed, all this would be thrown into the river to drift away.

Now the preparatory phrase was over and it was time to move the corpse. But first a hole had to be chopped with axes in the plank wall in the front of the family room, for the corpse could not be carried through the door that normally gave onto the veranda. This usage, so widely found in Southeast Asia and beyond, requires that the corpse have its own exit, not the one used by the living. Two men not closely related to Utan Nin were standing by to pick up the corpse with a simple stretcher made with a folded cloth, and emotional tension was again rising. But one of the older women remembered a small ritual that had to be carried out at this point. It had almost been overlooked. Tama Aweng first lay beside the corpse of his wife in a posture of sleep, then he sat up and was handed a cigarette of local manufacture, i.e., home-grown tobacco rolled in a leaf. He took a few puffs, and then held it to his wife's lips as if she too would draw upon it. The same acts were mimed out by their daughter and adoptive son. They express the shared residence and commensality of the now-disrupted family. Then, amid a new bout of keening, and with anxious glances to make sure that all was indeed ready, the two men slid their makeshift stretcher under the corpse and picked it up in more or less sitting position.

It was obvious that their load was pathetically light. Hurriedly they moved it into the kitchen, where it was seated on a gong near the hearth, with one hand on a large rice pot. Biló Kasi made a rapid prayer, asking the ancestors in general, and the dead woman in particular, to bring health and full rice pots to the family and to the longhouse. Then a little cooked rice was put into the corpse's mouth. Next it was off again, through the crowded room and the hole recently made in the wall, to the open side of the veranda. There the corpse was seated briefly, again on a gong, in the place where people so often sit idly in the evenings looking out over the open space in front of the longhouse and the river beyond. No prayer was made this time, although I am told that it sometimes is. After a moment or two the body was moved finally to the seat of the *tèlorèn*. It was secured in place by strips of cloth tied around the waist and under the chin. The knees were also loosely tied together.

The finery that had previously been assembled could now be arranged around the *tèlorèn*. Utan Nin's body was decorated sumptuously: a brocaded fabric draped about the shoulders, old beads around her neck, a fine bead headband, and a heavy embroidered skirt draped about the knees, one of the type employed by *orang ulu* folk before the Malay-style sarong came into fashion. All these valuables would be removed later before the corpse was inserted in its storage container. I kept close watch as the body was arranged, for I did not wish to miss a small rite that I had previously been told about: two old beads were slipped inconspicuously into Utan Nin's mouth, one in each cheek. These are to enable the soul to purchase its way over an obstacle in its journey to the land of the dead. At Batu Belah, a tiny bell was formerly put into the mouth, so that the soul could summon its dead relatives to help it pass the same obstacle. Another rite more obscurely connected with the passage to the land of the dead involved setting the feet of the body in a large gong, and pouring several pounds of rice over them. The hands were arranged in a shallow plate containing money, rice cakes, and sweets, and a cigarette placed between the fingers. In front of the corpse a small plate was suspended, on which food would be placed at regular intervals during the funeral. While this was in progress, other women were arranging all manner of valuable or decorative fabrics over the bamboo frame above the *tèlorèn*, and men and women bustled about fetching objects of value and stacking them around the catafalque: gongs and brassware, a sewing machine and a shotgun, even an old twelve volt car battery of obscure utility and origin (see plate 1).

The previous half hour had been one of incessant noise and bustle. Berawan say that it is necessary to get the corpse properly arranged on the *tèlorèn* before rigor mortis sets in. But, as noted above, this kind of intensity is characteristic of Berawan ritual in general. The sound of women wailing had been continuous, and virtually every adult woman had taken a turn, sometimes shifting rather suddenly from vocal grief to some practical preoccupation. There is an odd tension between the requirement to express grief, and the unlocking of real emotion that occurs because of the group display of grief. It is impossible, even within oneself, to sort out whether the emotion is causing the participation or vice versa. However, there is no doubt that it was intensely emotionally involving. But now that the corpse was in place on the death seat, where it would stay for a day or two, things began to quiet down, and the tension to ebb away with the crowd. A few women were left putting finishing touches to the display, but apart from that Utan Nin was for the moment abandoned. The initial ritual processing was complete.

Activity now became diffused between several neighboring apartments. In Tama Aweng's room the kitchen was being expanded and pots and plates collected from all over the longhouse in order to handle the catering for the funeral. In an adjacent room, mourning clothes of cheap white fabric were being sewn for the close kin (see plate 2). In another, the most serious business: a council of all those on whom the responsibility of organizing the funeral would fall, including all close adult kin of the deceased, and leaders of the community. In rapid order it was decided what ritual sequence to employ, whether to use a jar or coffin for storage of the corpse, who must be invited, how many days the funeral was to last, and a dozen other details. After that Tama Aweng would become incommunicado, boxed up in his mourning prison of mats.

But let us pause here in the account of the rituals to pose some analytical questions. There are no lack of them, since so many aspects of Berawan practice are strange to Western eyes. The public

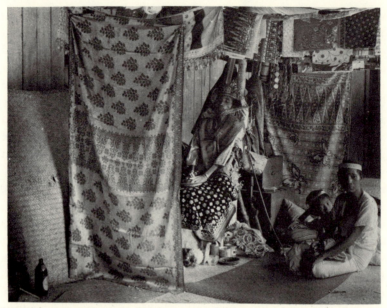

Plate 2. Utan Nin surrounded by her family. On the right sit her two children, wearing white mourning attire, and her grandchild. Behind the wall of mats on the left, her husband is huddled in his tiny cubicle.

nature of the events has already been remarked upon. In chapter one, we saw how death rituals are related to longhouse solidarity, and this is a case in point. But there are also ideological rationales for why it is the responsibility of the community to participate continuously from the moment of falling ill to the completion of the death rites, if the outcome is fatal. The same is true of the emphasis on the display of valuables with the corpse. We noted above that the scale of death rites, the amount of food and drink consumed by the visitors, is an element in status competition and confirmation. But that is not what is involved here: Utan Nin was not a woman of particularly high standing in the community. Nor were the goods involved to be consumed. They were simply loaned for the period of the funeral, to be stacked around the corpse, and it is not yet clear how that is thought to benefit either the deceased or the survivors.

But perhaps the most striking feature is that the corpse is treated in ways that seem to deny that it is dead after all: it is talked to, offered food and cigarettes, and even, on one occasion, spoon fed. What these gestures express, in the most direct manner conceivable, is continuity. Now we have to ask what it is, in the Berawan view, that goes on through death, and what it is that happens at death.

Notes

1. I have made no attempt to disguise the real names of people mentioned in the text. Short of using a pseudonym for the entire ethnic group, which would be a disservice to ethnology, I cannot effectively mask the identity of individuals because there are so few Berawan communities. In many cases I want to acknowledge the help given me by particular informants, and I do not believe that I have revealed anything that is damaging to anyone.

2. In his travels up the Rejang in the 1880s, H. B. Low found very similar arrangements for displaying the dead in use among the Kajaman (Low 1882:64). The Kajaman are one of many small groups distributed in an arc across central northern Borneo that practiced secondary treatment of the dead in recent times (Metcalf 1976b). On the other hand, the style of death seat used at Long Teru is closely similar to some traditional Kenyah designs, for example the one shown in Elshout (1926: plate opposite p. 60). The Kenyah do not practice secondary treatment. This detail illustrates the complexity of borrowing of ritual features characteristic of interior Borneo. Space does not allow me systematically to take note of all these similarities and differences between communities, let alone explore their ethnological significance.

CHAPTER FOUR

The Soul's Career

The Berawan define death differently than we do. This is not simply a matter of apparatus, of elaborate devices to detect vital signs versus the humble feather; rather it is conceptual. Death is not for them the final malfunctioning of the body as machine, but an irreversible act of the soul. This chapter has two analytic goals: To comprehend the Berawan conception of soul, and to arrive at a definition of death in terms of the fate of the soul. This is not easy because Berawan, as we saw, do not say directly what soul *is*. Consequently, I cast my net widely, examining practices that bear upon the notion and utilizing comparative material from other Bornean peoples. Moreover, death is not for them the matter of an instant; instead it is a process. For that reason, we must view death as a stage in the career of the soul.

I argue that the conception of soul comes most clearly into focus in the process of dying. It is also importantly mobilized in the etiology of illness and disease. As for the soul in life, that is only made apparent, and only understood by the Berawan, by a kind of retroactive logic, in contrast to conditions of morbidity. Concerning the origins of souls, there is no doctrine whatsoever. However, I present the material in the reverse order, working from the less defined toward the more defined, and following the life cycle of the soul from beginning to end. I begin by distinguishing between soul and spirit.

Soul and Spirit

When Berawan pray, they address their prayers to a spirit or spirits, *bilí*. The agency most commonly addressed is called, in the language of *piat, bilí puwong, bilí ngaputong* (*puwong* = to own, possess; *ngaputong* = to create). In common speech, it is the latter title that is used, so that I refer to him as the Creator Spirit.[1] He is unitary and supreme, and prayers made in front of a shrine are addressed primarily to him. Nevertheless, there are any number of other spirits that might be mentioned because they are relevent in a particular context. So the spirits of the omen creatures (*bilí aman*) might be summoned, or the spirit of a particular omen creature, usually *plaké*, the black eagle (*Ictinaetus malayensis*, see Metcalf 1976a). Alternatively, the spirits of the shrine itself may be summoned, *bilí tapó* (*tapó* = shrine). But this phrase, *bilí tapó*, does not imply that there is a special deity or presiding spirit associated with shrines that is distinct from other spiritual agencies. The same applies to the phrases, also commonly heard in prayers, *bilí tana* (*tana* = land) and *bilí atak tu* (*atak* = place, *tu* = this). Berawan are perfectly clear about this: It is not that there is a special spirit of the land, or that there are necessarily spirits peculiar to the place. It is simply that there *may* be spirits connected with or somehow present in the shrine, or the land, or some particular place. These phrases are catch-all terms designed to make sure that all benevolent spirit agencies have been invoked. This conception of the spirit world is not appropriately labeled animism. Berawan do not assume that objects, natural features, or creatures are inherently imbued with spiritual essence, but only that they may be.

Where animism implies the certainty of a one-to-one relationship of essences and things, Berawan ideology is full of uncertainty. The Berawan spirit world is unbounded, and they do not claim to have knowledge of all of it. Shamans, for instance, in the course of their psychic journeys, often learn of new spirits, and the information is stored away for what use it may be later. These spirits may be good or evil; if the former, they may be added to the repertoire of familiars to whom the shaman looks for assistance. If the latter, their malicious characteristics are noted. It is this willingness to concede that their knowledge is incomplete that causes the use of such phrases as "spirits of the land" and "spirits of the place." At the same time, there is no agnosticism. Berawan believe that they know the major features of the spirit world, including the Creator Spirit, the spirits of the ancestors, whom we already met in chapter two, the spirits of the omen creatures, and other well-known and frequently invoked spirit agencies.

For present purposes, this will serve as an introduction to the Berawan notion of spirit. But people, living human beings, are not said to be or to have *bili̇́*. That would be a contradiction in terms, unless one were referring to the very special circumstances of shamanistic inspiration. Moreover, when a death has occurred, when the small rituals are being performed that involve talking to the corpse, giving it cigarettes, and feeding it, *bili̇́* is not the word used to refer to the evanescent nonmaterial component of the deceased person. What living human beings have, and what persists after death, is *telanak*.

Animals, plants, and objects do not have *telanak*. In accordance with what was said about animism, or the lack of it, they *may* have spirit. For example, when a pig is about to be sacrificed, it is first of all spoken to in the formal language of prayer *(piat)* and charged with a message to bring to the Creator. At such times it is addressed as *bili̇́ bikui*, spirit of the pig, and this is so precisely because the pig is being assigned a spiritual mission. But, as a counter instance, I was once asked to name a large bird that was flying in front of the longhouse. I recognized it as the eagle commonly used in augury, and so I replied: *bili̇́ plaké*. This answer brought laughter. The bird that was flying by was merely an eagle, *plaké*, not the spirit of *plaké*. A similar logic applies to spirits in objects. There was once at Long Teru a large utilitarian jar of the type called *gusi* that suddenly began to move around in the middle of the night in a mysterious way, and to emit low moaning sounds. People began to refer to *bili̇́ gusi*, the spirit of, or in, the jar. Later a shaman found out more particulars about the spirit, including its proper name. It would have been merely eccentric to have referred to *bili̇́ gusi* had the jar not manifested extraordinary behavior. By contrast, living human beings inherently have *telanak*.

The etymology of the word offers, as far as I have been able to discover, few clues as to its meaning. The term is unusual in the region. It may be derived from *anak* (child), suggesting perhaps a small replica of the owner. *Anak* is also used in a manner that implies something that is a necessary part of a whole, as for example in *anak konci*, a key (*konci* = lock). Rodney Needham has suggested to me that there may also be a connection with the Malay *tela,* meaning a passageway.

The *telanak* is associated vaguely with the pupils of the eyes, where, it was pointed out, a tiny human face could be seen. *Telanak* is also associated with the fontanel, through which it is supposed to exit from the body. This is particularly the case with young children, whose heads are shaved when they are very small, leaving only a tuft of hair around the crown, where the *telanak* is said to "sit." However, another tuft is left at brows also, with a similar stated purpose. These beliefs reinforce a general association between *telanak* and the head.

The obvious gloss for *telanak* is soul. In many ways the match between the terms is nice, because there is about the English word an indeterminateness that is similar to the Berawan. A dictionary definition includes the following diverse list: "the immaterial essence, animating principal, or actuating cause of an individual life . . . a person's total self." Different streams of Christian thought, ranging from the folksy to the theological, see the soul variously as an immaterial replica of the living body, warts and all, or as a sublime and completely abstract moral force, or some compromise between these extremes. In similar fashion the Berawan *telanak* appears in some contexts as particulate, in others immaterial; sometimes anthropomorphic, sometimes not. At shamanistic rites the adept may occasionally claim to have captured a soul on the blade of his or her *parang* (sword),[2] and the audience will crane to catch a glimpse of it before it is returned to its owner by pushing it back in through the crown of the head. At other times, as for instance during the soul's journey to the land of the dead, we find it paddling a canoe, stopping to cook rice, and even singing a lament. In this guise, the soul is a homomorphic counterpart of the dead person, a "shade" perhaps.[3]

But the Berawan notion of *telanak* is different from the English "soul" in two important respects. First, we do not normally think of the soul as divisible from the body in life. The soul may perhaps be damaged, diminished, or "blackened" by evil acts, but it does not wander about independently. The Berawan *telanak* does. As we might say that a group consisted of twenty souls, the Berawan say cautiously, twenty bodies. Second, we normally think of the soul as immortal, whether its final destination is pleasant or otherwise. But the same is not true of *telanak*. Certainly it continues after death. But we have already seen that the ultimate fate of souls is to become *bili"* as in the ritual formula used to refer to the ancestors collectively in prayer. The *telanak* has finite existence, with a beginning and an end.

As regards the beginning, Berawan are noncommittal about when a soul enters the body of an infant. Some think it is present at conception, others that it arrives when the fetus has discernable eyes, which they believe is at about three or four months of gestation. This echoes the association between soul and the eyes that we noted above. Others again feel that even at birth the infant might not have a soul, and justify the extremely casual burial given to still-born children in this way. The Melanau, a numerous people to the south of the Berawan, and related ethnically to them, have more precise notions about soul acquisition. They say that an unborn infant receives its soul in the seventh month of pregnancy, and there is a ritual that occurs at that stage of gestation (Morris 1953:120, personal communication). Berawan have no such rite, and the only thing that Berawan agree upon about the origin of souls is that it is the Creator Spirit that assigns them to human infants. They are not sure how or when.

Body, Soul, and Name

The most satisfactory direct statement that can be made about the nature of *telanak* is that it is an essential component of the living human being. It was a proposition that I could get Berawan to assent to, but not to offer spontaneously. (I have already pointed out what response Berawan give if asked directly what soul is.) I borrowed it from Rodney Needham's description of Penan ideas of the composition of the individual.

The Penan are a hunting and gathering people who live in small seminomadic groups, some of which are associated with, and politically dominated by, Berawan communities. These bands have adopted much of Berawan culture, even preserving items that have now fallen out of use in the dominant group. The Penan conceive a human being as consisting of three components: body, soul, and name. The terms for these (in the Eastern Penan isolect) are *usab*, *sabe*, and *ngaran* respectively. The equivalent Berawan terms are *usa, telanak*, and *ngaran*. The body is spoken of by the Penan as the "container" occupied by the soul, and the combination of body and soul is denoted by one or another name. The body contributes to the identity of the individual, but it is relatively immutable, except for such processes as aging. The soul has a persistent character also, but it has a liberty of motion possible only to the immaterial. It is the conjunction of a particular body and soul that is marked by a name:

> The name is a component of the personality, for without a name there is no person, and the name by which an individual is known can affect his bodily and psychic state. But the name, unlike the body, is infinitely changeable; and, unlike the soul, it has no independent existence. The name is not a mere designation, but even to the extent that it is such it is not just a social convenience; it is the crucial identification of the individual, not only for men but also for the innumerable and unseen spiritual powers *(balei)* to which men are always subject. (Needham 1971:206)

Needham's account of Penan ideas of the constitution of the individual is a preamble to a further discussion of naming, which is a sufficiently complex subject to have occupied several articles (Needham 1954a, 1954b, 1959, 1965, 1971). A person may have more than one name at a time, and many over the course of a lifetime. Every Penan possesses a personal name *(ngaran usab)*, but may change it under certain circumstances, such as serious illness. When he or she becomes the parent of a child, and later a grandparent, teknonyms are assumed to mark that fact, and the personal name is only infrequently used. Whether married or single, when certain relatives die a special name is taken specific to the nature of the relationship *(ngaran lumo)*. In addition, there are friendship names *(ngaran ai')* that are used reciprocally between two people (Needham 1971:206–8).

Clearly, the institutions of naming are an essential element in the definition of the social person among the Penan, and hence in the construction of the individual identity and social solidarities. The same remarks apply to the Berawan: Their system of naming is as complex as, and moreover closely resembles, that of the Penan. Interesting as it would be to contrast the details of the Berawan system with that of the Penan, it would involve us in a lengthy detour. For present purposes, our concern is not with "name," that is, social personality, but with the other elements of the triad, body and soul.

Here again, Berawan conceptions correspond closely with Penan ideas. The combination of a particular *telanak* and a given body produces the character traits of the individual, including temperament and mannerisms. Someone who is known to be stingy, chronically bad tempered, or otherwise antisocial is described as *jat unyin* (*jat* = bad, *unyin* = feelings, disposition), or more emphatically as *jat telanak*. The latter term implies an evilness of character so deep as to be unchangeable. Sometimes a child is given as a personal name the name of some forebear, because it is believed that the soul of the dead individual has returned in the child (see chapter fourteen). It is then expected that the child will manifest some of the character traits of the forebear; but no one will be surprised if the looked-for similarities fail to occur, or only partially occur, because, after all, the soul is present in a different body. I conclude that, for the Berawan as well as for the Penan, it is the conjunction of soul and body that constitutes the living human being. That statement provides us with a working definition of Berawan ideas of the soul.

Maturation of the Soul and Multiple Souls

Given the indefiniteness about the origins and nature of soul, it is appropriate to compare Berawan ideas with those of other peoples of Borneo, and Indonesia generally, to see if the latter can clarify the former. In particular, there are two notions that are commonly found: First, of a supernatural maturation that parallels physical growth, and second, of souls that are somehow subdivided into parts.

In many parts of Indonesia, botanical analogies are used to describe the life history of the individual. James J. Fox (1971b) describes the elaboration of metaphors of taking root, flowering, and producing fruit, that are employed in ritual language on the island of Roti in Eastern Indonesia, in order to describe the life cycle of the individual. This idealized image of growth towards a prime, followed by a dignified withering, is highly formalized.

Hints of something of the same idea can be found in Berawan ideology. Infant mortality is high, and Berawan express that by saying that the souls of children are "light" or "not strong." Parents of children under, say, one year of age often do not want them photographed for fear that somehow the picture will dislodge the child's soul.[4] Adults are not at all shy about being photographed, with one significant exception: Shamans in trance, whose souls are also in a tenuous state of connection with their bodies. Old men who stay robust in health are regarded as having particularly "strong" souls, and they are consequently asked to perform supernaturally dangerous tasks. I was told that previously if there was a need to move the heads, for instance to a newly constructed longhouse, then an old man would volunteer for the job. It was said that, being old already, he did not mind taking the risk. But there was more to it than that; the risk he took was less.

Turning to the conception of multiple souls, there are many instances reported from Borneo. For example the Dusun, a numerous people of northern Borneo, say that each person has seven souls. I. H. N. Evans (1953:70–79) reports an account offered him by an informant at Kadamaian village. The first soul, by this appraisal, dwells always with the male deity, Kinorohingan. The second returns to the sky when the individual dies, and is welded together with the first by Kinorohingan in his capacity as blacksmith. At intervals these combined souls become worn out, and Kinorohingan reforges them. Finally, however, they wear out to the point that they cannot be reworked, and Kinorohingan then makes them into winds, which he keeps in a cave. When these winds waft through the flowers in Kinorohingan's garden, they talk to each other. The third soul is the one that is most active in life. It wanders about in dreams, leaving by the big toe or the crown of the head. It may also be stolen by evil forces. At death, the third soul may appear to humans, and is prone to play tricks. But after seven days of license it must depart for the long journey to the summit of Mount Kinabalu, the highest mountain in Borneo, which lies some twenty miles to the south of Kadamaian. About the remaining four souls, Evans' informant was vague. He had heard that they became beetles. Others were of the opinion that they were transmuted into butterflies or birds, or that they become the souls of wild animals such as deer.

In effect, then, there are three souls about which definite statements were made. But even concerning them, there were differences of opinion between authorities within the village. At Sensuron, a village about thirty miles away, on the other side of Kinabalu from Kadamaian, the doctrine of the seven-part soul is found, but almost all the other details vary (Williams 1965:44). Beautiful as were the images of the first and second souls conjured up by Evans' informant, they evidently cannot claim any wide orthodoxy. Significantly, it is concerning the third soul that opinions were most firm, and it is this one that most resembles the Berawan concept of *telanak*. It is also the one that is the focus of most ritual activity.

A similar lack of concensus is found in the views of the Penan about multiple souls. They distinguish three manifestations of soul:

> . . . *sahe bok*, the soul of the hair (of the head); *sahe anak maten*, soul of pupils of the eyes; and *sahe usah*, soul of the body. The Eastern Penan have no orthodox doctrine of the soul, and reports differ on the question whether these are three separate souls or whether they are (as I take to be the preponderate view) three aspects of spiritual identity. Even by the former interpretation, however, the three types of *sahe* are not independent but live and die together, so that the *sahe* component of man may be considered as unitary. (Needham 1971:205)

Each of the three types of *sahe* has a Berawan correspondence. We noted already the association between *telanak* and the pupils of the eyes, and also the crown of the head. I was consequently interested to hear a Berawan speak, on one occasion, of *telanak tuké* (*tuké* = guts, innards). I inquired as to whether this implied a second soul, a "stomach soul". There was a division of opinion, and some desultory debate, but the answer appears to be in the negative. As an adjective, *tuké* means fat, and the context in which the expression was used was a derogatory remark about someone not present, to the effect that he had a "fat soul," that is, he was lazy and inactive. It was simply an example of the manner in which character traits are attributed to a conjunction of body and soul.

Indonesia is a cultural area of considerable ritual integrity. It comes as no surprise to find that ideas of multiplex souls found among other peoples of the region are echoed in Berawan ideology. Unfortunately, these echoes do not sharpen our vision of the concept of soul. Rather they emphasize its lack of definition, for even in those neighboring cultures that claim explicitly that the soul has several aspects there is very little doctrinal uniformity about, or ritual consequence of, the differentiation. Similar remarks apply to the growth of soul. Although clearly formulated in some Indonesian societies, the notion is weakly developed in Berawan ideology. The emphasis lies instead upon the stability of the soul, its greater tendency to slip away from young children than adults. Old men are supernaturally hardy simply because their prolonged vigor indicates that they have souls that are firmly attached. It is not that the former conception is totally inapplicable, but rather that it is not significant.

Charles Hose, who wrote about the peoples of the Baram watershed based on his service there as an administrator at the turn of the century, employs a philosophical argument to suggest that the Kayan distinguish, albeit "vaguely," between two souls:

> ... on the one hand the ghost-soul, which in a live man wanders afar, in dreams and abstractions; and on the other, the vital principle, which possesses the 'conatus in suo esse perseverandi', which is Life. As long as the latter remains in the body, the ghost-soul may return to it; but, when death is complete, the vital principle departs and the ghost-soul with it. This interpretation is borne out by the use of the word *urip*, which in common speech means 'to be alive', but may also be applied to a person recently dead, as if to mark the speaker's sense of the continuance of the personality, in spite of the death of the body. (Hose 1926:206)

But Hose's account is inconsistent: if the "vital principle" *(urip)* persists after death, and if the ghost-soul *(blua)* is merely off wandering, then we still have no understanding of what death is. Nothing differentiates the individual who is dead from one who is merely asleep. Moreover, it is unnecessary to posit a belief in two souls. The word *urip* has its counterpart in the Berawan *ulong*, to live, alive.

Using a nominal inflection of the verb, one might say that an individual "has" *mulong* (life), but that phrase would no more imply a second soul in Berawan than it would in English. Lacking any body of doctrine or ritual that turns upon a bipartite soul, we are better served by the more parsimonious statement: life is the conjunction of unitary body and soul. It remains to define the nature of that conjunction.

Illness, Dreams, and Soul Loss

The most revealing context in which to observe the conjunction of body and soul is in the diagnosis and treatment of illness. There are, in the Berawan view, three possible etiologies of illness. Two involve supernatural causes, the other does not. Of the former, one is the result of breach of a taboo, the other, the ensnarement of the soul.

Some common complaints are attributed directly to physical circumstances. Such things as skin rashes and tropical ulcers are regarded as an inconvenience of everyday life, like mosquitos, and no other attention is paid to their causality. This despite the fact that they may result in serious conditions. A tropical ulcer occurs when some small wound becomes infected, and it may spread until it becomes very ugly, painful, and debilitating. The skin disease *karap* is also called "headhunters disease" because it is so itchy as to make sleep virtually impossible, supposedly an advantage for the headhunter. Treatment for these conditions involves traditional herbal remedies, and there were formerly people known for their expertise in this lore. Western medicines, now available from government dressers, is so effective at curing these conditions that the herbal lore is now little regarded. Malicious use of toxic herbs is also known, and there will occasionally be suspicions of the use of poison if someone falls violently ill with diarrhea and vomiting. The shaman may be summoned, but only to identify, if possible, the poisoner. The action of the poison is purely physical. Normally members of the longhouse community do not accuse one another, but they are suspicious of some of their neighbors, especially the Iban.

The second etiology involves breach of a taboo. For example, there are dozens of acts that are proscribed *(ñilèng)* for the husband of a pregnant woman. Usually the symbolism of these prohibitions is obvious: He may not tie knots, or drive nails, lest he symbolically stop up the birth canal. Nor may he kill certain kinds of lizards, for fear the child is born with a birth defect, specifically lizard-like hands and feet. Infraction of these rules places the husband, wife, and child in a state of ritual danger, called in this case *palé*. There are several other states of ritual danger *(sijang, padju, tulah, parit)*, each provoked by the breach of some rule. Some rules are highly specific, such as the one about tying knots. Others are general, for instance, that children should obey their elders. Sometimes the affliction that results is predictable from the nature of the offense (although the logic proceeds in the other direction). So, if a woman is having a difficult labor, the husband will rack his brains feverishly for any oversight on his part. At other times, there is simply a heightened risk of some misfortune, an accident, attack by a dangerous wild animal, or an illness, which might happen immediately or months later. Whatever the particular affliction thought to have resulted from a breach of tabu, the only recourse is an appeal to the Creator Spirit, *Bili' Ngaputong*. Since he made the taboos at the creation, only he can alleviate their inexorable and automatic effect. If the victim has already succumbed, it is too late to do anything. But if he or she is seriously ill but still alive, then the appropriate response is to construct a shrine *(tapó)* and offer up prayers. If the condition does not improve, all that can be done is to renew the appeal; no other ritual action can bring relief.

That is, if the condition is definitely a result of a state of ritual danger. But in any serious case the alternative supernatural causation will be considered, and perhaps, nonsupernatural causes as well. This classification is of etiologies of illness and not of illnesses, and that explains why Berawan often attempt several modes of cure simultaneously, and also why they seldom decline Western medicines, even when they are confident that the cause is supernatural.

But despite the fact that in many illnesses several possible etiologies may be cited, it remains the case that in the Berawan view soul loss is the single most important cause of illness. It is the most frequently cited, the most likely to cause fatal outcome, and the one for which there is the most complex battery of defenses. In fact a major segment of Berawan religion—shamanism—is concerned with little else.

Harm does not necessarily result from a temporary absence of the soul from the body. As we noted above, the notion of the soul wandering about independently has no place in the English concept, but it is an important aspect of *telanak*. Among other things, it constitutes a theory of dreaming. In sleep, the soul may wander into spirit worlds that lie outside the usual waking experience of human beings. There are hazards in this, but there is nothing to be done to prevent it, and it is not in itself bad. On the contrary it may be useful, because it provides information about events in those other worlds. Berawan take dreams seriously. Dentan (1968) reports that the Semai of Malaya frequently discuss their dreams, and in this way deal with all manner of interpersonal tensions. In contrast, the Berawan are generally reticent about the contents of their dreams. A certain amount of folk psychiatry is accomplished through them because close kin will speak up if they have troubling dreams about one another, and I was even told that one can be fined for repeated hostile acts in someone else's dreams. But their usual import is as omens. On one occasion an elderly woman had several dreams about her father, who had died only months previously. First she dreamed that she encountered him out hunting in the forest, and then that she saw him dressed in warrior garb. Meanwhile a friend from another house sent a message to say that the dead man had appeared to him in a dream and announced his intention of returning home. Alarmed by these portents, the woman consulted a shaman. On his advice, a miniature house (*meligai*) was built to accomodate the shade, and offerings of food were put inside it so that no harm would result from the visit. But not all omens received in dreams are threatening. On another occasion, a middle-aged man dreamed that he had made a huge catch of fish. The interpretation placed upon this was that the man would achieve personal wealth. Delighted, he hastened to "own" *(puwong)* the dream by making offerings and inviting his neighbors in to drink.[5]

After an absence in dreaming, the soul should return promptly to its owner. If it be tardy, or if it is captured by some evil spirit (*tekena*, bewitched), then illness results. Precisely how so many and varied maladies are brought about by the same cause is not clearly expressed by Berawan. One interpretation offered was that soul loss, like *palé* and the other states of ritual danger, is a condition of heightened vulnerability to sickness. This view implies that the soul loss is a precondition, and that particular illnesses are due to natural causes and agencies. It is supported by two explicit items of belief. First, in cases of soul loss, as with *palé*, there is no fixed period after which sickness of a particular kind or intensity is inevitable. Sooner or later harm will befall the abandoned body, but no one can say just when. Second, most people feel that it is worth using herbal cures, and nowadays Western medicines, even when soul loss has been diagnosed. This is not simply a matter of hedging bets; the implication is that it is possible to alleviate the symptoms without removing the underlying cause. There were instances where curing rituals were conducted for a person who had already apparently recovered, and the logic of the procedure was that sickness would only recur if its preconditions were not removed. An alternative interpretation is that the type of illness depends upon the particular circumstances affecting the soul. So, for instance, people with chronic diseases are often described as having habitually truant souls, ones that return frequently enough to maintain life but not enough to produce a cure. Again, in the curing rites it is sometimes suggested that the nature of the sickness will be understood when the malevolent spirit that ensnared the errant soul is identified. There is no need to choose between these interpretations, but the former has the advantage that it explains why there has been so little resistence to Western medical techniques among the Berawan (and other upriver folk), even where shamans remain active.

Berawan concede that one does not always fall ill when asleep. Evidently the soul also wanders away from the body when the owner is awake, and the same circumstances apply as in sleep, that is, no harm results unless the soul is overlong away. This is consistent with casual attitudes about waking up sleeping people. Unlike other folk who have a theory of soul loss (Tylor 1878:5), the Berawan do not fear to disturb the body while the soul is absent, because the soul can just as well be absent from the waking body. At funerals, when no one is supposed to sleep, it is considered great sport to startle into wakefulness those who have conspicuously dozed off. The most interesting aspect of this is the relationship between soul and sensory experience. In dreams, the individual is made aware, if only hazily, of the journeyings of the soul. It is as if some thread or filament connected the two, along which messages could flow, and this is a metaphor that Berawan themselves employ. But the waking person is not conscious of the soul's whereabouts, and the first warning of danger to the soul is symptoms of sickness. Presumably the raw sensations of this world blanket out, as it were, the thinner signals arriving from the distant soul. However this is expressed, it is clear that, for the Berawan as for us, there is no direct connection between soul and consciousness.

For those who are thought to be ill because of some irregularity of the soul, curing practices center upon restoring it to the body. This is the special province of the shaman *(daiyung)*. The shaman is able, by the assistance of spirit helpers, to discover the where-abouts of the sufferer's soul, and what is detaining it. He or she may in addition be able to recover it, and so restore the patient to secure health. The curing rites and seances in which this is attempted were a frequent occurrence at Long Teru during the period of my field-work, perhaps the most common of all religious observances. This was not immediately apparent because my hosts were at first secre-tive about these sessions. It was several months before it was finally admitted that they occurred, and I was allowed to attend one. This reticence was partly due to the disapproval that missionaries had expressed in the past, an opinion that was assumed to be common to all Westerners. But more significantly, shamanism is a branch of Berawan religion that invokes, and tries to control, powers that are as dangerous as they are potentially useful. It was not until my hosts were confident that I would not do something to disrupt the sha-man, which could endanger not only his or her life, but also that of the patient and the entire community, that I was admitted. Even then I was warned not to take photographs, because the flash equip-ment of the camera might cause the spirit to depart so suddenly that the shaman would fall dead on the spot.

Often there would be seances for different people on several nights in a row, or even on the same night. On rare occasions, such as when a family suspects that it is subject to supernatural attack by someone within the community, performances are held in private in the dead of night. But almost invariably they are open to anyone who wishes to wander in, and held during the day or in the evening. This is consistent with the Berawan view that shamans cannot act maliciously. Should they attempt to do so they simply lose their powers. There are ineffective shamans, but no evil ones. Consequently, it was possible after the first few months to observe many shamanistic sessions. The first hint that one was planned was often the sight of small boys ransacking the roosts of hens for eggs, which are necessary for the offerings prepared for the spirit helpers of the shaman. Berawan allow their chickens to roam freely in the gardens around the longhouse, and finding enough eggs to keep up with the demand was often difficult.

Even in the houses that are now Christian, shamans still operate. At Long Teru there was in the early 1970s one very prestigious male shaman, Tama Ukat Sageng, and six others, three male, three female, of varying prestige and activity. At Long Jegan there were seven, of whom five were women. Aggregating the two communities, there was a ratio of one shaman for about fifty people. Among these many adepts there were considerable variations in style of operation. Most of them operate in a manner comparable to the classic examples from central Asia, described by Mircea Eliade (1964). For example, Sadi" Miri, a woman of Long Jegan, became a shaman in her thirties as a result of a prolonged illness, which was inflicted upon her as a sign that she should accept inspiration. She still suffers from the "shaman's illness" (*sakèk daiyung, sakèk* = illness). She is assisted in her performances by her husband, Sadi" Pejong, who looks after her and interprets her messages. He sets the seance in progress by strumming a special tune on a stringed instrument called *sapé,* and his wife sits with her head in her hands until a shudder passes through her body and she enters a trance. She has many spirits that come to her while she is in trance, and some choose to sing, using her body, others to dance, and others to give advice. Sometimes her words are incomprehensible, and even Sadi" Pejong is obliged to give up. But usually he can discern the spirits' message, which will be for curative measures, or rituals that should be performed. Sometimes she will attempt the recovery of a soul, and its reinsertion into the owner's body. After anything from twenty minutes to two hours, she resumes her initial posture and comes out of the trance. Invariably she appears dazed and tired.

It is not clear who or what is considered responsible for the recovery of souls. Sadí' Miri reports that the experience is, for her, very much like waking out of a dream—it is hazy and soon escapes from memory. But apparently it is her soul, along with those spirit helpers that are not at that moment in her body, that make astral journeys to locate the soul of the sick person and to wrest it away from whatever has seized it. That is why the experience is so draining for her. In this way, Sadí' Miri's style of shamanism is in accordance with the classical pattern—she is a psychopomp.

In contrast, the style of *daiyung* originated by Tama Ukat Sageng and borrowed by other shamans at Long Teru does not fit this pattern. Eliade's minimal definition of shamanism is that it is a technique of ecstasy (1964:4). By that criterion Tama Ukat Sageng, most famous of Berawan *daiyung*, was not a shaman. As he described it to me, he remained fully conscious during a seance, and was able to conduct a conversation in the normal way with anyone sitting in the room, perhaps to clarify some point about the sick person's symptoms. But in addition the room was, for him, also filled with other beings whom we could not see, spirits of all shapes and sizes, who sat beside us and between us, and to whom he talked in the language of spirits. The props that he uses are usually simple, a tray *(pǎkan)* with various offerings to the spirits, including candy, rice cakes, rice wine, and the hard-to-find eggs, now hard boiled. After the spirits have left, those sitting there may sample the candy and eggs. The remainder are hung under the eaves at the back of the family apartment. On all the occasions that I saw him perform, Tama Ukat Sageng's style was unsensational, almost inconspicuous. He merely sat beside his patient, nodding and muttering incomprehensibly to his invisible friends, and shooting the odd benign smile at us. I was told that as a younger man he engaged in a wide range of shamanistic rites, some more energetic, but that the basic format had always been the same. However that may be, he continued to command the greatest respect until the day that he died. He suffered no shaman's illness, in fact he was very seldom sick. He learned his skills from no other *daiyung*, but acquired them independently in his youth. And as we shall see below, even the manner of his passing demonstrated his charisma.

These two examples show the range of variation in personal style of operation. But beyond that, there are a host of special curing rituals that are elaborations on the basic format of each practitioner. Sometimes *daiyung* work together in teams. Sometimes their spirits decide that special apparatus must be constructed: spirit houses of various kinds *(meligai* and *beran),* swings *(ayun),* little boats *(along),* posts hung with leaves like those used in the headhunting cult *(belawing),* and barriers of vines *(rèrng).* Each has its own mystical uses.

In all of these different contexts, the *daiyung* are seen working to preserve or restore a correct relationship between souls and their owners. They constitute the focus of Berawan reactions to illness and disease, and as such they provide an answer to the universal problem of the origin of evil. The misfortunes of men largely come to them because of the malice of anonymous spirits that steal their souls. The shamans, members of the community, struggle to recover them. In this scheme of things there is little room for witchcraft, which locates the source of evil within human society. It is because of the centrality of the doctrine of souls that the Berawan have so little interest in magic. We can go one step further. The death rituals are also centered upon the soul and its fate, so that they reinforce the same tendency. It would be tendentious of me to argue that the great importance of death rites in so many phases of Berawan life, which was pointed out in chapter two, causes the cultural emphasis on shamanism and away from magic. But certainly the two institutions interlock neatly in this respect.

Terminal Soul Loss

In the end, all fatal illness is, in the Berawan view, a matter of soul loss since it is the conjunction of soul and body that brings life, and the disjunction that ends it. But it no more follows that there are no other etiologies for illness in the Berawan conception than it would in Western medicine to argue that all illness is caused by brain malfunction. Certainly, if an individual dies, we know that his or her brain waves have ceased. But not all fatal maladies begin in the brain, they just end there. Moreover, to say as we do that bodily death is brain death is not a biological statement, but a medical and legal definition, and a tricky one at that, as the celebrated case of Karen Anne Quinlan proved.[6] As we noted in connection with Hose's discussion of the "soul" versus the "life principle," what still eludes us in the conception of soul loss is the equivalent definition of death.

The death of Utan Nin, which I described in the previous chapter, was pronounced on the basis of "loss of breath." In her case, it was hardly necessary to apply any test of the condition, either by means of a feather placed on the lips or by attempting to hear any heartbeat. But in the emotion of the moment, it is not impossible to make an overly hasty pronouncement. About fifteen years before my fieldwork, a woman at Long Teru had been declared dead, and had already been placed upon the death seat when she suddenly revived. Evidently her breathing and heartbeat had been depressed, but had not actually stopped. This was recounted as an extraordinary event, but not an incomprehensible one. After all, the woman had only begun to die. It was not as if a long dead ancestor had suddenly returned to the world of the living. The interpretation that was offered was that the woman's soul had indeed departed for good, but then a powerful spirit had snatched it back from its last journey, and carried it forcibly back to its owner so that she could become the spirit's medium. Consequently the woman immediately became a shaman, and at her spirit's behest lived another ten years. It was in hope of a similar match that all the *daiyung* at Long Teru went on performing for Utan Nin to the very end, even though they knew that without unusual spirit intervention of this kind she must die.

But what is it that causes "loss of breath" to occur? If the soul can wander in dreams, and be detained for long periods with harmful but nonfatal consequences, then what is it that causes death? The unanimous and immediate answer was that if the soul continues to stray, and if eventually it strays so far that it enters the land of the dead, then at that moment the bond between body and soul is broken forever. Sadí Pejong, the headman at Long Jegan, was one of the people who gave me this answer, and he illustrated it with this story.

When he was a young man, he had been seriously ill and had lapsed into unconsciousness. He dreamed that he was paddling up the river Tinjar, and turned into a tributary stream that he later realized was the Lamat, that is, he was following the route to the land of the dead. He paddled up the stream, beached his canoe, and started up a steep hill. On top of the hill were beautiful people dressed in fine clothes, harvesting rice that shone like gold. They gestured to him to go with them, and together they descended the further side of the hill. Reaching the bottom, they were about to cross another stream when suddenly Sadi′ Pejong realized that these were spirits of the dead, and that to cross the stream would be to enter their land. So he turned away from the entrancing vision of the spirits and fled. Later he regained consciousness, and having passed the crisis of his illness, soon recovered.

We now have a clear statement of what death is in terms of the soul, of which "loss of breath" is only an epiphenomenon. In dreams, and in illness, the soul wanders away from the body into unknown spirit realms. The outcome is not fatal unless and until the soul strays so far as to arrive at the land of the dead. When that occurs, there is no longer the possibility that the soul may return to its owner. Then vital signs disappear from the body, and the process of dying has begun. Fundamentally, it is an irreversible act of the soul.

This account can now be set in contrast to my original statement of the nature of soul, which was borrowed from Needham's description of Penan conceptions of the individual: That it is the conjunction of body *(usa)* and soul *(telanak)* that constitutes a living human being. It was pointed out above that the Penan are ritually conservative, and preserve practices that have fallen into disuse among their dominant Berawan neighbors. But there is no need to argue that the statement of dogma that Needham reports is something that has been forgotten by the Berawan. Rather it is, from their point of view, irrelevant or implicit. It represents nothing more than an inversion of the conception of death. The vagueness of Berawan about the soul in life underlines the fact that it is in sickness and finally in death that the doctrine of souls comes sharply into focus.

Many years ago, W. H. R. Rivers pointed out how wrong is the commonsense view that death is one thing that must surely be experienced by all people everywhere in essentially the same way:

... on looking up any Melanesian vocabulary you will find that some form of the word *mate* is given as the equivalent of dead, and that dead is given as the meaning of *mate*. As a matter of fact, such statements afford a most inadequate expression of the real conditions. It is true that the word *mate* is used for a dead man, but it is also used for a person who is seriously ill and likely to die, and also often for a person who is healthy but so old that, from the native point of view, if he is not dead he ought to be. (Rivers 1926:40)

But the conceptual difference runs deeper even than that:

... while with us death is an event which sharply marks off one durable state from another, *mate*-ness is itself a state, rather than an event, which may last for a long time, sometimes for years. (Rivers 1926:47)

In Berawan eschatology, the difference is even more marked, because death is not so much a prolonged state as a continuing process. Notions of a journey that the soul makes in death are found in all parts of the world.[7] What is special about the Berawan case is the extension of, and the emphasis that is laid upon, the liminal phase of the soul after death. In the following chapters, it is the Berawan view of the progress of the soul that provides the key to understanding the external form of the rites.

Notes

1. There is no real reason why I should refer to the Creator Spirit as "him." The third person pronoun in Berawan does not distinguish gender. Consequently, there is no way to know whether the Berawan think of any spirit agency as male, female, or neuter. The same is true of souls. Although I am not entirely consistent about this (the Creator is an exception), I generally refer to souls and spirits as "it."

2. Rodney Needham points out to me that, in Malay, the point of a blade is called *mata*, the "eye," echoing the previously noted connection between eyes and the soul. The way that the blade is used, however, is as a mirror, the metal being brightly polished. As it was described to me, the shaman is able to catch in the blade images from the spirit world, and it is in this way that she "catches" the soul. It was not clear what the image was supposed to be: Some people thought that they would see a small image of the patient; others a minute particle, the soul in material form. Though I never saw it done, I was told that in the past shamans would sometimes

produce the "soul" in the palm of their hands, and skeptics described it as made of a small piece of wax with some fine hairs attached to it.

3. There is a Berawan term meaning a soul that makes itself visible in the form of a human being. The word is *uted*, and I think it is best glossed as "ghost." *Uted* is not a word that is heard frequently, as is *telanak*. It usually crops up in stories where a ghost appears (often not recognized as such at first) with the purpose of reminding the living to carry out their duty to provide rites of secondary treatment for the deceased. There is no equivalent in Berawan to the much more general Penan concept of *ada*, which Rodney Needham tells me means not only shade and shadow, but also invisible counterpart of material things (Needham 1964:279, personal communication). I did not ask whether Berawan were familiar with the Penan notion of *ada*.

4. In a note in the *Times Literary Supplement* (May 28 1976, p. 647), Rodney Needham points out that it is a stereotype of "primitive man," and a largely inaccurate one, that he believes that "the little black box" will steal away his "soul." Where this stereotype originated remains a mystery. Clearly, the Berawan were not familiar with photography before Westerners appeared upon the scene. It seems likely, if ironic, that they also acquired this piece of "primitive" folklore from Westerners.

5. Edward Burnett Tylor erected an entire theory of religion on the basis of dreams. He argued that a certain level of "mental evolution" was marked by the elaboration of notions of the soul and the afterlife, deduced from the common human experience of dreaming. Some of his key evidence came from Spencer St. John, who was one of the first Westerners to travel up the Baram. He visited Kayan houses in the mid reaches of the river in the 1850s. Tylor summarizes him:

> Mr. St. John says that the Dayaks regard dreams as actual occurrences. They think that in sleep the soul sometimes remains in the body, and sometimes leaves it and travels far away, and that both when in and out of the body it sees and hears and talks, and altogether has a prescience given to it, which, when the body is in its natural state, it does not enjoy. Fainting fits, or a state of coma, are thought to be caused by the departure of the soul on some distant expedition of its own. (Tylor 1878:5)

He goes on to remark:

> How like a dream is to the popular notion of a soul, a shade, a spirit, or a ghost, need not be said . . . a man who thinks he sees in sleep the apparitions of his dead relatives and friends has a reason for believing that their spirits outlive their bodies, and this reason lies in no farfetched induction, but in what seems to be the plain evidence of his senses. (Tylor 1878:5–6)

"Dayak" is a cover term frequently used to describe all the peoples of interior Borneo.

6. The case of Karen Anne Quinlan attracted much publicity. She fell into a coma in which her autonomic nervous system failed to keep her vital bodily processes functioning. It was believed that her life could not be maintained without mechanical means. However, she continued to show some minimal brain wave activity, and so to switch off the machines would technically have been murder. Her body became shriveled and the doctors concluded that there was no chance of any improvement in her condition. The parents sued for the right to remove the machines and allow her to die. After a protracted trial, they won. But when the machines were eventually turned off, she did not, contrary to medical opinion, immediately die. So she continues to be maintained partially by mechanical means. It will be a matter of the nicest technical distinctions to say how or when Karen Anne Quinlan died or will die.

7. As one example, Owen Rutter collected the following story among the Tagal Murut of northern Borneo:

> . . . when he had been ill with smallpox, he had fallen into a trance. He found himself on top of (Mount) Antulai and saw an immense log leading down the farther . . . side. He began the journey down, but awoke when he was halfway—and recovered. His wife and a number of his friends continued the descent and all of them died. (Rutter 1929:223)

This account closely resembles the one given by Sadí Pejong. Yet the Tagal Murut do not have rites of secondary treatment of the dead. What is correspondingly lacking in Tagal Murut ideology is the elaboration of the subsequent fate of the soul, after the trip down Mount Antulai is completed.

III

The Season

of

the Soul's Menace

CHAPTER FIVE

The Funeral Rites

The hectic events of the first hour after "loss of breath" is pronounced—the emotional outpouring, the preparation of the corpse,
and its enthronement—begin the rites of the funeral, which may
continue for as long as two weeks. In this chapter, I pick up the
narrative where I broke off at the end of chapter three. The funeral
is sufficiently much of a piece that it is more convenient to recount
it from start to finish. Consequently, I postpone extended analysis
until the next chapter.

Funerals vary in scale; in the amount of cash expended on
them, duration, and the number of members of the longhouse and
guests from other communities who attend. But it is important to
note that their ritual format is similar however grand or humble
they may be. We may take the funeral of Utan Nin, whose death
was described above, as typical. She was not of particularly distinguished descent, nor was her family wealthy by the standards of
upriver life. They were respectable folk of the middling sort. I refer
to her rites as an example of the average, but they were not the only
ones that I witnessed. During fieldwork, I attended nine funerals in
all, of which five were full-scale events for adults, as opposed to the
much briefer ones for children. Of these five, two were at Long
Teru, two at Long Jegan, and one at Batu Belah. They were sufficiently uniform that it is possible to offer a generalized account.

Discussing Arrangements

After the corpse is installed on the death seat (tèlorèn), a meeting of
all interested parties is held to make the necessary arrangements,
and to go over details of the ritual so there shall be no confusion

71

later. At Utan Nin's funeral, the meeting was convened immediately that her body was in place, and while it was still being dressed and hung about with valuables. A quiet corner of an adjacent apartment was chosen, away from the bustle around the corpse. The talk was rapid, restrained, and purposeful. The participants, perhaps thirty in all, sat close together on the mat-covered floor, so as not to miss what was being said. The principal speakers at first were two men, close kin of Utan Nin, who had evidently decided to take on a major share of the organization of the event. Responsibility does not devolve upon any one person or category of persons, instead it is diffused among the whole range of affinal and consanguineal relatives. It sometimes occurs that someone closely related to the deceased hangs back, for his own reasons, and allows others to take the lead. Conversely, individuals more distantly related may push themselves forward, for instance if they wish to use the occasion for display and political maneuver. Tama Aweng, Utan Nin's husband, had his say, but he would not be able to play much part in organizing the event because he would be rendered immobile and incommunicado by the prescriptions of mourning laid upon him. As the discussion developed, it was increasingly a senior woman of the house, Biló Kasi, who held the floor. As widow of the most important leader of the community in the postwar period, and a woman of strong character in her own right, her opinion as to what was proper in this case held weight, even though she was not closely related to Utan Nin. In short order it was decided that the wake would last five days, and that only a few people would be invited from other houses. Secondary treatment *(nulang)* was out of the question. The only substantive area of disagreement concerned the container to be used for Utan Nin's body. Strict adherence to custom would have prohibited the use of a large jar in this case, because the death had been an ugly one, involving a slow wasting away, almost as if corruption had begun even before death occurred.[1] But Utan Nin, months before her death, had badgered her husband, unsuccessfully, to make provision for this day by obtaining a suitable jar. Having failed to comply with her wishes previously, he wanted now to find a jar. As it happened, there was one available, and it was argued that it would be much quicker to put the corpse, already wasted as it was, into the jar than to complete the heavy

Plate 3. A later stage in the funeral shown in plates 1 and 2. Utan Nin's body has been inserted in the jar, which sits at the foot of the *tèlorèn*, draped with the skirt and other fine fabrics that previously decorated the corpse, and hung about with beads and jewelry. Her daughter continues the vigil, and her husband is still inside his cubicle of mats.

work of constructing a coffin from a solid log. This argument won the day, but not without misgivings in some quarters. As the meeting broke up, messengers were sent to summon people back from the remote farms. Some would come immediately; others would wait until the all-important last night of the wake. But they would all appear sooner or later, even for a modest funeral of this kind.

The Widow's Wall

Having attended this meeting, Tama Aweng began the long incarceration inflicted upon widows and widowers alike. The "prison" (*diching biló; diching* = wall, *biló* = widow) is made of mats stood on edge, fencing off a little piece of floor next to the longitudinal wall of the longhouse directly in front of the corpse (see plate 3). The mats stand about five feet high and enclose an area too small to allow the spouse to lie down comfortably to sleep, or even to stretch the legs out straight when sitting up. In fact it is specifically tabooed for the widower or widow to sit with his or her legs straight out in front. These uncomfortable arrangements are maintained for as many as eleven days, when an important person has died. Moreover, only the poorest rations are provided for the bereaved spouse: sago served in half a coconut shell, and water. It is not surprising that the victims are often unable to walk when they finally emerge, because of cramped limbs and general weakness. There are other discomforts too. They are not allowed to wash themselves, a privation keenly felt by the Berawan. They must wear filthy clothes. They must defecate through a hole in the floor inside their tiny cubicle. In the midday heat, the unventilated cell becomes stifling. Finally, they may not talk to anyone except unmarried young people of their own sex, and then only sparingly. A hole about eight inches in diameter is their only view into the outside world, and it faces directly at the dead person.

An event some years ago at Long Teru caused the partial relaxation of these rules. An elderly woman died, and her sick husband was cooped up as custom prescribed. After four days, and without having voiced any complaint, the husband expired also. This double death shocked public sentiment, for, as we shall see in the next chapter, the ordeal of the spouse is designed to avert death, not cause it. Thereafter the spouse's ability to cope with the physical trials of incarceration has been taken into account. Women who have been widowed twice are not cooped up. But still they must stay near the corpse all the time that it is in the house, wear dirty clothes, eat poor food, and refrain from washing, and talk to people only in a reserved manner.

The discomfort of other kinsmen is much less than that of a spouse. The children of a deceased person, in particular the eldest and the youngest child, are next most hedged about by taboos. They eat a restricted diet, maintain a sober bearing at all times, and spend most of their time near the corpse. But they can drink coffee, smoke, and go out of the house briefly to wash and defecate. They may also talk, but not laugh or joke. Other close relatives follow the same restrictions with varying degrees of conscientiousness. Siblings and parents, if still alive, may be caught in a dilemma, wishing at once to observe the mourning usages and also to assist in the work of the funeral. A brother, for instance, might want to lend a hand in the preparation of the mausoleum. The death restrictions bear only lightly upon more distant relatives, who laugh and play games, eat all the foods that are prepared for the guests at the wake, and go in and out of the house freely. They observe only the minimal restrictions that apply to the entire community: no dancing, no singing of songs other than death songs, and no engagement in ritual or festivities unrelated to the funeral.

Soon after the corpse is seated on the veranda, a sewing machine is certain to appear, together with a hoard of coarse white cloth that may have been kept in store for months. Relays of women fashion loose simple garments for the bereaved family to wear: baggy shirts and trousers for the men, blouses and sarongs for the women, and narrow headbands made from white material. By the end of the funeral, these clothes are dirty and worn out. The widow or widower wears clothes that are dirty to begin with, often an old mosquito net crudely stitched together.

Why these trials are visited upon the close kin is an issue to be taken up in the next chapter. Meanwhile, there are two sociological questions that are best dealt with briefly here: Who are the "close kin"? And why is it the spouse that is singled out for the principal role?

I was never provided with a set of rules for who precisely must wear the white clothes of mourning, or how long it is permissable for a person of a given relationship to be absent from the longhouse while the funeral is in progress. There is a measure of freedom for personal choice, and moreover, individuals vary in the rigor with which they observe the prohibitions. But basically, the "close kin" are, first, the parents, siblings and children of the deceased, and second, the coresidents of the family apartment *(ukuk)*. Between these two groups there is often considerable overlap. If the deceased is an adult woman, then her mother, father, unmarried siblings, and children may very well also be coresidents, because of the frequency of uxorilocal marriage. For the same reason, if there are grandparents alive, the maternal ones may also be *ukuk* members, and so adopt the white garb, whereas the paternal are probably not, and will refrain. The husband may be the only nonconsanguineous relative to enter full mourning. If the deceased is an adult male, his parents and siblings are likely to be living in other apartments, perhaps even another longhouse. If the *ukuk* group into which he married is large, then some of its members may choose not to wear mourning clothes. For instance, his wife's mother will do so, while his wife's mother's husband may not, unless there was a close bond of affection between the two men.

What these two categories of people represent are the principles of blood and residence. It is not difficult to see why, in a cognatic society, all first degree relatives are considered close kin. Regarding the latter category, we must remind ourselves that the *ukuk* coresidents comprise the only corporate groups in Berawan society, other than the longhouse communities themselves. Moreover, Berawan lay stress on the commensal aspect of the *ukuk* group. It sometimes occurs that what appears to be one apartment within the longhouse contains, by Berawan reckoning, two or even three *ukuk*. What this signifies is that the people living within the same physical space do not in fact share one store of food, but instead make separate farms. It usually occurs because an elderly couple have several married children living within their room at once. The parents attach themselves to one or other of their children for farming and sharing food. When, in due course, a new longhouse is constructed, the old apartment will spawn two or three adjacent rooms in the new structure.

In the words of Robertson Smith, there is "a connection thought to exist between common nourishment and common life" (1885:177), so that commensality creates a bond similar to consanguinity. This principle of common substance affects all the members of the *ukuk* group. But no relationship is closer than that between husband and wife; they share more than the same rice pot, to a great extent they share the same life. Hence the special role of the spouse in mourning. It is a feature of mourning in societies the world over, whether or not they posses unilineal descent groups, and everywhere its roots lie in the cosubstantiality of husband and wife.[2] In Berawan society it is reinforced by the makeup of the *ukuk* group, in which links through marriage play a predominant role. In affective terms, Berawan expect marital relationships to be close, and also, unfortunately, stormy, much as Westerners do.

The Days and Nights of the Wake

In the first twenty-four hours, the rhythm of the funeral period is established. The house steadily fills with people, and becomes noisy both day and night.

As new mourners arrive, they go directly to the corpse surrounded by its finery. There the women keen in the formal manner described above, and often they are joined by other women who happen to be nearby, so that the chorus of dirges is constantly renewed throughout the days of the wake. The flow of arrivals is augmented by relatives from other communities and often some inquisitive Iban from nearby houses.

During the day only close kin remain near the corpse continuously. Others keep them company from time to time, and then wander off to attend to their tasks. Teenagers and older children amuse themselves playing the gongs and drums that are set up near the body. The close relatives, being largely confined to the longhouse, must rely heavily upon more distant kin and other longhouse residents to take care of the major work. Almost every adult in the house will somehow contribute labor or assistance at the funeral of an important person, and even for lesser men, each household within the longhouse will be sure to send some help. The men are largely absent from the house during the day, off preparing the coffin, fetching food and stores from the farms or the nearest Chinese shops, and building the tomb. The women are engaged around the house preparing rice wine *(borèk)*, cooking meals to be served to the guests in the evening, and attending to the chores of the household. Those for whom the pace of activity has been too much are meanwhile trying to nap in the quietest corners that they can find.

For the nights are not restful. At my first Berawan funeral I was told flatly that no one may sleep at night while the corpse is in the house. The rule is never completely observed. Children and the sick are absolved, and there are always those who simply stay in their rooms at night. Also, napping on the veranda near the corpse is perfectly allowable. At Utan Nin's funeral, the gatherings were poorly attended for the first couple of nights. There was a lot of work to do at the farms, and many people delayed their return to the longhouse. On the third day people began to flood back into the house, and the nightly vigils took on a less mournful air. At the funeral of an important person, a high percentage of the community will be seated on the veranda adjacent to the corpse every evening, and bright pressure lamps burn all night.

There is nothing solemn about these large gatherings. In fact, it is *de rigueur* to make them as festive as possible. Berawan say that the community's duty is to entertain the dead person during the last hours in his or her home, and to beguile the kin in their grief. People sit chatting in circles, or engage in games and tomfoolery. The young girls are often conspicuous in these antics since they have license to rub soot from the bottoms of cooking pots onto the faces of unwary bystanders. Partly this is a religious usage, since it is judged appropriate that everyone at a funeral have a smudged or dirty face and clothes. So the game consists of ambush by the young girls and retaliation by the men, and no one may take offense at these attacks. There is also an element of flirtation in these frivolities, and funerals are a recognized opportunity for young men and women to meet their peers from other villages. The older folk applaud these sallies, and rice wine is passed around among the crowd.

Another major activity of the nights is the singing of the death songs. The nature and content of these important songs will be the subject of chapter twelve. Suffice it here to say that while many of them have a serious ritual purpose, others are more in the nature of games or competitions. Between songs, the large drums (*genèng*) used only at funerals may be played, together with an ensemble of gongs which are hung from a special frame. Card games are also popular at these vigils. Coffee and cookies are served at regular intervals. In this way the party often manages to remain lively until two, three, or even later in the morning. Towards dawn, however, only the staunchest remain jovial. The majority are napping on the mats on the veranda or blearily playing cards. The lively ones wake up the sleepers as they see fit, or play jokes upon them. One is called "fishing," and involves trying to lower a piece of putrescent pork tied onto a thread into the open mouths of snoring sleepers.

When the first rays of the sun illuminate the veranda, the party ends in a final burst of noise as those who have persevered all night let the slowly stirring longhouse know of their fortitude.

The Status of the Deceased and the Length of the Wake

The diurnal cycle of work and play may continue for more than a week in the case of a person of some age and respectability. Toward the end of that time, the people principally involved begin to take on a zombie-like air, and sheer physical exhaustion provides an effective palliative for emotional stress.

At Long Teru and Batu Belah, the corpse may remain in the house no longer than ten nights and eleven days. But normally eight nights would be considered sufficient, since modesty would prohibit taking the maximum time allowable. However, should the mausoleum not be ready on the morning of the ninth day, then a further extension of two nights on grounds of necessity would not excite unfavorable comment. For people of lesser status, shorter funeral rites are appropriate. Four or five nights within the house would be sufficient for a man or women of no particular distinction, but of respectable family. All this implies that status is fixed, and it is merely a matter of figuring out the appropriate time for each individual. This is an oversimplification, since the length allotted for a funeral is one way of negotiating status. But the generalizations will serve for present purposes.

Less than four nights in the house, assuming that the deceased was an adult, would clearly indicate a person of inferior status: an incorrigible reprobate or descendent of a slave. No such funeral occurred during the fieldwork. For Utan Nin, the period selected was five nights.

At Long Jegan, initial death rites last a maximum of eight nights, but if a mausoleum is not quite completed they can be extended for another eight, and in theory at least, another eight after that and so on. If it is decided to perform the rites of secondary treatment, then such extensions are unnecessary, since the corpse simply goes into temporary storage after eight nights.

A child's funeral is much simpler than an adult's. Two nights in the house would normally suffice, allowing enough time for the preparation of a simple grave and a coffin fashioned from planks. For an infant of less than a year of age, who has barely taken on a social personality, the corpse remains in the house overnight only, and is taken off to the graveyard without pomp at dawn. Its passing is barely noticed by the community as a whole.

Jars, Coffins, and Corpses

The corpse does not stay on the death seat for the duration of the initial rites. One night is sufficient to comply with custom, but two are not uncommon. Delays in removing the corpse from the *tèlorèn* are usually for practical reasons, such as failure to complete the coffin, or tardiness of mourners in returning to the house. However, as the days go by the urgency increases, for the corpse needs to be placed inside a container before it reaches the condition known as *melarak*, when the flesh begins to sag away from the skeleton.

Work begins on the coffin *(lungong)* as soon as possible after death occurs. It is a laborious task since the coffin must be carved from a solid log—a practice designed to make them sturdy and durable. A work party goes off into the jungle to select a hardwood tree of suitable size, at least three feet in diameter. A chicken is sacrificed before work begins. After felling, a section about eight feet long is selected and roughly worked *in situ*. This is in order to reduce the weight of the log for easier portage. A team of at least six men is needed to carry it to the longhouse, where it is first hollowed out in much the same way as is a canoe. Indeed, the coffin is a boat, for the journey of the dead is a voyage, but this symbolic identification is not emphasized by Berawan as it is among other Bornean peoples. Having cut out a recess sufficient to hold the corpse, the outside is shaped so as to leave the sides and bottom at least two inches thick. A top is fashioned from a separate plank. Coffins are usually rectangular in plan and cross section, with the corners chamfered. Time does not allow of any elaborate, carved design on them. After the corpse is inserted, they are often painted with simple scrollwork designs, or covered with a valuable cloth.

If the corpse is to be put in a jar *(sitong)*, it is necessary first to cut the jar at its "shoulder" or widest point (see plate 4). Several ingenious methods for doing this have been described (Hose and McDougall 1912:II:49). The Berawan method is simply to chip away slowly at the pot using an iron chisel, repeatedly working around the circumference. In this way the jar can usually be cut cleanly. The Berawan do not make glazed ware of their own, and jars for mortuary purposes have been obtained for more than a century by trade with the coast. Many are of Chinese manufacture. Some are old and valuable, with elaborate designs. But cheaper jars are also available, even of the biggest variety. A Chinese pottery on the coast near the mouth of the Baram River makes jars large enough for primary storage of a corpse, and the cost is modest, about Malaysian $30 (U.S. $12). Jar burial is consequently not, as has been suggested, the prerogative of the rich (Moulton 1912:94). Old jars are often found in longhouse apartments, and many have a utilitarian function such as storage of rice wine. But sometimes one is kept upside down, indicating that it is being saved for the funeral of some elderly member of the household. Old people are comforted by the notion that their jar is ready, but will sometimes part with it if there is a need, on the condition that it be replaced as soon as someone can be sent to the coast to purchase another.

Before the corpse is put into the coffin or jar, the valuable things that it has been wearing are removed, such as the beads and golden jewelry, but it retains the fine clothes in which it was dressed soon after death occurred. Usually the only things put in the coffin or jar with the corpse are some small, crudely carved statuettes about six inches long, representing male and female figures (*butong lamulong, butong* = figurine, *lamulong* = human). An important man may have as many as eight, a lesser person one or two. Berawan offer no explanation for this usage. One may hypothesize that it is a survival of a former practice of sacrifice of slaves to accompany the dead person to the afterlife, concerning which I shall have more to say in chapter seven.

A gong is sounded as the body is inserted in the coffin or jar.

Plate 4. Jars inside an old mausoleum. The fine fabrics and rattan lashings in which they were once covered have rotted away, to reveal how the jars were cut at the shoulder to allow insertion of the corpse. The thick beads of damar used to reseal the cut are still in place, as are the plates used to close the mouths of the jars. The jar on the right is smaller because it houses the remains of a child. The mausoleum contained seven such jars in all.

Coffins are constructed so that the corpse may lie on its back without being cramped. For insertion in a jar, the knees are tucked up under the chin, the arms folded flat against the chest, and the head allowed to fall forward onto the knees. Strips of cloth are used to tie the limbs in these positions. Usually the corpse can then be slipped easily into the jar, but occasionally the jar is too narrow at its base to allow the feet to fit in properly, and it may then be necessary to cut the tendons at the heel with a sharp knife so that the feet can be folded upwards against the shins. The top half of the jar can then be placed over the head and shoulders and tied on securely with rattan or wire. A plate is used to close the mouth of the jar, and likewise secured with bands of rattan. Finally all holes and seams are sealed by a liberal application of damar gum. Coffins are similarly lashed shut with rattan bands, and carefully sealed with damar.

The valuables that were stacked around the corpse remain in place, and food continues to be put in the plate, now sitting on the coffin or beside the jar.

It is entirely possible that in former times less care was taken to seal up coffins and jars. P. C. B. Newington offers this recollection of a visit to a longhouse of the Tabun people, once neighbors of the Berawan to the north who shared similar mortuary practices:

> In 1912 I came across the last of the Tabuns, a dying race. This was in the Madalam River, or Madahit (I forget which; it was so long ago). The old chief had died and they had him sitting in a large jar, the neck of which had been removed. He was squatting with his knees up to his chin,—what was left of him, —and had been dead for weeks. All the same, he occupied the place of honour alongside the family cooking place. Most of his flesh had gone and his skull, which rested on his knees, had the eye sockets stopped up with boiled rice. His condition did not allow me to remain long in the house; and his son was the last (aristocrat) of the group. He was sick too. He said the house was built on *tanah panas* ("hot land") and was unhealthy; but more likely the "heat" was produced by the juices of his father, which ran down a bamboo pipe from the bottom of the jar, into the earth below the house, where the domestic pigs were rooting about . . . (Newington 1961:107)

Newington's memory may have been faulty, but it is not likely that he would have mistaken the condition of the corpse, or its position inside a jar. Many details are similar to Berawan practice. At Batu Belah and Long Teru the option existed of keeping a corpse inside the longhouse to await secondary treatment, instead of removing it to the graveyard, provided that it was stored in a large jar. The jar was equipped with a drain tube, just as Newington describes, running from a hole in the bottom of the jar to a sump in the ground below. This alternative has not been employed at Long Teru since the 1950s, probably because of the disapproval expressed by government officials. The jar that Newington saw had clearly been cut at the shoulder to allow insertion of the corpse, just as are Berawan jars.

Hertz (1960:32) admonishes us not to impute to Borneans our notions of hygiene. Nevertheless, it was not my experience that contemporary Berawan are indifferent to the sight and odor of corruption. There was a definite anxiety about getting a corpse securely stowed in a jar or coffin. The bottoms of coffins are often filled with concoctions of earth and ashes designed to soak up the products of decomposition and prevent their escape. The Long Jegan folk are particularly skilled at preparing these compositions because it was their practice to keep coffins inside the longhouse awaiting secondary treatment. Unlike jars, wooden coffins were prone to rot, especially as they were not fitted with drain tubes. But the sturdy construction of coffins and the liberal use of damar usually prevents the escape of any foul odor. At only one of the funerals that I attended was any smell noticeable, and it was a source of embarrassment to the close kin. People wrinkled their noses, and tried not to sit too close to the coffin.[3]

No early traveler in the Tutoh or Tinjar Rivers reports seeing decomposing corpses openly displayed in Berawan longhouses in the manner that Newington describes. But even if Berawan have always been as fastidious as they are now about stowing them away before corruption is too noticeable, it remains the case that they keep around the house for extended periods corpses that have not been preserved in any way. This is enough to indicate sensibilities unfamiliar to Westerners. As we shall see, the process of corruption itself has for them mystical connotations.

The Climax of the Funeral: Ichem Mugé, *Entombment,* *and* Liang Kijí"

Tardy mourners continue to arrive until the final and most important night of the funeral, *ichem mugé* (*ichem* = night, I could elicit
no meaning for *mugé*). The festivities are more hectic than previous
nights and continue unabated until dawn. The crowd on the veranda is larger than before. Activities are much the same as previous
nights, except that the death songs are more important. They climax on this night with an important sequence of songs whose
function is to bring the soul of the deceased to the land of the dead.
They are described in chapter twelve. At Long Jegan no death songs
of any kind are sung during funerals; they are reserved for *nulang*
only.

Food, comprising rice, fish, and pork is served once or twice
during the night, and coffee and cookies between times. At the
funerals of important men a large pig may be sacrificed just before
dawn, and its meat used at the banquet that precedes the departure
of the corpse for the graveyard. This special pig must be white in
color, and its spirit is charged with carrying a message to the ancestors, imploring their protection. In addition a pair of chickens may
be sacrificed, one white and one black, and charged with the same
errand. Nowadays, at the funerals of government-appointed chiefs
(penghulu), occasions when there are likely to be dignitaries from
other villages present, formal speeches are made eulogizing the dead
man. Sometimes there is one purporting to have been written by the
dead man, in formal Malay, urging tolerance and justice in the
affairs of men, almost as if the dead man had already achieved his
place as spirit guardian and arbiter. To balance these prim sentiments, there is throughout the night heavy drinking and people
may get thoroughly drunk, even to the point of quarreling.

At dawn the men primarily involved in the work of the funeral
summon their energies for a final effort. They have to prepare the
barge that will carry the coffin or jar to the graveyard, and the ramp
down which it will be carried, for the corpse may not leave the
house by the ordinary exists. The ramp *(achīn)* is a light structure,
about ten feet wide, leading from the veranda in front of the coffin

or jar to the ground at an angle of 45 degrees or less. It is made out of poles cut from the jungle, with lateral pieces lashed on to form steps. Above it, leading from the veranda right to the river bank, is stretched a long white cloth. From the foot of the ramp to the water's edge, a line of inverted gongs is placed on which the pall-bearers will step as they go down to the funeral barge. The ramp is sometimes built the day before the corpse is due to leave if an early start is desired on the day itself.

For transporting the cortege to the graveyard a stable vessel is constructed by lashing three canoes together side-by-side, using beams that run across their gunwales. The barge (*magun* or *kenaga-din*) is equipped with a canopy of white cloth supported on a bamboo frame, also red and white triangular flags on poles raked aft at about 60 degrees, a large elaborate banner painted with curlicue designs that will later be hung on the mausoleum, and various gongs to make a noise with as the vessel goes to the graveyard. Nowadays the *magun* is propelled with an outboard motor.

Meanwhile, in the house the women are preparing the final large meal before the departure of the deceased, and the guests are drinking coffee, bathing, and otherwise trying to revive themselves. A brief rite performed at this time is called *kanan biau* (*kanan* = food, I could elicit no gloss for *biau*). Cooked rice is sprinkled on the veranda, and thrown around playfully by the guests. Berawan had no explanation to offer for this custom, but they claimed that previously, presumably in some golden age of wealth, rice was thrown about by the potful until the walls were white with it. *Kanan biau* is a ritual of excess, intended to ensure abundance by extravagance.

When all the preparations for moving the coffin or jar have been completed, the last large meal of the funeral is served. The food is laid out in trays, running in a straight line along the veranda, and it is at this moment that the size of the funeral is judged and recorded in peoples' minds. Sometimes there may be as few as fifty people sitting there. But on grand occasions Berawan will proudly report that the double line of seated male guests (people sit on either side of the row of trays) went the full length of the longhouse veranda—a truly impressive congregation. After the men have eaten, the trays are cleared, and an identical display is set out for the women. It is this meal that constitutes the death feast.

At Utan Nin's funeral things had begun slowly, but on that final morning about two-thirds of the entire community must have been present to share in the corporate meal. There were few outsiders. The final death song had dragged on into the morning, and it was nearing noon. As the trays were cleared away after the meal, preparations began to move the jar out of the house. The crowd became more animated, the great funeral drum was played for the last time, and tension began to mount. A section of the balustrade along the outer side of the veranda was hastily smashed down with axes, so as to allow access onto the ramp, and a number of men, not close relatives of Utan Nin, began to pick up the jar. The wailing at this time was the most unrestrained heard during the funeral, more emotional even than that which had occurred in the minutes after death. Nerves were strained by the many sleepless nights, and, moreover, the crowd was now much larger than on the previous occasion, and packed in close together on the veranda, so that the effect of the emotional outpouring was correspondingly greater. As the sweating pallbearers struggled to get a firm grip on their heavy and cumbersome burden, they were obstructed by the crowd. A man standing nearby decided to secure the blessings of the deceased for the small children hanging onto their parents or peeking between the legs of the grownups. He grabbed up a child and waved him round above the jar, calling out a prayer to the ancestors to protect the tot from harm. Then he swung around and plucked up another, and after that another, so that the wails of the alarmed children joined those of their elders. No sooner had the jar finally been lifted up than a woman relative threw herself on top of it, screaming that she could not bear to be parted from her loved one in this fashion. Berawan express the sentiment that it is unkind to remove their dead relatives from the house, and cite this motivation in justification of their extended funerals. The pallbearers, struggling to maneuver in a confined space against such opposition, reported that the jar seemed at that moment animated by a will of its own, pulling this way and that, as if unwilling to depart.[4] In all the confusion, the jar was picked up and put down several times, and turned around, so that there was little chance of keeping track of whether the corpse was leaving face forward or not (see plate 5).

The jar was preceded down the ramp by young men carrying the grave goods, and a large iron pot containing smoldering brands, the stated purpose of which is to keep the corpse warm in transit to the graveyard. The jar emerged finally from the longhouse, and was carried as rapidly as possible to the waiting barge, trailing a procession of weeping women. A man standing atop the river bank fired off repeated blasts with his shotgun. Others threw ashes into the air in the wake of the jar so that the soul of the deceased would not be able to see its way back to the longhouse. Only a small company climbed into the canoes to escort the body to the grave-yard. The rest, including most close kin, stood on the bank and watched the barge move off. Then they slowly dribbled back to the longhouse, where Tama Aweng was still cooped up in his house of mats, hardly aware of what had been going on.

As it went along the river, the barge was made to loop around three times, turning through a full circle while moving away from the house. This device, called *pusing naga* (*pusing* = revolve, *naga* = water dragon; both words borrowed from Malay, though the latter is of Sanskrit origin), like the screen of ashes, is designed to make it harder for the soul to find its way back. The party in the barge was extremely noisy, drinking and beating gongs all the way to the graveyard. They said that this was to avoid hearing or seeing any adverse signs from the omen birds (see plate 6).

The graveyard to which the barge was headed is on the banks of the Bunut stream (see map 5). Long Teru is exceptional in having cemeteries upriver from the longhouse, and in having several in use simultaneously. The most prestigious is on a small island in the middle of the large lake that lies inland behind the house. It is used only by those descended from important people of the Lelak, the original inhabitants of the area around Long Teru, now assimilated into Berawan society and culture. The one on the Bunut stream, which leads out of the lake, is used by families that remember their Lelak heritage, but who are not of noble lineage. A third cemetery on the Chet stream is used by people of purely Berawan descent, people whose ancestors immigrated to Long Teru from Batu Belah. Yet a fourth is located just upriver from the longhouse on the opposite bank. It has the advantage of being much the most easily accessible, and is consequently used for burying children. But there

Plate 5. Utan Nin's jar leaves the longhouse on the morning after *ichem mugé*. The bearers in the foreground are stepping carefully on the ramp to avoid slipping with their heavy load. At the top right, two women are being restrained from holding back the departing jar.

are also one or two grand funeral edifices there, because of the prominent location. When one of the graveyards on a side stream is used, it is necessary to clear out of the watercourse, which is in places very narrow, all the driftwood that obstructs it, so that the wide funeral barge may pass freely. After a freshet, or alternatively when the water level is low, the rivers can become clogged with debris, so that it is difficult to get to the lake even in a single canoe. Clearing out a path is then a major chore for the menfolk during the funeral, involving hundreds of man-hours of work. The principal graveyard of Long Jegan is just downriver from the longhouse, and always easily accessible (see plate 7).

On this occasion, a recent rain had raised the level of the water just enough to make the passage easy, and in an hour or so the canoes arrived at the graveyard, which had been carefully cleared of brush all around the tomb. A handrail had been prepared to make it easier to climb up the muddy river bank. Sometimes a sacrifice is made beside the mausoleum, if there are already occupants, so as to avoid provoking their ire, and also to dedicate major new edifices. But Utan Nin's tomb was a simple vault, albeit constructed with concrete sides and floor. Her jar was inserted, with a long strand of rattan tucked underneath it and leading up out of the tomb. The grave goods were tucked in around the sides of the jar: A wide sun hat, a *parang* (work knife and sword), a paddle, and some cooking pots—all things that Berawan would normally put into a canoe when going on a journey. I have also seen tin trunks with cloth in them, china, and all manner of possessions of which the deceased was fond, put into the grave. Sometimes small wooden replicas are substituted for real *parang* and shields. Pots and china are always chipped or broken before insertion in the mausoleum.

When the contents of the vault were organized, planks were placed across the top and a concrete slab poured over it. Meanwhile, other people were hanging up the banner that was previously on the barge, using a tree near the grave. The long bamboos with their red and white pennants were staked into the ground around the tomb, so as to make a brave show when viewed from the river. Finally, when all was ready, all those who had gone to the graveyard took hold of the strip of rattan leading down through the soft concrete to the jar. Together they pulled it out and went straight on down to the canoes to return home. The name of this rite explains its purpose: *kilan telanak mulei*, "to pull the souls back." The return trip was quieter than the trip out, but there was still a little something to drink tucked away in the canoes, and everyone had to be thoroughly splashed by his companions to separate them from the contact with the dead.

When the graveyard party arrived back at the house, they found it silent in contrast to its former confusion. Many people had left already, so as to avoid being caught inside the longhouse by the taboos of the following day. Those who had stayed at the house had cleaned up the veranda, throwing out all the things associated with the funeral, such as the timbers of the death seat, and all the bedding and clothes used by Utan Nin during her long illness. The ramp had been thrown down too, and all this rubbish lay in a heap in front of the house. Later it was thrown into the river to drift away. But the valuable objects still stood outside Tama Aweng's apartment, and he himself was still inside his mat house. That night a very small crowd collected on the veranda to keep him and his children company, a mere handful, but they kept lamps burning all night. As always, there were one or two who wanted to drink and engage in horseplay, but the great majority wanted only to sleep. The night is called *ichem nitèng* (*ichem* = night, *nitèng* = damar). Damar is used to seal up gaps, and so the implication of the phrase is that the dead should be properly sealed up in the tomb. The gathering, such as it was, was explicitly to protect Tama Aweng and his children.

The next day, the final day of *patai*, the funeral, is called *liang kijí*. Usually it follows directly after *ichem nitèng*, but sometimes a day is allowed to elapse between them. The name is difficult to gloss. *Kijí* means simply great or big. *Liang* is used to describe a gun that fails to shoot game, or a hunting dog that suddenly loses its skill. The basic notion seems to be inactivity, for *liang kijí* is a day when normal activities are greatly circumscribed. Most importantly, no one is allowed to leave or enter the house from the first trace of dawn until the following morning. Large white flags are hung up at the landing places in front of the house, a signal widely used in the Baram district to indicate that stopping is taboo. If strangers, such as Chinese from the lumber camps, enter the house or so much as touch the landing stage, they will be obliged to pay a fine on the spot.[5] A community member, or a Berawan from another house, who commits the same indiscretion is in more serious trouble. It is felt that he should know the custom, and that the insult is therefore intentional, and in theory he may be fined the entire cost of the funeral! Berawan who are traveling up or downriver are expected to stay close to the opposite bank and make no noise as they pass. Those within the house must remain quiet: they may not gather in large groups, laugh, chatter noisily, or play transistor radios. Children are hushed if they cry, and yapping dogs chased away. People may bathe only on their own, never more than one person at the same landing, and they must enter the water slowly, without diving. *Liang kiji'* is a day of silence. No one may touch a sun hat, a paddle, or a canoe. The structure of the longhouse takes on a different character. Normally so noisy, it seems now to brood at the edge of the jungle, like a place abandoned. That night, people gather outside the dead person's room only to talk in a subdued manner. *Liang kiji'* is not observed for children.

The following day is called *liang umī* (*umī* = small, little). On this day only the immediate family of the deceased go on observing the taboos of the day before. The widow or widower is finally released from the house, and allowed to wash, but the description of that rite belongs to chapter eight.

Notes

1. Berawan had no explanation to offer for why jars are not allowed to those who die in this way. It is not, as noted below, because there is any association between upper class people and the use of jars. My understanding of the matter is as follows: Previously, when corpses were put in jars, it was often because it was planned to keep the corpse on the veranda of the longhouse during primary storage. But people who have died ugly deaths are dangerously similar to the bad dead (see chapter fourteen), that is, their souls are especially malicious. Consequently it is not good to have their bodies stored within the house, but better to remove them as far as possible from the living.

2. For example, Christopher Crocker (personal communication) reports that the Bororo of Brazil are fascinated by their observation that couples who have been married for many years come to resemble one

another, as if they were siblings. Like the Berawan, they assign the major role in mourning to the spouse.

3. A similar set of attitudes are reported among the Penan of the Kemena River, who have been in contact with the Berawan of Long Jegan for at least a century (Yap 1963:95–6). One group of them claims to be descended from an ancestor who was found in a durian fruit. Consequently, they claim, the corpses of their dead smell like durian, and this is a source of pride because people are willing to sit near their coffins. This state of affairs they contrast to the shame of having people avoid the funeral because of bad smells emanating from a coffin. Durian has a strong smell, which many people unfamiliar with the fruit find unpleasant. But it is a great favorite in Southeast Asia. This group of Penan use the timber of the valuable durian tree to make their coffins, and the same practice occurred among the Berawan of Long Jegan as a mark of elite status.

4. Coffins that run about in the night are a familiar theme of Berawan folklore, and I am told that the Kajaman people on the Belaga River carve feet on the coffin, thereby making the notion specific.

5. The irreverent now make a sport of this, cheerfully dunning any non-Berawan passerby who happens to fail to see the frequently small and dirty white flags. The usual fine is Malaysian $15. In former times the matter was taken more seriously.

CHAPTER SIX

The Ambiguity of Death

The great day of silence, so much in contrast with what went before, brings the funeral to a close. With the whole sequence of public rituals now in view, from illness through "loss of breath," to (at least temporary) storage in the graveyard, it is time for interpretation. The analytical questions that I take up in this chapter all turn upon the way that the soul of the deceased is conceived, and how that conception shapes the character of the rites. In particular: What is the nature of the funeral as an extended party? It lasts longer, and assembles more people, than any other festivity in Berawan society, and it is not yet clear why that should be so. Why are such privations visited upon the bereaved spouse? It would seem more logical that they receive comfort and support, rather than discomfort and ostracism. What, in eschatological terms, is the reason for the completely public character of the events? We have already noted some of the sociological consequences of this publicness, but there is, as yet, no ideological rationale for why they have to be so. And why the constant association between wealth and the soon-to-decay corpse?

The Link Between Body and Soul

Let me begin with a proposition: That the character of the soul in the period following upon death is best understood by viewing it as metaphorically linked with the corpse. The connection is not physical; the soul is not in any sense in, or tied to, the body. Indeed, as we have seen, even in life the soul is thought to be able to separate itself from its mortal vehicle and travel about in other worlds. At death, the physical association only becomes looser. Now the soul

94

cannot reenter or reanimate the body; that is what makes it a corpse.

Instead, the relationship between body and soul becomes one of shared fates. As the abandoned body sinks into ruinous corruption, the soul also changes its nature, and not for the better. Progressively it takes on a dreadfulness of its own, a quality of lurking menace. As the corpse is formless and disgusting, so the soul is homeless and miserable. It no longer has a place among the living; it is not yet pure spirit, *bili*, and is not acceptable to the dead. It can only wander alone in alien spirit worlds, or hover on the fringes of human habitation. From the dank, comfortless margin of the jungle, it looks upon the living with mounting jealousy. However good-natured the individual was in life, this test is likely to prove too much for his or her soul. It may inflict illness, so that death follows death. Only the passage of time can alleviate this condition; the slow ebbing of putrescence, leaving dry bones, hard and imperishable.

This proposition constitutes the nub of a classic essay by Robert Hertz entitled "A Contribution to the study of the Collective Representation of Death" (1960, original 1907). It is a study of rituals of secondary treatment of the dead, based principally on material from southern Borneo. About the death rites of that area there was already an extensive literature in Hertz's day. But that literature was not, needless to say, based upon extensive participant observation in the modern manner, and consequently the Berawan case provides a suitable test of Hertz's insight. It is worth quoting the passage in which this insight occurs:

> These tribes thus explicitly connect the dissolution of the corpse and their belief in a temporary stay of the soul on earth, together with the obligations and fears that derive from this belief. . . . This representation is linked to a well-known belief: to make an object or living being pass from this world into the next, to free or to create the soul, it must be destroyed. . . . As the visible object vanishes it is reconstructed in the beyond, transformed to a greater or lesser degree. The same belief applies to the soul and body of the deceased. (Hertz 1960:46)

The "well-known belief" that Hertz refers to is borrowed from an essay by two of his senior colleagues in the *Année Sociologique* group, Henri Hubert and Marcel Mauss. Called *Sacrifice: Its Nature and*

Function (1964, original 1899), it was well known to Hertz, having appeared nine years before his own. Hertz's originality lay in putting the ideas that he had learned about sacrifice together with the data on secondary burial that he had accumulated by bibliographical research.

His formulation has two elements. The first is that the immaterial component of the living person (Hertz uses "soul" in a much wider sense, including the "souls" of objects and animals) goes through a protracted transitional stage after death. This was the part of Hertz's formulation that caught the attention of Arnold Van Gennep, who allows that Hertz had thereby foreshadowed his notion of the liminal (Van Gennep 1960:190). It is not a notion that is restricted to Borneo, or to societies practicing any particular kind of ritual. To take an example at a good remove from the Berawan, Evans-Pritchard tells us that the Nuer have extremely brief funerals, and an "almost total lack of eschatology" (Evans-Pritchard 1956: 154). Yet even they have some minimal notion of the persistence of the social person after death:

> . . . the mortuary rites. . . . send the dead man away to join the ghosts and cut him off formally and finally from the living. Only when that has been done can his property be taken by his heirs and his widows cohabit with those with whom they have decided to live. It follows that the dead must be thought to be in some way still among the living till he is dispatched by these rites to the community of the ghosts. (Evans-Pritchard 1956:160)

In a footnote to the last sentence, Evans-Pritchard points out that it was Hertz who was "the first to draw attention to the universality of this idea and to show the great variety and complexity of its forms."

One of these complexities of form is exemplified by the Berawan case, where the second element of Hertz's formulation is operative: The transition that the immaterial component goes through is linked in peoples' minds with the changes that are simultaneously overtaking the corpse. This is a much more demanding element. It is common for people to conceive of some kind of continuity through death, but this form of the conception is not common. Moreover, it has specific ritual and ideological corollaries. Beliefs about the body are reflected in rituals concerning the soul, and vice versa. There is, as Hertz says, "a kind of symmetry or parallelism between the condition of the body . . . and the condition of the soul" (1960:45).

This conception of the soul in death is made manifest in Berawan funeral rituals. Also the anxiety engendered by a death is made plain enough, in whispered comments and knowing looks. Is a child sick in the house? Everyone knows the probable cause, and it would only be tactless to say the obvious. That much of the account is explicit. But the metaphorical relationship of the soul to the rotting body is not explicit, and given the tacitness of Berawan ideology, it is too much to hope that it would be. Nevertheless, I was able to gain some confirmation of it.

The question that I pursued my informants with was this: If the soul enters the land of the dead at the moment of losing breath, what was the point of the funeral? What good did it do for the soul of the deceased, or for the living for that matter? My quizzing produced only reiteration: The funeral is to entertain the soul of the dead person. The soul only goes to the land of the dead later. Then what is death?—and so back to square one. Their replies were earnest, but they simply did not see my problem.[1] I had the feeling that we were somehow talking past each other. There had been an occasion when the roles had been reversed. When a friend visited Long Teru, I had been repeatedly asked why he did not speak Malay. I replied that he had only been in the country a short while. But that answer did not satisfy them, and the question was posed again. Finally someone rephrased the question with great deliberation. How, he wanted to know, does he buy things? In Borneo, Malay is a lingua franca, the language of trade. What I had failed to explain was that in his country everyone, including the traders, speaks English. That was the answer for which they were searching.

In the same manner I rephrased my question with care, trying not to lead my informants. The man that finally put the missing piece in place was Sadi' Pejong, headman of Long Jegan: The soul does indeed arrive in the land of the dead at the moment of "loss of breath," but it does not *stay* there. When he, and the others sitting there, realized that this simple response was all I needed to remove my problem, the relief was mutual. Sadi' Pejong launched expan-

Plate 6. A funeral barge on its way to the graveyard. It is made of three canoes lashed together athwartships, and propelled by a small outboard motor. Over the coffin is rigged an awning of red and white cloth. The bamboo poles, with their pennants of the same fabric, will be set up around the mausoleum. The square banner covered with black and white curlicue designs will be hung on the tomb, around which the jungle has been cleared down to the water's edge.

sively into an account of the career of the soul. In illness, he explained, the soul may wander far away, into worlds unknown by men. Only if its wanderings should somehow lead it into the land of the dead, to which there are many possible routes, will death ensue. Meanwhile, the soul continues to wander, but on returning finally to its body it finds that decomposition has begun. The soul cannot reanimate the putrescent corpse. To do so would breach the order of things established by the Creator. But now the soul cannot easily find its way back to the land of the dead, where it previously arrived by accident and along an indirect route. Even if it can find its way back there, it will certainly be rejected by the dead, because it is as disgusting to them as the corpse is to the living. It has yet to become a bright spirit, as they are. So it must stray in unfamiliar spirit realms, or lurk on the margins of human society, foul and friendless. In the days after death occurs, the soul's condition worsens steadily, and in its desperation it becomes malevolent and a threat to the living. After some weeks the worst is past, and there is a slow improvement until it can at last gain access to the land of the dead.

Sadi̋ Pejong was pleased with this account, but clearly it was not one that he would have put together in so many words for himself or for any other Berawan. It was not a piece of esoteric lore, hidden from the uninitiated, but something novel. Consequently, it could hardly be regarded as a part of any universal Berawan dogma. This impression was confirmed when I heard, through a third party, how Sadi̋ Pejong had made everyone laugh in reporting the interview. On the other hand, mimicking someone's personal eccentricities is a perfectly standard Berawan mode of entertainment, and I must have been the butt of such humor a hundred times. What had bemused Sadi̋ Pejong on this particular occasion was the earnestness with which I had pursued my topic.

What he had produced was a synthesis, an indigenous analysis, informed by his intimate knowledge of Berawan custom. That he had never had cause to verbalize it before did not necessarily mean that it was false. What is striking is the emphasis that is placed in Sadi̋ Pejong's account on the linked fates of body and soul at each stage of their common career. Putrescence begins in the body because the soul strays that one step too far. Having begun, it shuts out the soul from returning to the body, and the world of the living. By the same token, it renders the soul unacceptable to the ancestors, the truly dead. Unable to go forward or backward, the soul's condition grows only worse, in parallel with the body's.

When is this unhappy state of affairs terminated? To that question everyone, not just the old and wise, knew the answer immediately: When the bones are dry. That formula *is* universal doctrine, and it contains cryptically the whole metaphorical identification that Sadi̋ Pejong elaborated for me.

The Equivocal Nature of the Festivities

In the first hours after "loss of breath" it is the simple continuity of the soul that receives the clearest ritual expression. People make a show of talking to it and offering it food, and these attentions continue throughout the funeral and beyond. But after the corpse is stored away in a coffin or jar, and decomposition has certainly begun, the level of this activity decreases. Instead of direct interaction, it is anxiety about the soul that predominates. It could be argued that fear of the recently dead is a projection of guilt. But this cannot be the principal factor because, in the case of an important person, not only the close kin but everyone in the longhouse feels threatened. Nor does this seem to vary much with how the deceased was regarded in life.

Those who are felt to be especially at hazard are the young and the ill. As we noted, Utan Nin died only a few doors away from a family that had a newborn child and a sickly man. Both were carefully kept away from close interaction with the death rituals. It was the grandmother of the child, wife of the sick man, who went to sit every evening by the corpse and represent her family at the gathering there. Pregnant women also avoid too close involvement with the funeral rituals, although they may help with the cooking, husking of rice, and other endless domestic chores that a major funeral involves. They will especially avoid going near the cemetery; in fact most Berawan avoid graveyards most of the time. Only when the working parties of men go there to build a new tomb, or prepare an old one to receive another occupant, are the graveyards cleaned up, and the encroaching jungle cut back.

If there has been any irregularity in the mode of death, or the death ritual, that serves to increase anxiety. Some deaths are so inauspicious that nothing can be done to soften the calamity, and all ritual is abjured. These "bad deaths" are discussed further below. But any slight thing might exacerbate the soul's malice. Before Utan Nin died, she had asked her husband to ready a jar for her. He failed to do so, and would have had to use a coffin instead, had he not been lucky enough to borrow one on short notice. When they came to cut the jar so as to allow the corpse to be inserted, they found that it was unusually hard to chip through the glaze. With increasing foreboding (for it was too late to start making a coffin), relays of men tapped away at the strangely unyielding jar. Tama Aweng could hear these goings-on from inside his cell, and made everyone all the more nervous by announcing the obvious: that it was his wife that was causing the problem, and that it heralded worse to come.[2] The evil that is expected is more death, and Berawan say that one death will cause another. The infant mortality rate, unhappily, tends to make their predictions come true.

Meanwhile, there are also anxieties revolving around the corpse. It is easy to see why the corpse is the object of disgust, but why fear? The answer is because souls are feared, and souls are metaphorically identified with corpses. Berawan do not imagine that the dead body has in itself any power to work harm. Their dread is that it will become reanimated by some spirit not of human origin, and rise up out of its coffin in partially decomposed condition. We noted the case of the woman who was supposedly snatched back from the jaws of death by a spirit that wished to make her into a shaman. But this occurred only a matter of minutes after "loss of breath" had been declared. To imagine such a thing happening a few days later is the stuff of nightmare. There is a spirit called *telasak* that tries to get inside the bodies of dead people, and if it succeeds a monster is created, that, it is said, will consume the populations of seven longhouses before it is satiated. On two occasions during fieldwork, panics occurred when a coffin was thought to have emitted a noise, or moved on its own. Men rushed to the scene grabbing whatever weapons lay at hand, and calm was only restored when Tama Ukat Sageng, the senior shaman, declared that all was well.

Corpses should never be brought *into* the longhouse. When someone dies suddenly or unexpectedly at the farms, his or her body is brought to the river bank in front of the longhouse and housed there in a small shed especially built for that use and afterwards destroyed. In all other respects the funeral continues as normal. Even at a rite of secondary treatments, the mortal remains of the deceased are not quite allowed to enter the longhouse proper, but their little shed is built on an addition to the longhouse, as if to acknowledge their much reduced dangerousness. Sometimes this rule is broken by a subterfuge. When "loss of breath" is detected outside but near the longhouse, then everyone near is warned to make no sound. With all haste the body is brought back to the house and carried in in silence. Then after a short pause, the wail goes up and the gong is sounded. But it would be unthinkable to bring a coffin or a jar containing a corpse into the house. If someone dies sufficiently far away from the village that he or she cannot be brought back within a few hours at most, then the body will be stored in any convenient graveyard and brought back only when the process of putrescence has ended, that is for *nulang*. If the other place is not a Berawan village, it may be impractical to conduct a funeral there. Hence the desire to bring home rapidly any sick person who seems likely to die.

People do not care to sit alone near a coffin or jar, even in broad daylight. But neither should the body be left unattended, and that is why all day long women bring their chores to do in a crowd sitting near it, and some of the close kin are there at all times. Towards sundown large mats are hung up on the open side of the veranda, and remain up all night. Part of this is color symbolism: The sunset is too "busy," too full of threatening red hues. Berawan do not care to look at the spectacular sunsets that occur in the tropics, and their objection is to the different hues that we find so pleasing. The motif of the danger of mixing primary colors is found throughout Borneo. For instance Evans (1953:146) recounts a myth that explains the prohibition on bringing meat and/or bamboo shoots into the house when women are dyeing cloth. He explains that to juxtapose meat (red), bamboo shoots (white), and dye (black), is to create a storm—white for the rain, red for the lightning, and black for the clouds. In this way all manner of prohibitions become attached to the thunder deity. The rationale that Berawan give for their antipathy toward sunsets is that it is the beginning of the day for the spirits, who are often attributed characteristics that are the inverse of human ones. The corpse is best masked from the view of spirits outside the longhouse, beginning at sundown.

I have already described the gatherings that are held every night that the corpse is in the longhouse, and we are now able to see what they are about in ideological terms. There are two reasons for them. The first, and the one that Berawan will give if asked, is that they play and enjoy themselves so that the last hours of the dead person (they will refer to him or her by name) in the house may be joyful, and that they do it out of attachment and respect. These sentiments are an extension of those most forcefully expressed immediately after death—that the individual has only just begun to die, and remains in some way sentient. But there is a second, darker reason for the wake. The living must be protected from the recently dead. Especially at night, there must be people around to keep a vigil over the corpse. At the same time, the soul's malice must be deflected, and for all but the close kin this is done by distracting it with noise and games. Hence the manic quality that these festivities take on. One may *not* sleep, one *must* play, night after night.

For some no doubt the amusement is straightforward enough. If the deceased was not an important member of the community, some men not closely related to the bereaved may delay appearing at the house until the final night or two, and then enjoy a boozy vacation from farm life. The unmarried young people relish the opportunity to flirt with members of the opposite sex, and perhaps meet teenagers visiting from other communities. But they have no small children to worry about. For many of the adults there is anxiety, and exhaustion. In any but the smallest funerals, a good proportion of the community is drawn into the work involved, and into keeping the vigil. For them the festivities become compulsive, an excess that mocks the declared aim to entertain the dead. Even the little games, like "fishing," have a punitive quality. It is because the wake is not simply a party that it becomes the most extended of parties.

The Widow's Ordeal

If the wake is ambiguously festive for many, it is overtly an ordeal for some. The strategy of the longhouse as a whole in dealing with the uncertain temper of the errant soul is to focus communal attention upon it, a vigil masking as a fete. For the close kin to do likewise would be foolhardy, directly provocative of the soul's jealousy. Consequently, they must observe a colorless mourning, clothed in white, dirty, tired, and constantly in attendance upon the corpse. Each of them is vulnerable, liable to have his or her soul stolen away to keep the deceased company. Of all the kin, the one that is most vulnerable is the spouse. The terrible discomforts visited upon the widow or widower are not a punishment, they are a defense.[3] Severe as they are, nothing less can be expected to dissuade the soul of the deceased from dragging down the living partner into its misery.

This applies with equal force to widows and widowers. However, women tend to be more careful about their observance of mourning usages. Men last out their ordeal behind the "widow's wall," but after that are not punctilious about avoiding sociality. Perhaps full mourning is inconsistent with male notions of vigorousness, or alternatively it may be implied that the souls of recently deceased males are more deadly than those of females. Certainly not all dead persons are equally dangerous: Children present little threat, whereas important men are a greater hazard than unimportant ones. In any event, the prohibitions of death are more keenly felt by women, and consequently I refer below mostly to the widow's role. The reader may take it that the same remarks apply to widowers, with somewhat less force, unless stated otherwise.

The widow's ordeal in the house of mats is such as to make her into a kind of corpse. She is given filthy clothes to wear. In the heat of the day, she sweats profusely in the stifling confines of her mat prison, a wetness not unlike that overtaking the corpse, and similarly stinking and repulsive. Her body is, in short, made a burden to her. The sago that she is given to eat is grey and watery, suggestive of decay, and inferior to the rice put out at the same time for the corpse. She is forbidden the company of other people, just as is the dead man's soul, for she cannot interact with anyone except under very restricted circumstances. When she looks out of her only window on the world, she sees the corpse. Finally, her confinement in the cubicle of mats parallels the body's in the jar or coffin. This state of affairs is something that is done to her; it is not the result of any spiritual change within her. The same applies with equal force to a widower. The spouse is made to share as much as possible of the fate of the deceased, precisely so that he or she will not in actuality have to share that fate.

The Communal Responsibility

The widow or widower, waiting out the days inside the little house of mats, is preventing harm from befalling himself or herself by mollifying the bitter envy of the soul of the deceased. But by the same token, others are also being shielded. If the soul were to become enraged, it might unpredictably take the life of a small child, or a sick old man, instead of striking at the most obvious target of its malice. In this way, the surviving spouse is defending the entire community.

Berawan funerals are public affairs in two senses. First, every phase of the proceedings, starting with the onset of illness, continuing through the crowded deathbed scene, and on into the wake, is completely open to the whole community. There is never any suggestion that the death or funeral is private, or the business only of the family. No invitations need be sent out to community members. The reason for this accessibility is now plain: from the moment when a death becomes a possibility, it is the vital concern of everybody within the longhouse. Should a death occur, the soul of the deceased will become a threat to every family there.

But if no one needs to be invited, then equally no one can refuse to participate, and this is the second sense in which funerals are public events: they are a communal responsibility. The time and energies of the close kin are constantly sapped by their duties to the dead. The husband or wife of a dead person can, needless to say, play no useful part in anything. But a sibling, son, or daughter is only slightly less restricted. Their obligation is to sit by the body all night long, perhaps napping in the hour or two before dawn, but only fitfully because of the bright kerosene lamps that are kept burning and the inevitable presence of at least one or two late revivers, who want to yarn or carouse. Meanwhile during the day, there is far more work to do than any one family can manage. This is true not only of the large-scale events for people of high status aspirations, but also those for ordinary respectable folks. There is the preparation of the tomb, or at least the place of temporary storage. Nowadays concrete is preferred for tombs, and even a modest below-ground vault involves hundreds of man-hours of labor. Someone, moreover, will have to go downriver to the bazaar to fetch the cement (not to mention supplies to feed the participants),[4] while others prepare the forms to hold the concrete, or head upriver looking for usable sand to mix with the cement. Others again must clear the encroaching vines and jungle growth from around all the edifices in the graveyard. If a cemetery at some distance from the house is being used, then the streams leading to it will have to be cleared of driftwood so that the funeral barge can get through. And someone should be out hunting for game . . . but enough, the point is made. The close male kin, even were they fully rested and able to spend all their time at it, could not do all the work that is necessary. As it is, the man who is principally organizing these things, and who probably is a close kinsman, can at best make a visit to the work site to see how things are going, and help out for an hour or two. For the rest, he can sit in his accustomed place by the coffin and worry about whether everything is going to work out on time. By the conclusion of the funeral, this poor man is exhausted. For the womens' tasks, the situation is the same. Even for a small funeral, the labor of more women than are found in any one family apartment will be required just to pound sufficient rice, and in fact close female kin do not normally do this work during the funeral at all. For a major event, the catering is impressive, with groups of women cooking up great tubs of rice, or preparing various side dishes, or making rice wine in kitchens that are extended for the purpose to take up just about the whole apartment.

The observances of mourning combine with the requirement of entertaining the lurking soul to ensure that the funeral is a communal effort. Not everyone participates to the same degree. If the funeral is small, a family that is only distantly related to the bereaved will send perhaps one member to help with the labor, and another to sit with the crowd in the evenings. A larger funeral will draw in a considerable proportion of the available manpower resources of the village. In either case, the ideological position is the same. Everyone in the longhouse has an interest in the proper execution of the rites, and everyone carries a responsibility to help to that end.

Plate 7. A funeral party at the graveyard of the Long Jegan community. The sturdy hardwood coffin, covered with a rich cloth of gold, and with bamboo carrying handles still lashed to its sides, has been set down while the tomb is being readied. Most of the group that went to the graveyard is out of the picture to the left, mixing the concrete with which the modern-style subterranean vault will be sealed. Meanwhile others are resting under the shade of an old-style mausoleum (*salong*). It is about thirty years old, and modest in size and decoration compared to others of the Long Jegan folk. The pennants of colored cloth have just been set up. The longhouse lies behind the trees across the river.

The Dead as Sacrifice

Hertz's insight was that where secondary treatment is found the dead are thought of in a manner analagous to the classical description of sacrifice: they must be destroyed in this world (by rotting away) in order to be transmitted into the next (as spirits of the dead). The Berawan do indeed have sacrifice in this classic mode, and blood sacrifice of chickens or, on more important occasions, pigs make up a part of many Berawan rituals. As Lévi-Strauss points out (1966:224), the fundamental principle of sacrifice is substitution,

stitution, which creates an intermediary between the sacrificer and the spirit world. The following is a section from a prayer said over a pig before it was sacrificed at the calendrical ritual called *papi' lamèng* (prayers for the house). It is spoken in the formalized parallel language called *piat*, as described in chapter two. As the prayer opens the speaker is singeing the hair on the back of the pig's neck to produce a pungent smoke that ascends heavenward:

Oooooou — (noise to attract attention of spirits)

tu bi'o suroh letó bikui — this is the smell of the burning pig

sakingan bili" puwong bili" ngaputong — let it arrive at the Creator Spirit

ra ko ngajui ra ko ngalarui — I'm not shouting, I'm not yelling

kam bili" lum luvak — to you spirits of the place
ngan no bili" bikui — and you spirit of the pig
sebarang — carelessly
pukú a an ko ngajui a an ko ngalarui — the reason that I'm shouting I'm yelling
bili" bikui — to you spirit of the pig
ka no selawèt kelajiu — don't take the wrong path
bili" no bikui — you spirit of the pig
ka no pabé — don't get it wrong
bili" no biku — you spirit of the pig
atan no ngalinga jiu ko — listen to what I say
piat ko paté ko — I pray, I talk about
ngan no bili" no bikui — to you spirit of the pig
chi' no bili" bikui — hasten you spirit of the pig

pulo bili" ngaputong — go to the Creator Spirit
ñi lo puwong kame lamulong — he who owns us human beings
atan no tiló kiu ngan ñi — you tell what they say to him

yo kame lia long teru — because we people of Long Teru

kapi kame — we ask
mulong jin mulong genin — a good life, a restful life
mulong luya mulong mida — a slow life, a healthy life
mulong tanyit mulong la'it — a safe life, a sound life

wong denga wong ada	to have reputation, to have belongings
wong kata wong tuah	to have influence, to have luck
ichung mateló beluri siju penod	let them obtain, give (us) a lot of fish
beluri ligit beluri duit	give money, give cash
beluri wang beluri parai. . . .	give wealth, give rice. . . .

This talk of obtaining wealth strikes another responsive chord in the funeral rituals. Let us take the equation literally, and say that the death is a kind of sacrifice. Granted, no one planned the immolation, and it is a decidedly inconvenient one. But it nevertheless fulfills the criterion of sacrifice that Hubert and Mauss arrived at: The death establishes "a means of communication between the sacred and the profane worlds through the mediation of a victim, that is, of a thing that in the course of ceremony is destroyed" (Hubert and Mauss 1964:97).

The corpse in the longhouse and the soul fluttering outside are principally a source of danger, but it is undeniably also the case that they are a potential mode of communication with the long dead, those immaculate spirits to whom the community constantly looks for special supernatural beneficences: health, safety, possessions, money—just those sorts of things mentioned in the prayer quoted above. The theme of the soul as potential bringer of wealth and protection is especially emphasized at the very beginning of the death rites, in the small rituals that go on immediately after "loss of breath," and, as we shall see, during the rites of secondary treatment. These are the times before the putrescence of the corpse has noticeably begun, and after it can safely be assumed to have ended. This logic accounts for the way that Utan Nin was taken into the kitchen and asked to send abundant crops to feed the community, and why all manner of objects of wealth were stacked around her as she sat in state on her death seat. But even at the end of the funeral, a less auspicious time, the notion is still expressed. When little children are waved over the coffin or jar just before it is removed, the prayer that accompanies the act implores life and wealth for the infants. It might seem that the malicious soul is likely to bring just the reverse, and that it is foolish to bring the infants to its attention. But, at the moment of departure, it is communication with the sacred dead that takes precedence.

Liminality and Ambiguity

I have argued that the equivocal nature of the wake, the ordeal visited upon the widow, the inherent communal quality of the rites, and the association of the corpse with wealth are all manifestations of the conception of the soul in the period following death, and further, that the conception has to do with the continuing link between body and soul.

The observation that the sacred has an ambiguous quality goes back at least to Robertson Smith (1889). It may sanctify, but may also pollute. It has the power to heal, but also the power to harm. It is necessary, and it is dangerous. Certainly a Berawan funeral is a sacred event, and a period of liminality, and it possesses the ambiguous character of those two qualities in full measure. But there is a special equivocal nature in these death rites. The corpse and the soul are likewise the object of fear, hope, and solicitude. The corpse must be protected lest it become some terrible monster, and is feared for the same reason. The soul is pitied because of its discomfort, and feared because of what its discomfort might lead it to do. The character of the funeral, half party and half ordeal, like the nature of the soul, both useful and dangerous, is a consequence of the state of the corpse, which demands attention and repels it at the same time.

Notes

1. I also had the question turned back on me, in the manner we noted in chapter one. Westerners are associated with the dead, because their white skins are said to resemble a corpse a few hours after death. Consequently people often behaved as if I knew all about the land of the dead, even to the point of asking me if I had met their dead relatives there. One old woman at Long Teru used to throw ashes off the veranda when I left to go downriver, as when a corpse leaves the house. I do not believe that she intended any ill will; only that she did not want me to take any souls with me, or worse yet, bring any back. The technological powers of the West are

also a factor in the assumption that Westerners have access to supernatural realms. Sadi' Pejong once told me that if I happened to die at Long Jegan, a plane would surely come that same day and bomb the longhouse.

2. A more spectacular instance occurred some years ago at Long Jegan, and it was recounted to me by a sophisticated young man who had completed secondary school and who said that he witnessed the events himself. An old man requested before he died that he be put in a certain mausoleum with many of his kinfolk. But his wishes were disregarded, and a concrete tomb was constructed for him alone at a graveyard just across from the longhouse. The vault was measured to accomodate the coffin, but when the funeral cortege arrived, amid the sounding of gongs and the waving of flags, they found to their consternation that the coffin was a little too long to fit. So they took it back to the long house and sawed a few inches off—a procedure which is practicable because the ends of the heavy Berawan coffin are very thick. Then back to the graveyard, where it was found that the coffin was still a shade too long. So they repeated the process, this time cutting the other end of the coffin. But to no avail, still an inch or so too long. Finally they took it back to the longhouse and kept it a further night, during which sacrifices and prayers were made. The next day the coffin fitted into the vault with several inches to spare.

3. It is impossible to deny that there is *any* punitive quality about the widow's ordeal. In Dobu, for instance, similar privations are visited upon a widow for several months, and the rationale is that she is likely to have killed her husband anyway, by sorcery (Fortune 1932:57,153). But, as noted in chapter four, the Berawan do not concern themselves with sorcery or black magic at all. Moreover, in no case did I hear it suggested either that a spouse was directly responsible for a death or that punishment was appropriate. It is, on the contrary, sympathy for the bereaved individual that is expressed. Whatever punitive motive may be subconsciously felt is not given verbal or ritual expression.

4. I do not here discuss the costs of all this, only the need for manpower support. I have written elsewhere about the economics of Berawan death rites (Metcalf 1981).

CHAPTER SEVEN

Mourning: Headhunting and Vitality

Mourning and the Elaboration of Liminal Symbolism

While the corpse is in the longhouse, it is the object of intense ritual attention. But when the funeral comes to a close and the body is removed, the metamorphosis of soul to pure spirit is not complete. Long and exhausting as Berawan funerals may be, they cover only the opening days of a process that requires months. As was noted at the end of chapter four, this is the special feature of Berawan eschatology. It comes as no surprise that the rites that, with reduced intensity, continue to be addressed to the dead are shot through with symbolism of transition and liminality. The interplay of these symbols is subtle and complex. It involves notions of vitality, sexuality, and pollution. In my description I continue to follow a chronological format, but particular symbolic themes are not restricted to one segment of ritual. Instead they are woven together, appearing here and there in various contexts. Consequently, the analysis must move back and forth in the ritual sequence in order to isolate them.

In the usages of mourning, the division of labor between close kin and the rest of the community persists. There is one series of rites that lifts the death restrictions from the longhouse as a whole, and another for the spouse and immediate family of the deceased. The latter is a continuation and slow relaxation of the proscriptions of the funeral period, but the former introduces a new element, namely headhunting.

It may seem strange that headhunting should be involved with the mortuary rituals. There is no obvious reason why the two should be related. But headhunting is a considerable mystery anyway. It would take a separate study, and a voluminous one at that, to come to grips with the structure and meaning of head-hunting beliefs. Needham (1976) shows the inadaquacy of much of the theorizing on the topic, which envisages something called "soul stuff," a limited resource that can be stolen from others and added to the aggressor's stock. The difficulty is that, in Borneo at least, there is no evidence of any such conept in indigenous thought. It is only recently that there have been any substantial modifications of the "soul stuff" theory (McKinley 1976; M. Rosaldo 1977, 1980; R. Rosaldo 1980).

Current Status of the Headhunting Rites

Hose gives some description of headhunting practices in Baram at the turn of the century (Hose and McDougall 1912:I:185–90, II:20–22). Most of what he has to say refers to the Kayan, and it is clear that the mourning observances for an aristocratic Kayan were strict and severe, so that the need to obtain heads was keenly felt. But we must be careful in generalizing from the Kayan case: We know that there were real differences between ethnic groups in the practice, and presumably the ritual significance, of taking heads. C. Hudson Southwell, a missionary who traveled through the upper Baram in the period just before and after the Japanese occupation, and who converted many people in the far interior to protestant Christianity, made an interesting observation (personal communication). He noted that Kenyah houses varied considerably in the number of heads that they had. Some kept clusters of them, evidently ac-cumulated over many decades, hanging from roof beams every-where. Others seemed content with only a few, and disposed of older ones. Southwell did not pursue the matter further. But his observation is confirmed by Hose, who remarks that the "Kleman-tan tribes," among whom he classifies the Berawan, are:

> . . . on the whole far less warlike than Kayans, Kenyahs, and Ibans. Their offensive warfare is usually on a small scale, and is undertaken primarily for revenge. Their warlike ambition is easily satisfied by the taking of a single head, or even by a mere

hostile demonstration against the enemy's house. Nevertheless, like all the other tribes, except the Punans, the Klemantans need a human head to terminate a period of mourning. (Hose and McDougall 1912:I:187)

As one of the first Residents in Baram District, Hose played a large part in the suppression of warfare and headhunting. He displayed diplomacy and ingenuity in accomplishing this without himself causing bloodshed. One of his devices to channel warlike energies in other directions was to hold a regatta. As he describes it:

> Some thirty years ago it was my privelege to be present at a meeting at Marudi (Claudetown) in the Baram District, and in the presence of an overwhelming force of the tribes loyal to the Government of Sarawak, of all those tribes whose allegiance was still doubtful, and all those who were still at variance with each other. The object was to abolish old blood feuds and to persuade the tribes to aide the Government in keeping the peace. In calling this conference, I felt that in order to suppress fighting and headhunting, the normal young Bornean's natural outlet, it would be well to replace them by some other equally violent, but less disastrous, activity; and I therefore suggested to the tribes a sort of local Henley, the chief feature of which would be an annual race between the war canoes of all the villages. The proposal was taken up eagerly by the people, and months before the appointed day they were felling the giants of the forest and carving out from them the great war-canoes that were to be put to this novel use. . . . (Hose 1926:148)

Hose's "local Henley" is still held and occasions much excitement, although it occurs now only every second year.

Another device that Hose mentions was prompted by the realization that heads were ritually necessary to release a house from mourning. In order to remove the necessity for actual homicide, he tells us, heads were kept at "some of the remoter forts" and lent out to villages that needed them (Hose and McDougall 1912:II:38n). The heads were obtained by confiscation from rebellious longhouses, and then lent out to well-behaved ones. This piece of institutionalization has its farcical side; one has visions of a district officer sorting through his collection, looking for a nice head to give to a favorite chief, and then perhaps noting the details on a file card for future reference. What is surprising is that upriver folk were prepared to go along with these modifications in traditional practices. Through them, Hose initiated a process of reritualization that gradually distanced the rites of headhunting from the bloody realities of former times. Although there were occasional lapses, it seems that the people of the Baram watershed, in contrast to the Iban to the south, readily cooperated in this process. Why they took this attitude would be an important question to answer were we studying headhunting per se, but for now I note it without further elaboration.

At Long Teru the process is well advanced. It is eighty years since the Rajah's administration began the suppression of headhunting, and over thirty years since the last heads were taken during the closing phases of the Second World War, when interior folk harassed the retreating Japanese to some effect. That was the last occasion on which the great headhunting festivals were held, ceremonies that were intended to reinvigorate the whole community. It was possible to obtain detailed descriptions of them, but the generation that remembers them is growing old now. It is hard to imagine circumstances in which the rites will occur again, unless perhaps they were arranged for my benefit. At one point in my fieldwork, there was some enthusiasm for doing this, premised on my ability to furnish the necessary heads. But unfortunately Hose's convenient service was no longer in operation.[1] It is true that the martial past is still very much alive in Berawan consciousness. Epic deeds still provide the material of extended song cycles, and it is surprising how many men have at hand the full accountrements of traditional warfare, including sword, shield, spear, war cloak, and bonnet. The modal male personality is still that of a warrior: vigorous, alert, stoical, and capable of an incendiary temper if provoked, a kind of beserk for which the Berawan are infamous. It is also true that people sometimes talk as if they expected the modern centralized state to collapse and leave them to run their own affairs as they did before the Rajah's administration came to interfere in them. But the only context in which headhunting still appears is mortuary rites, and then in attenuated form.

Indeed, it is not immediately obvious that these rites concern heads at all, for none appear during the performance. In the early seventies the Berawan possessed only a couple of heads. The Batu Belah and Long Jegan folk threw theirs out when they adopted the

Bungan revivalist cult in the 1960s, a religious change that was partly motivated by the desire to be done with restrictions such as those surrounding the heads. The Long Terawan community lost theirs when their house was burnt down by the Japanese as a reprisal against guerilla actions in 1945. Long Teru also lost its heads because of a fire, an accidental one that occurred in the late 1930s. Long Teru folks say that there was no great desire to replace the lost skulls because, even in this conservative community, their cult was considered bothersome.

Nevertheless, the headless head rites continue to be performed and we must conclude that they continue to carry a ritual significance. Nowadays at Long Teru they are held more or less directly after the conclusion of the funeral, and completed in one day if possible, so that the community as a whole is released from mourning a matter of two weeks after the death that occasioned them. Thereafter other rituals such as weddings, may be held, although a further lapse of a couple of weeks is tactful. Social gatherings may once again involve dancing and the singing of lighthearted songs that are proscribed during communal mourning. At Long Jegan a very similar set of rites was held prior to 1960, but the scheduling was different. There they could not occur until after the next harvest, and this feature made the Long Jegan usages more nearly approximate to the realities of headhunting. Headhunting parties could not normally be organized at short notice, but were instead left until a slack time in the agricultural cycle. However, the inconvenience to members of the longhouse was not great, because festive occasions such as weddings are normally held over until the same period, which constitutes an informal ritual season.

Nowadays the headhunting rituals are performed after the funerals of virtually every mature adult. They are not carried out for children or unmarried young people, and I was told that they would be omitted in the cases of those who are less than respectable. It is not possible to say what the usage was in the period before pacification, when the rites required fresh heads. Given Hose's report that the Berawan and other "Klemantans" were less warlike than their Kayan neighbors, it seems unlikely that heads were taken after the deaths of every adult member of the community. Certainly, as among all the peoples of central northern Borneo, the need to obtain heads was more strongly felt when important leaders died than for less eminent folk. It may be that in some cases the rites were never performed, and the death restrictions placed upon the whole community were lifted after some arbitrary period.

What follows is a brief account of the rites as they were performed at Long Teru in the early 1970s.

Ngachang: *The Reenactment of a Headhunting Raid*

A couple of hours before dawn on the third or fourth day after the removal of the corpse from the house, the young men of the community are shaken from their slumbers by an older man who is leader of the ceremony. Sleepy and shivering they collect at the riverside bearing whatever items of military equipment came to hand as they left: a sword, spear, war bonnet, or shield. Embarking in the largest canoes available, they paddle upstream in silence until well out of earshot of the village. They draw into the bank, and some go looking for *chang* leaves, from which the rite takes its name.

Chang appears in several religious contexts and is the most prominent of a range of plants embued with ritual significance. *Chang* is the pinnate leaves of a relatively common feather palm. Mature palms grow about fifteen feet tall, but near longhouses they are seldom allowed to reach that height because of depredations on their leaves, which have practical as well as ritual uses. As the fronds emerge, they pass through a stage when they are long, thin, and rectangular in cross section, made up of the neatly folded leaves lying along a boxshaped stem. If the frond is shaken vigorously the leaves separate from the stem so as to resemble a cat-o'-nine-tails. If an individual leaf is examined, it is found to consist of many layers uniformly pleated along the spines of the leaf and stacked on top of one another in concertina fashion. If one leaf is carefully opened out it reaches a width of eight inches or more, and after carefully drying and flattening supplies the raw material for the Berawan sun hat *(sakiong)*. These wonderful hats are shaped like a segment of a sphere and are often as much as three feet wide, providing protection from sun and rain, a veritable portable environment.

When employed ritually, the leaves are torn along the spines, producing a cluster of ribbons. This artifact is referred to below as a *chang* "whip." As the strips dry they curl up, producing a decorative effect, and it was pendants of this kind that were formerly used to decorate heads hung in the longhouse. Thus it comes about that *chang* is associated with heads, and in the ritual of *ngachang* it substitutes for them.

While *chang* is being obtained, those not engaged in the search sit in the canoes chatting. Perhaps they light a fire, and the mood becomes more jovial. When their comrades return with *chang*, it is first of all made into whips and then woven together in a special manner, to form a rough triangle with fluffy tails hanging off it. This represents the head, and two or three of them may be constructed. Not too long ago, I was told, it was the custom to hang these "heads" in the jungle and then to sneak up on them and spear them with light sticks. Nowadays the "heads" are, without further ado, tied onto a pole that is erected in the center of the canoe, the putative "head rack" *(lachan)*. Sometimes the more stoical members of the party jump into the water at this juncture and use a *chang* whip to splash water onto their backs, and this is the occasion for horseplay and laughter. The sun is up by this time and the canoes return to the longhouse making as much noise as possible, in the manner of a returning war party. Gongs are beaten, and the peculiar shrieking war cries *(lalu)* go up.

The din is answered by gongs within the house, and as the canoes come to the landing place in front of the house, a reception committee of young women rushes down from the house to intercept them. A wild melee ensues at the water's edge, with the women splashing the men thoroughly and pelting them with mud and any other refuse that comes to hand. The canoes are capsized as the men leap to the counterattack, and the usual restraints about body contact between young men and women are forgotten as they hurl each other into the water and roll in the mud.

Meanwhile, some sober older person has taken charge of the "heads" and planted the rack in front of the house. The widow or widower of the deceased person comes down from the longhouse, aided perhaps by a young son or daughter. Taking a *chang* whip, he or she splashes water on the backs of the returning menfolk, muttering a prayer for their health and safety. Then he or she retires to a discreet spot a little away from the scrimmage, takes off the dirty clothes worn throughout the funeral, hangs them on a forked stick, and bathes. The old clothes are simply left where they are to rot. Having washed, the bereaved spouse puts on new clothes of the same coarse white stuff and returns to the house collecting the "heads" on the way. This is the signal for the mud fight to cease. While this has been happening, other senior people of the house have carried wet *chang* whips through the longhouse and adjacent gardens flicking droplets here and there and muttering a benediction. Sometimes a *tapó* (formal prayer site) is prepared while the spouse is bathing, and a chicken sacrificed at it with prayers to the Creator Spirit.

If the site of the mausoleum of the dead person is close by, one of the "heads" may be taken there directly and hung upon the tomb. If this is not convenient, some more suitable opportunity will be found later.

Meanwhile there has also been activity within the house. As soon as the returning "war party" is heard coming down the river, the gongs are played, and the great funeral drum *(genèng)* is sounded, but in a new manner: It is hung up from a roofbeam and a rhythm unlike the ones used during the funeral and employing a drummer at each end of it is beaten out. All of the remaining apparatus of the funeral catafalque is put away. The valuable cloths are folded, and the sewing machines, brassware, and what have you, are put inside the rooms. The veranda is swept and new mats put down.

Having washed themselves clean of mud, the young people reenter the house. As the men of the party come up the steps to the veranda, each must pass between two married women, who hold over his head a shallow sieve of the kind used to separate leaves and stalks from rice after the harvest. It contains a broken egg, and while one woman holds the sieve the other pours a little rice wine over the eggs, letting it drip down onto the head of the man crouched below. This rite lifts from the returning warrior all the prohibitions that must be observed on warlike expeditions. These taboos are numerous, but the one specifically referred to is the proscription against eating eggs.[2] The men than take their ease for a while on the veranda, drinking coffee and smoking, another luxury forbidden them while they were engaged in hunting heads. Gradually they drift off to change into dry clothes.

The women meanwhile have another ritual to perform called *ngalai*. Utilizing this propitious opportunity, they attempt to rid the longhouse of all malign influences lurking within it. The method is as follows: A group of older women assemble at the upriver end of the house armed with paddles or bamboo poles. Shoulder to shoulder they advance along the veranda thumping the poles or paddles down rhythmically and sweeping all the evil spirits before them, both those that caused the previous death and any others in residence. For good measure, they go up and down the house twice in each direction.

Ngalaké: *The Taking of Omens*

The next task is to obtain a favorable omen, indicating that no more deaths will occur, from the most important of the omen birds, the eagle *plaké*. The technique for calling *plaké (ngalaké)* has been described in detail elsewhere (Metcalf 1976a:101–107). Suffice it to note that *plaké* is particularly associated with war, and that the length of time required to obtain an omen cannot be predicted in advance. At one funeral I attended, a completely favorable reading was obtained within ten minutes from a pair of eagles that showed up exactly on cue. Naturally, the augur was very full of himself after this amazing success, but at other times I have seen him sit through the heat of the day, and perhaps for a second day too, before receiving a sign. Unless the omen is of the most damning variety,[3] the next stage of the ceremony can begin at once. If the augur is lucky enough to obtain his omen in the morning after *ngachang* has been made, then the rituals can be completed on the same day. The medicinal water *(pi plaké)* dedicated during the calling of *plaké* is placed on a shield suspended horizontally under the eaves outside the room of the deceased person.

When news of a successful calling of *plaké* spreads, a crowd once more assembles on the veranda near the room of the deceased person, and coffee and cookies are served to them while preparations are made for blessing the war swords *(belilik takèng)*. Great bundles of *chang* are prepared for later use, and to hang in festoons over all the ritual gear. Piled three deep in an inverted shield, the swords look hoary with age, and each is equipped with its fight magic, mysterious-looking bundles containing stones and boar tusks and other charms (*gimad*) obtained by supernatural means over the years. Other swords are suspended in a cluster from the roof above the shield. Some blades are reputed to "sing" or jump from their sheaths if an enemy is near.

The air of bustle and excitement is regenerated, and the crowd amuses itself with playing the large drum and by performing a line dance. The dancers snake up and down the veranda, led by a man playing a *keluné* (a wind instrument that sounds like a harmonica), and stamping rhythmically as they proceed. In former times, a special dance (*makoi*) was performed in honor of new heads, and I gather that women dominated this performance, and that lewdness and transvestism were features of it.

The climax of the blessing of the swords is the sacrifice of a chicken, accompanied by suitable prayers. The men huddle around the swords, each holding on to the person on his right, and thus forming a chain to the elder making the prayers. The bloody sword used to chop off the chicken's head is touched onto the wrist of each participant. Blood from the chicken is put on the swords and fighting charms also. This completed, they turn their attention to the next stage of the ritual.

Ngalăp: *The Initiation of Warriors*

Ngalăp is not included in the ritual sequence of every funeral, and it can occur in other contexts, whenever new heads are obtained. Of the funerals that I attended, *ngalăp* was performed at only one, that of an important old man at Long Teru. Previously, when the head rites had a more autonomous place in the mortuary sequence, the martial emphasis was more pronounced. The rituals of initiation of warriors, now seldom bothered with, lasted several days.

There are two classes of initiates, those who are entering for the first time, mostly young boys, and older men who wish to advance to higher ranks. The present practices are only a shadow of the former festivals. It is now difficult to get agreement among informants concerning the details of ranking, but it is clear that there were at least five grades, each marked by a distinctive style of dress or decoration. A Batu Belah informant related to me the following details: At first participation in *ngalǎp* the novice receives the right to decorate the lower end of his sword sheath with a long tuft of human or animal hair; after the second time, two of the long black-and-white tail feathers of the rhinoceros hornbill, *temmenggang (Buceros rhinoceros),* may be worn on the war cap *(tebutong);* after the third, feathers of the helmeted hornbill, *tepion (Rhinoflax vigil),* may be worn on the back of the war cape *(lai'a);* after the fourth, a full complement of eight hornbill feathers may be worn upon the war bonnet; and finally after the fifth occasion, the upper lobes of the ear may be pierced for the wearing of tiger teeth, or a facsimile thereof *(udang).* Some people claimed that the fourth stage was collapsed in this account, and that in fact feathers were added to the war bonnet one at a time, making ten grades in all. These feathers, in the full array, should consist of three as long as possible (the *dorg*), sometimes as much as three feet in length, and five shorter ones. A man who had actually taken a head was allowed immediately to assume all the warrior insignia, irrespective of how many times he had entered a *ngalǎp* ceremony. Young women can also participate, and they win the right to use the beaded headband *(labong)* and the most valuable cloths, those with an interwoven gold thread *(kain songkèt).* Women join the rites once only, and are not "bloodied" as the boys are. Galvin (1966:302) lists a similar set of grades alloted by the Lepo Tau Kenyah as part of their *mamat* ceremony, and the Sebop evidently had yet another version (Madang and Galvin 1966:312).

The first step in the rite as performed at Long Teru was to line up the boys on the veranda on the left-hand side of the young man for whom the procedure was initiated, in this case a grandson of the deceased elder. Each was decked out in items of military dress—war bonnets, swords, and capes. Only a handful of girls wished to participate, and they stood to the right of the boys. The boys were told to turn and face the wall, and place their hats and swords between their feet. The girls sat upon gongs. Then a large black pig was brought in, its feet trussed together in the usual fashion, and an elaborate prayer made over it. The pig's head was rapidly cut off, the entire carcass was lifted up with great war cries, and quantities of blood were spilled on each boy in the line. As each was bloodied he jumped into the air *(tepurok)* and let out a yell *(nekèng)*, and then he stamped four times on either side of his hat. The adult men then began to splash each other with blood, in the meantime dancing about and shrieking. When the supply of blood from the pig began to dry up, chickens were hastily decapitated so that more blood could be thrown on the participants, the military equipment standing on the veranda, the fight charms, and even the walls and floor. Waving their bloody swords around recklessly, and running hither and thither in wild-eyed confusion, the men reproduced in a way that I, at least, found convincing, the bloodlust of real hand-to-hand combat. When they eventually quieted down, the boys' hats were collected and hung up beside the swords. Water was brought to wash the floor, and the pig and chicken carcasses whisked away to be cooked. Coffee was brought, and the men sat down to chat. Ideally, the items of military equipment worn by a boy at the *ngalăp* become property that no one else may use or even touch, for they are invested with power benevolent only to their owner.

The principal value of *ngalăp* at Long Teru today is that it allows free use of hornbill feathers. Particularly among the young people, little regard is paid to the rules about use of insignia. The sanction against their use is a mild one: people who intentionally use inappropriate badges of rank, who give themselves airs, will be punished by making fools of themselves; specifically, they are liable to defecate involuntarily. The older men still take some of the symbols seriously, such as the pierced upper earlobe, and all who went through this painful operation had been involved in warfare or entered *ngalăp* many times.

Ninung Ulèng: *Standing Up the Effigy*

The final rite in the sequence is necessary after every funeral, except those of children. It consists of standing up a decorated post (*ulèng, ninung* = erect). The post is about eight feet long, and has two crossbars, the "arms" and "legs" of the *ulèng*, each about three feet long. The upper end of the post is cut off at an acute angle, and a crude representation of a human face is carved on it. The whole is covered with *chang* leaves. Those principally involved in the funeral stand the *ulèng* up in front of the longhouse next to the room of the dead person, and a crowd looks on from the veranda above. The post is planted in a hole in the ground and supported at an angle of about 60 degrees by means of two bracing struts. One of the woven "heads" is hung from the end. While the men are raising the post, they are liberally doused with water by the women. A boy, if possible a son or grandson of the deceased, climbs up the pole, aided by the older men, and, with a war whoop, chops off the head of a chicken held against its upper end. After that, other participating menfolk stand astride the post as if to climb it, and mutter a prayer. The head and liver of the chicken, plus one green leaf, are skewered to the top of the post with a sliver of wood.

Most obviously, the *ulèng* is an effigy of the victim of the head-hunting raid, erected outside the house as a memorial and reminder to the lurking soul of the efforts taken on its behalf. So the effigy is covered with *chang* leaves, which are associated with the heads, and it is symbolically vanquished by the men and boys who climb astride it. The first of these, a lineal descendent acting as proxy for the deceased person of the longhouse, reproduces the killing in miniature, using a chicken. So the rituals that begin with the taking of heads also end with the taking of heads.

But there are other possible associations for the effigy. It could be taken as representing also the subject of the rites. His or her body has only recently been removed from the longhouse, so that the effigy might be seen as a substitute, distanced only slightly from the longhouse. The effigy is not removed after the rituals, but allowed slowly to fall into disrepair and eventually collapse when the rattan lashings rot through, paralleling the fate of both corpse and soul. It is the same with all the props associated with the funeral, the shamanistic devices made during the final illness, the timbers used to build both the death seat and the ramp down which the corpse was carried, and the spouse's clothes; all are simply left to rot. Since this pile of detritus is inconveniently large, what in fact usually happens is that days or weeks later someone with a little time to spare casually throws it in the river, like other rubbish. But biological decay remains the imagery of the gradual ebbing of death.

There is a further possible association of the effigy, and that is with the widow. She has until recently been cooped up in the house of mats, in a state of symbolic death, so that the effigy can be seen as taking *her* place. She is associated with the "heads" which she carried into the longhouse. Moreover, their "death" removes her "death" because the introduction of the heads into the house lifts a state of mourning in which she is seen as corpse-like (see plate 8).

While the men are mounting the effigy, women haul water from the river and throw it over them by the bucketfull, so making a muddy patch in front of the longhouse. High-spiritedly, they pelt the men and boys with mud, provoking them into retaliation. Goaded on by observers from the veranda, the men try to seize the girls, and in the process often slip over, so that there may be a whole pile of bodies writhing around in the mud, clothes in disarray, men's and women's bodies pressed together in total disregard of the usual rules of decorum. The women shriek in delight, and the men roar with mock fierceness. Sometimes individuals who get mud in their eyes or mouths go to the river to wash it out, and then come back for more horseplay. But gradually the action slows, and people drift away to the river to wash. The unmarried young men and women often carry the scuffling to the river bank, and go on with their ambushes long after the adults have had their fill.

Sometime later a meal is served for all those who have participated. It is the last public event of the abridged mortuary rites. Guests from other houses seldom stay for these rites, and the mood is intimate and relaxed.

The Connection Between Headhunting and Mourning

The stated purpose of the headhunting rites is to lift a condition of *lumo*. *Lumo* is a term of wide reference embracing a range of restrictions and usages consequent upon a death. Some personal possessions of a dead person are considered *lumo*, and they cannot be given away or sold. These things are not normally valuables such as beads or brassware, but things that had an intimate association with the deceased, such as favorite items of clothing or a musical instrument, perhaps. There is no particular supernatural sanction that enforces

Plate 8. Termination of the ritual of "standing up the effigy." The effigy is covered with *chang* leaves, and two crossbars comprise its "arms" and "legs." Water was carried from the nearby river and splashed over the participants while the boys and men were mounting the effigy. Now everyone is playfully smeared with mud. The man standing in front of the effigy is holding a war bonnet and making a prayer for the safety of the community.

this usage; it is instead a matter of sentiment. Names assumed because of the death of a close kinsman are sometimes referred to as *ngaran lumo* (*ngaran* = name). But the most common use of the word is in connection with the restrictions placed upon the entire community after the death of anyone other than children or those of the most lowly station. What is prohibited is other public ritual, such as weddings, and parties, and the secular singing and dancing that goes with them. Consequently, a state of *lumo* disrupts the life of the longhouse.

But how does the performance of the rites, and previously the taking of heads, bring about the lifting of *lumo?* I pursue two approaches to this question, which in turn depend upon two premises, two statements of dogma that may be taken at face value. The first is the explicit aim of headhunting. In common with other peoples of central northern Borneo, the Berawan claim that the taking of heads brought increased vigor to the community, so that people were more healthy, more children were born, and crops grew more abundantly (Haddon 1901:397, Furness 1899:15). Just how those actions were conceived of as bringing about these ends is, of course, the central conundrum of headhunting. But it is not the problem that concerns us here. The second piece of dogma is that, for the Berawan, death has a chain reaction quality to it. There is a considerable anxiety that, unless something is done to break the chain, death will follow upon death. The logic of this is now plain: The unquiet soul kills, and so creates more unquiet souls.

As currently conducted in connection with the mortuary sequence, there are only three episodes in the headhunting rites that usually arouse much popular enthusiasm or concern: The two mud fights, and the calling of the omen bird *plaké*. Calling *plaké* is the most serious act of divination that the Berawan observe. It occurs after the "heads" have been brought into the longhouse, and what it reveals for them is whether or not there will be more deaths in the near future. From our point of view, the taking of heads is murder, and pretending to take heads is an evocation of death. For the Berawan it is just the opposite. The taking of heads somehow breaks the chain of death, and that is the first thing to understand about it.

At one funeral I attended, sickness struck the small children of the house before the funeral was even over. On *liang kiji*, "the day of silence," a child died, and the next day another. The headhunting rites were accordingly cut to the barest minimum. Two or three men went to fetch *chang*, but they simply washed themselves when they arrived back. There was no mud fight then, or later when the effigy was quietly erected. No attempt was made to summon the omen bird *plaké*, since an omen of the worst kind had already been received.

The first approach is to see the headhunting rites as basically a continuation of the strategy of the funeral, that is, another in a battery of techniques designed to deflect the malice of hovering souls.

Sacrifice to the Dead

In the last chapter, we viewed the dead as a kind of sacrifice in themselves. Now we reverse the roles and see them as the object of sacrifice. Close kin of the deceased are most vulnerable to attack, but the jealousy of the soul may fasten upon anyone in the community. The object of the headhunt is to provide a victim, and thereby assuage the soul's vindictiveness. Close kin would achieve this most effectively, but that would defeat the purpose of the maneuver. Victims were taken from the nearest available source, often, evidently, the inoffensive Penan.

The arrival of a new head lifts the state of *lumo* by reducing the risk of spiteful attack by the soul of the deceased community member, and so making precautions against such attack less necessary. But what about the victim's soul, is that not also malicious? It is; but the danger is less for the sinners than for the sinned against. It is the relatives of the victim that are most threatened, and that is the gain.

Headhunters do, however, bring upon themselves a state of *lumo* as a consequence of their success. In the context of mourning, they cast off the condition, only to enter into it again immediately. This second state of *lumo* is less hazardous than the first for the reason noted above, but it is removed in the same way, by the killing of a victim. There is a second headhunt, one that, even in the period before headhunting was suppressed, was carried out only in mime. It occurs at the very end of the sequence of rites, when a boy chops off the head of a chicken whose neck is stretched across the upper end of the inclined post *(ulèng)*, with its crudely carved face. So there is another persona for that amibiguous effigy, that of second headhunting victim. In this way, the state of *lumo* created by the original death ebbs by degrees.

There is some evidence to suggest that the taking of heads as part of a mortuary ritual sequence may be a substitution for a prior practice of human sacrifice. We noted in chapter five that small statuettes *(butong)* are put into the coffins or jars of important people, and my informants claimed that these represent the slaves who were previously killed. Historical examples of such homicides are on record. Hose and McDougall (1912:II:46) report a case of the ritual killing of a slave at the tomb of an important man from a community adjacent to present day Batu Belah in the lower Tutoh. The murder occurred near the turn of the century. A slave was purchased for the purpose from Brunei, and it is interesting to note that the head of the victim was severed and hung upon the tomb, just as it would have been if it had been the product of a headhunting raid. Berawan say that the last occasion on which they made such a sacrifice was in the 1920s, and that they were able to keep it a secret from the District Officer. If they had taken a head, they said, there would surely have been a complaint from the community of the victim.

Echoes (or presages) of headhunting practices are also found in another well-attested variety of human sacrifice. Berawan claim that formerly when the main post of a large mausoleum *(lijèng)* was ready to be erected, a slave would be placed in the hole, bound hand and foot. As the post was hauled into an upright position its weight crushed the victim to death. The sacrifice ensured peace for the occupant of the mausoleum and sturdiness for the structure. Recently, the foot of an extremely old *lijèng* that stood on the banks of Loagan Bunut, the lake near Long Teru, became eroded, and human bones were discovered at its base. Exactly the same value is placed on heads. To ensure firmness of the structure, heads were hung on the posts of a new mausoleum, and also on the first post of a new longhouse. The belief persists to this day, long after human sacrifice and headhunting have been suppressed. Interior folk still fear *penyamun*,[4] mythical headhunters who are supposedly in the pay of the foreign-owned firms on the coast, or even the government. The heads are needed, it is said, to hold up the oil rigs that stand so precariously in the sea.

These clues suggest that the sacrifice of some lowly member of the group may have preceded the taking of heads as a means to terminate mourning. Berawan say that in the distant past opportunities for headhunting were limited because their nearest neighbors lived far away. If this is correct, then the nineteenth century, just before the Europeans arrived and when the migrating tribes were pressing closer upon one another, may have been the apogee of headhunting in central northern Borneo. Be that as it may, human sacrifice forms an appropriate stepping-stone to headhunting, in terms of the ideology of the mortuary rituals. The malicious soul must be appeased, but it is foolish and futile to kill a kinsman —that will only produce a new angry soul. The next best thing is an unwanted member of the community who lacks kin to suffer from his or her demise—a slave. After that some weak or unwary member of another group is the best target.

However, there is a problem in all this. By relating the need to take heads to the appeasement of the angry soul, I may be guilty of explaining the general from the particular. The maliciousness attributed to the recently dead is a special feature of Berawan eschatology. But other peoples in the Baram, including those that did not have secondary treatment of the dead, practiced headhunting. What for them is the connection between securing new heads and terminating mourning?

There are three possible answers. First, it may be that other folk had different ideologies concerning headhunting. I have already noted that the practice of headhunting was evidently not everywhere the same in the Baram: some communities retained large stocks of skulls, others only a handful. The second possibility is that the interpretation of Berawan headhunting as it relates to mourning is wrong, and that there is some other explanation that can be applied equally to all the peoples of the Baram. The third and most likely possibility is that the Berawan ideology of headhunting is both different and the same; it has its own peculiarities, but is a variation on some pattern of belief that is found across the entire culture area. The Kayan say that the victims of their depredations went to provide servants for the departed great man in the land of the dead. The Berawan say that the victim's soul was company for that of the deceased community member in its miserable transition, and those two statements are not irreconcilable.[5] If, as the Berawan claim, headhunting was a practice acquired from others, the Kayan or Kenyah, it need not surprise us that in the borrowing a peculiarly Berawan slant was placed upon it.

But even for the Berawan, the taking of heads did not occur exclusively in the context of mourning. Sometimes they were taken in the course of raiding or warfare not associated with any death ritual. In fact, the term for headhunting makes reference to just this kind of activity. Nowadays the Iban word *ngiau* is often used, but the Berawan term is *bawa ñiting*, literally to make war in small groups. It follows that there must be additional import to the headhunting rites, which augments rather than displaces what we have already discovered in them.

Vitality and Sexuality

The second approach is more general. It applies to headhunting both within and outside a context of mourning, and, *mutatis mutandis*, to the equally warlike but *nulang*-less neighbors of the Berawan. It sees the taking of the heads of enemies or outsiders as simply another "technique of life-saving," to employ the phrase that A. M. Hocart uses to characterize ritual:

> If life comes and goes it must come from somewhere and go somewhere. The more scientific among us carefully avoid the question where; but the greater part of mankind has not been so agnostic: they think they know in what objects life resides and into what objects it passes. Man has gone further: he has come to think that he can *control* that coming and going. He has worked out a technique to the end of controlling it. None of us has so far the remotest idea how this confidence first established itself, or how the technique was first worked out. We can only note that, like the concept of life, the technique of life-giving exists all the world over. Everywhere man goes through prescribed forms of words and actions in the persuasion that he can thereby transfer life from one thing to another. (Hocart 1936:33)

In defense of this universalistic notion of life, Rodney Needham argues that, contrary to what one might expect: "there does commonly seem to be a contrast between a relatively patent and apprehensible conception of life and a more obscure and perplexing conception of death" (Needham 1970:xxxv). That death is not universally perceived in a similar way is central to the purpose of this book. Meanwhile, the vast anthropological literature on "fertility cults" and the museums full of life-producing charms attest to the existence of a general category of life-sustaining ritual.

Certainly, the statement that the Berawan and their neighbors make about headhunting, that it promotes health and fecundity, places it squarely in this category. Its use to terminate mourning is a special application of this quality, one in which it operates as an antidote to the death that preceded it, and serves to halt the repetition of death after it. This quality makes comprehensible the persistent association between headhunting and sexuality.

I have already noted that the phases of the headhunting rites that arouse most public attention are the calling of the eagle *plaké* and the two mud fights. The former is the most serious; it tells whether death has been contained for the moment or not. But the latter is the more exciting. The young men in particular are expected to demonstrate that they know how to be *sagem*, "fast" or "vigorous," rather than *maport*, "slow." It is acknowledged that there are times when being *maport* is necessary, as when performing some tedious task such as weaving a net. But it is the *sagem* young man who draws all the admiration from the young women and the old folks alike. He represents the warrior ideal, and it is often expressed that he is the life of the community. This is literally true, since without such men the longhouse stands in risk of dissolution (Huntington and Metcalf 1979:133–41). But there is not only vigorousness in the mud fights, there is also sexual license. Just how marked this license is can only be judged when contrasted with the propriety that Berawan usually display concerning body contact between people of opposite sexes. Here the rules are not only being broken, but all the senior people, those who would normally frown at the slightest infraction, are now wildly cheering the young folk on. The dance previously performed by the women when a new head was brought into the house, the *makoi*, was so lewd that I could never get any of my informants to talk about it except in innuendos, accompanied by a rolling of the eyes. The *makoi* formed an appropriate complement to the headhunt itself; it displayed the vigor of the women, which was as necessary as that of the men. On the basis of their conjoined energies depended the reproduction of the community from generation to generation.[6]

The theme of vigor as an antidote to death strikes a responsive chord from another corner of the Malayo-Polynesian world. The Bara of Madagascar, described by Richard Huntington, conceive of life as a balance of the contrary principles of order, symbolized by bone, and vitality, symbolized by flesh. Life begins because the formless chaos of the mother's blood is given order by the father's semen. It ends when flesh loses out to bone, and ultimate order is achieved in the tomb. The purpose of the mortuary rites is to restore the correct balance, upset by the death. In the long run that is accomplished by storing the bones of the deceased where they belong, in a neat pile in the ancestral mausoleum, after a rite of secondary treatment. But this rite must await the completion of decomposition. In the meantime the morbidity of the rotting corpse must be offset by the ritual generation of vitality. The principal modes of forwarding vitality are in the emphasis on vigorousness and sexuality. Unlike some of their neighbors, the Bara stop short of incest, but intercourse is common and lewd behavior positively enjoined:

> An important aspect of the representation of vitality is the idea that it is chaotic, as opposed to the order of the ancestor cult. In one of the songs, the girls call upon the boys to act crazy, unrestrained, and shameless during the funeral fete. It is in this regard that rum takes on special significance. Rum is served not merely because intoxication is pleasant, but because disorderly conduct is essential. (Huntington and Metcalf 1979:114)

This obligatory excess is reminiscent of the manic quality of Berawan funerals. There are moments in the funeral when the emphasis seems to be upon spontaneous vitality. For example, in the games that involve rubbing pot blacking on peoples' faces, a young man who has been ambushed will chase his shrieking female assailants along the veranda, out into the kitchens at the back of the family apartments, and even up into the rafters of the longhouse. When he catches one, he grabs hold of her in a manner that would normally be considered scandalous. He tries to blacken her face in turn, while she wriggles and yells for help from her age mates. The din when one of these games is in full cry is considerable. Even one person running down the veranda is noisy because of the echoing clatter of the massive floorboards. A dozen or more, with the yelling included, produce bedlam. While the action is thick and fast, all other activity in the longhouse comes to a halt. Older people play a vicarious role, pointing out which way the girls have gone, joining in on the edges of melees, and getting their faces smeared in the process.

Everyone thoroughly enjoys these sudden uproars which break out especially during the day, when many people are busy at the routine chores of housekeeping such as pounding rice and hauling firewood. The elderly clap and cheer and shout encouragement all the while, and after it is over all the participants and onlookers laugh at each others' begrimed faces and recount who ran where and what kinds of ridiculous looks they wore on their faces.

The same elements are present in this game as in the mud fights during the headhunting rites: dirt, vigorousness, and sexuality. Pot black is the favorite way of making people grimy because it is irritatingly difficult to remove from either clothes or skin. But other things that come to hand are also used, such as flour from the pounding of rice. Certainly no one should be allowed to walk around unmolested in clothes that are too bright or too neat. They are a hazard, for they might arouse the jealousy of the lurking soul. But the game goes beyond that. In chapter one I noted that noise, confusion, and hilarity are viewed as essential elements in any major public ritual. Not to have them would indicate that the event had been a failure. In the funeral, there is an extra intensity to this sentiment, a tightening of the screws, that goes beyond what is normally found. This I attribute to the equivocal nature of the festivities, which are as much to protect the community from an immediate threat as to provide amusement. Now we observe a third element, the need to generate raw vigor and vitality, the clearest evidence of which is the exceptional freedom between the sexes. That freedom hardly goes as far as it does in Madagascar, but it is unmistakably there. Old folks, watching the fun, remark to each other that the longhouse must prosper now that there are so many energetic young people. "Soon there will be more children," they say. On one occasion, a grizzled old man nodded towards a chase in progress, and made a remark that took me by surprise at the time: *Bawa ñiting dé*, "They are headhunting."

In Madagascar, among the Bara, this theme of the generation of vitality as an antidote to death is the principal one running through the mortuary rites. The principal theme of the Berawan rites is different, even though there are many similarities of ritual sequence. What is interesting here is the resonance between the two; the dominant motif of the Bara rites emerges as a counterpoint

in the Berawan rituals. However, the passage in which the secondary theme is developed is less the funeral itself than the subsequent
headhunting ceremonies. That among both the Bara and the Berawan, sexual license should be associated with mortuary ritual at first
surprises us, but is comprehensible in terms of a restoration of
vitality. The association of headhunting with the termination of
mourning among the Berawan takes us a stage further in the same
argument. For us there is nothing invigorating in ritualized murder. That there is this significance for the Berawan derives from the
premise that the headhunting rites have the power to break the
community free from the grip of death.

Notes

1. There is a darker side to this. As noted below, there are occasional
panics when it is rumored that headhunters in the pay of the government
or European interests are operating in the interior. For me to have allowed
that I could get hold of heads for their ceremonies would have had odd
implications.

2. This is not the place to set out or explain all the restrictions placed
upon headhunters. It may be noted, however, that eggs are used in a variety
of ritual contexts. They are needed in the preparation of a shrine *(tapó)* to
the Creator, where they are used in a group of four or eight, each egg
supported by the split end of an upright stick. They are also often used by
shamans as offerings to their familiars.

3. At one funeral I attended a clearly bad omen was obtained. It caused
considerable consternation, and brought the proceedings to a halt. The rite
of *ninung ulèng* was performed the next day, but on a small scale, almost
furtively. All other ritual activity was curtailed. The death of another adult
in the community occurred within a few weeks.

4. *Penyamun* is a word of Malay origin, meaning robber, marauder, or
pirate. But throughout central Borneo it implies a headhunter.

5. The practices reported among the Melanau in the last century provide an interesting mediating case. Slaves were tied to the uprights of
mausoleums and left to die of exposure. Here we have human sacrifice as
among the Berawan, but the mode of death is different. The Melanau
believed that people who died violent deaths went to a different region of
the afterworld than those who died natural deaths. If the sacrificed slave
was to serve his master, a notion similar to that given for Kayan headhunting, then he could not be mercifully executed with one rapid blow, but had
to be subjected to the slow death of exposure (Jamuh 1949).

6. This aspect of social reproduction is illuminatingly discussed in Michelle Rosaldo's (1980) account of headhunting among the Ilongot, an egalitarian, swidden farming people of Northern Luzon, Philippines. Her account is especially valuable because the Ilongot were still actively engaged in headhunting during her first period of fieldwork. Many Ilongot conceptions of the makeup of the individual assign considerable objectivity to emotions. In particular, young men tend to be ruled by *liget*, which Rosaldo glosses as "anger" or "passion." It makes them moody, sullen, and inclined toward sudden violence. Its expression, *par excellence*, is the taking of a head. This "passion" must be channeled by mature men, who ideally possess *beya*, "knowledge." Without "knowledge," "passion" is socially destructive, even self-destructive. But the acquisition of "knowledge" means the taking on of adult roles of responsibility, and that, inevitably in the Ilongot view, cools youthful ardor. Consequently, the two are in dynamic balance:

> . . . a good deal of what Ilongots see as beautiful and exciting in the act of killing has to do with the dynamics of social reproduction; because adults, constrained by physical weakness, "knowing" bonds, and nets of obligation, cannot themselves be lovely, filled with "focused" energy, and inclined to violence, they look for their vitality to the *liget* of the young. Headhunting is the moment in which youth's *liget* finds fulfillment; invigorating to the social body, it is a token of the ways in which civil society depends for its liveliness and renewal upon the initiative of youth. (M. Rosaldo 1980:219)

CHAPTER EIGHT

Mourning: Pollution and Transition

For the community as a whole, mourning is terminated by a festival that, like the funeral, is public and exuberant. By contrast, the close kin of the deceased, and especially the widow or widower, are released only by degrees, in a protracted series of small, intimate rites. Simple though they are, they utilize a range of symbols of transition, including dirt, water, noise, food, and hair. Needless to say, the use of these symbols is not restricted to the familial mourning rites, and I draw together here instances of their employment from the funeral and the headhunting rites as well.

The Mourning Rites of the Close Kin

The close kin continue in a spartan style of living for some months after the funeral. Widows and widowers in particular have a long list of restrictions to observe. They may not rise early in the morning but must lie abed until a couple of hours after dawn; for it is said that anyone who gets up after the bereaved spouse is liable to suffer the sickness that killed his or her partner. Their social life is much restricted: they may not dance, sing, or attend parties, and they must not visit other family apartments in the longhouse other than their own, even the adjacent ones that house their children and grandchildren, if they have them. They may not go to the farms, or anywhere far from the longhouse.

These restrictions are observed by the surviving spouse for four, five, or six months, until he or she begins to feel "ordinary" again, that is, not tearful or strained in the company of others. Widows tend to be longer in mourning than widowers, and more obviously so. This is not a matter of prescription; it is just that men soon feel the pressure to return to everyday affairs at their farms. Men and women alike are circumspect in their contacts with the opposite sex during this period, for fear of public censure, and there is a special illness *(pengusan)* that afflicts those who too soon take an interest in flirtation. A full year should elapse before plans to re-marry are entertained.

Other kin observe a weaker form of these taboos, for periods that largely depend on their feelings about the deceased. At a mini-mum, they will avoid dancing and singing for a month or two.

In addition to these restrictions, there are rituals that the fam-ily, that is, coresidential group, of the dead person must perform. The widow or widower is usually the principal actor in these events. They begin three of four days after the interment, when the family observes a private day of silence, after the great day of silence observed by the whole community. On this day the widow or wid-ower is finally released from the house of mats, and on emerging he or she receives a haircut. Widowers merely trim their hair neatly in the traditional fashion, but a widow's hair is cut in a special style. The front half of the head is shaved in a straight line over the top of the head from ear to ear, and this tonsure is the distinctive mark of a widow. Also, a few inches are cut from the long hair at the back of the head. Other kin simply cut their hair neatly in their usual style.

The widow or widower is then ready to perform the rite of *katong achīn* (*katong* = drift, float, *achīn* = steps, stairs). A simple ladder is prepared by cutting notches out of a pole, and the floor planks are removed from underneath the recently vacated mat en-closure. Then the surviving spouse lowers the ladder to the ground, and descends. Usually the assistance of a child or grandchild is necessary, because long internment in cramped quarters has im-paired the use of the legs. Older widows in particular become very weak during their ordeal. The pair of them, adult and child, hobble shakily to the river to bathe, carrying with them the crude ladder, which is thrown into the river. Other bathers should avoid the spot, allowing them a modicum of privacy. Having washed and put on new mourning clothes, they return to find the floorboards replaced, and they enter by the normal steps.

A day or two later the widow takes a further ritual bath, in connection with the rites of *ngachang* described in the preceeding chapter.

Another series of small rituals is associated with the phases of the moon. At each new moon for several successive months, the family must arrange for a formal dirge to be sung. The scene is the riverbank outside the family apartment of the dead person. The performer is either the widow herself, or if she is not skilled, a stand-in can be employed. Men usually call upon the help of a woman known for her skill in this verbal art form. The dirge tells how the deceased's soul is fairing in the land of the dead, how lonely and sad it is. The spirits of the ancestors are, for the most part, kind to it, and invent all manner of games and entertainments to distract it. Slowly it forgets, even as the living are forgetting the dead person. The audience is often moved to tears by this dramatic performance.[1]

At the first full moon after the harvest, a specially elaborate version of the nocturnal dirge is made called *tepá dulīt (tepá* = pestle used for pounding rice, I could elicit no meaning for *dulīt).* An elaborate ritual apparatus is prepared and stood up in the open space in front of the longhouse, adjacent to the dead person's apartment. It consists of a bamboo pole about fifteen feet tall, with the upper end split, and the split bamboo pried open to form an inverted cone. On top of this cone a roof is attached, made of wood or nowadays a small piece of roofing zinc, and covered with a red cloth. Inside the cone is a small tray with offerings for the dead person's soul: tobacco, sweet things, a little rice wine, and two crudely carved figurines *(butong).* All around the outside of the cone are hung ears of the new rice, arranged in geometrical patterns. Berawan say that this rice is the share of the new harvest offered to the soul of the dead person, who may well have lent a hand in planting it. The first eating of new rice is a joyful moment of family integration, in which only those belonging to the productive unit participate, and this rite enables the deceased to share in it. A time of full moon is chosen, I was told, so as to be sure of encountering the dead man's spirit. The rite is not completed with the erection of the pole. The surviving spouse must sing a dirge for the dead person, much as described above. Widows kneel at the foot of the pole and keen pitifully. No one is permitted to accompany the grieving spouse, and the lone mourner in the moonlight makes a tragic and dramatic figure.

One final familial rite remains to be described, the ritual washing of the widower or widow called *katé apok* (*katé* = to throw away, *apok* = dirt). He or she slips quietly away from the village alone, and paddles a short distance downriver to a place where there is tall grass by the river bank for privacy. There, the mourner climbs a small tree and vigorously shakes its branches, while making a quiet prayer for the health and safety of members of the family. Finally, he or she bathes in the river and goes quietly back to the house. There is no specific occasion for the rite, nor is there a specific number of times that it should be performed. Three or four times within the first two months of mourning would seem to be normal.

Since the widow or widower figures so prominently in the mourning usages, we must say a word about the death of unmarried persons. Though divorce is common among the Berawan, at any given time most adults are married. Few adults choose to remain unmarried, and it is most commonly people who have been predeceased by their wives or husbands who lack a principal mourner at their own death rites. In this case, there is no one to put into the cubicle of mats, or to make *katong achīn*. The dirges at full moon may be omitted, but the *tepá dulīt* will erected by other family members.

Mud and Pot Black

The widow's rite of *katé apok*, literally "throwing off dirt," draws our attention to the polluting aspect of death. There are several occasions in the mortuary rites when people are deliberately made dirty; specifically, the two mud fights during the headhunting rites, one when the new "heads" arrive at the longhouse and one when the effigy is erected, and the games during the funeral when the young men and women try to rub pot black on each others' faces. I have already discussed the significance of the vigor that is displayed, and the sexual license allowed, at these times. But the most obvious feature of them is that all the participants are made as filthy as possible, and there are various possible interpretations of this. I have suggested that to present too neat an appearance may arouse the jealousy of the hovering soul, so that, however flirtatiously done, the muddying or blacking serves to protect the over-clean individual. Alternatively, dirtiness might be seen as implying the carelessness of grief.

But this kind of behavior is not restricted to mortuary rituals. Similar scenes are enacted when visitors leave a longhouse, if feelings of friendship have grown during their stay. Many travelers in central northern Borneo have the same story to recount: In the early morning, after a night of partying with their hosts, they are wearily making their way down to the canoes loaded for departure. The young girls who were the ringleaders of the previous night's festivities follow them down to the river bank as if to bid a last farewell, while a smirking audience looks on from the longhouse veranda. Suddenly there is a melee when it turns out that the girls have hands covered with pot black and plan to smear it on the visitors' faces and bodies. As the latter beat a hasty retreat to their canoes, they are liberally splashed or pushed headlong into the river. A cheer goes up from the longhouse as the victims disengage themselves and struggle out into the stream. Clearly, making people dirty with mud and pot black is not only a feature of mourning.[2] It has some more general significance, having to do with arrivals, departures, and changes of state, in short, transitions.

Notice that water is employed along with the pot black. The Right Honorable Malcolm MacDonald, then Governor-General of Malaya and British Borneo, gives this account of his departure from a Kenyah longhouse:

> On the river bank we said our final adieus. Every Kenyah in the place, male and female, shouted a mighty "Salamat Jalan" as we went aboard our prahus. In the front rank stood Tama Weng and his wife, with Kallang and Nawang, Bungan, Lohong and Ubong. The girls waved their handkerchiefs and beamed enchantingly at us. As I lolled on the cushions in my boat, waiting for the crew to complete the last minute preparations for departure, I stretched my hands over the vessel's side, dipped my fingers in the water and playfully flicked a few splashes in their direction. I was sitting fifteen yards away from them, above fairly deep river, and they were not only on dry land but also in smart dresses and fine jewellery; so I felt sure that my trick

would not invite serious retort. That was, of course, an incredibly foolish mistake. I should have known better. With shouts of joyful belligerency Bungan, Lohong and Ubong leaped into the river, waded quickly forward until they stood immersed above their waists, and started to hurl great showers of water into the boat. For a while I could scarcely see them through the flying spray. I returned their fire as effectively as I could, but they did not seem to mind being nearly drowned in cataracts of river. Sochurek, sitting near me, joined in our defence, and a tremendous nautical engagement ensued. Soaked to the skins, with their long hair clinging to their lovely faces and floating around their trim figures, the girls appeared like outraged mermaids. . . . (MacDonald 1958:348–9)

Water and Noise

MacDonald's august position evidently inhibited the ambush, at least temporarily, so that he avoided the pot black. But the target of these attacks usually ends up both wet *and* dirty. We normally think of water as something that removes dirt, with the help of a little soap perhaps. But in this case both the wetness and the dirtiness have to do with departure, so that they appear, not as a sequence, but as coexisting symbols of transition. It may seem that the difference is one of splitting hairs, but it has this substance to it, that it changes our perception of the pollution of death. So let us explore further the ritual use of water.

There are some interesting comparisons to be made between the use of water and that of noise. Berawan mortuary rites are sometimes remarkably loud affairs. The general hubbub of a large funeral, with the longhouse packed with residents and guests and everyone socializing with gusto can be heard a half a mile away through the still forest. But not satisfied with that, the Berawan have additional ways to make noise at funerals. There is the great brass gong that is used initially to announce that a death has occurred. Its deep reverberations can often be heard several miles away. Then there is the large drum that can only be played during funerals. It booms out day and night, using rhythms that are proscribed at other times. The same rhythms are played on gongs large and small, which together make up an orchestra with several players. The larger gongs are hung vertically, and struck with a padded mallet to produce a deep, resonant sound. The smaller ones are strung horizontally in order of size on two strands of rattan stretched across a frame. The player holds a piece of firewood in each hand and plays rapid tinkling figures, further augmented by the staccato clatter of children beating on bamboo slit gongs.

But it is at the rites of secondary treatment that this noisiness reaches its greatest intensity. The crowds are larger, the socializing more intense and nonstop, and the playing of gongs and drums is more frenetic. In addition to all that, there are special games that are played at *nulang*, of which noise is supposedly only a byproduct. These are described in detail in chapter ten. Suffice it for now to say that they are cacophonous: one involves beating upon the floor of the longhouse with heavy wooden rice pestles that are as tall as a man. As in the games that involve the young people charging about the veranda, the floor acts as a great sounding board, and magnifies the din.

Finally, when the corpse is moved out of the longhouse to the barge that will carry it to the graveyard, a series of shotgun blasts punctuate the wailing of the women.

If one asks what all this noise *means*, then it is difficult to phrase a direct answer because the connotations are diffuse. Just how common is the use of noise in ritual was pointed out by Rodney Needham (1967). He expands upon an idea in a 1938 paper by Maria Dworakowska entitled "The Origin of Bell and Drum." Dworakowska hypothesizes that the use of bells and gongs at funerals derived from the use of drums, which in turn originated from "coffin logs," hence the association of these instruments with death. The historical speculation is untestable, but Needham accepts that the association does exist. However, it is too narrow: The list of instruments needs to include xylophones, rattles, rasps, metallophones, stamping tubes, sticks, resounding rocks, clashing anklets, and other objects as well as drums, bells, and gongs. Not all these instruments are capable of producing a melody, or even a rhythm. What they have in common, Needham argues, is only their percussive nature. Moreover, the use of these instruments is not restricted to funerals, but is also found at weddings, naming ceremonies, initiations, harvest festivals, and all manner of rites of passage. He concludes that it is a general feature of the human psyche that percussion is associated with transition.

In addition to their percussive quality, drums and gongs are able to make loud noises. In the din of the modern world, it is easy to forget how exceptional really loud noise is in technologically simple societies. It is often the result of the forces of nature, and has connotations of the sacred. In another paper, Needham writes of the impressiveness of thunder in the jungle terrain of Southeast Asia. It is "an appalling natural phenomenon, seeming to crack and reverberate menacingly on the very surface of the forest canopy and shaking the guts of the humans cowering underneath" (Needham 1964:141). For the Berawan, the spirit of thunder *(bili'gau)* is a powerful and dangerous spirit agency.

Our problem in dealing with the significance of noise is to cope with too many associations, not too few. Already we have three, of increasing generality: Drums and death, percussion and transition, and loud noise and the sacred. All three are in evidence in Berawan mortuary rites: There is the great drum that sounds only for death. There are the gunshots when the corpse is moved out of the house on its way to the graveyard. And there is the continuous tumult of socializing, games, and music that accompanies the sacred seasons of the funeral and *nulang,* with their hovering souls and ancestors. The contact with the sacred is broken off at the conclusion of each by *liang kiji',* the great day of silence. All these ritual uses of noise, or the lack of it, relate to liminality, but they do so in slightly different ways.

If we now compare the ritual use of water with that of noise, a similar succession of levels of association can be made out. At the first level, we see water associated with death. When the "headhunting party" returns to the longhouse shortly after dawn on the third or fourth day after entombment, it is liberally splashed as it approaches the river bank. What provokes this response is the presence of the "head," which connotes a second death, albeit one that was planned. The rite of *ngachang* is like an echo of the funeral; in the space of a few hours a new state of *lumo* is created and almost immediately cast off, in the rite of erecting the effigy. The effigy also represents a death, or several deaths, and it calls forth the same response: splashing with water.

But, as Governor-General McDonald testifies, horseplay at the riverside is not restricted to mortuary rituals. Moreover, even at funerals it may have more to do with transition, our second level of association, than with death per se. For example, when the party returns from taking the corpse to the graveyard, everyone in the boats is thoroughly doused. This expresses, not contact with death, but separation from it. A nice instance occurs in the rite of "drifting steps" *(katong achīn)*, in which the widow (or widower) leaves the house like a corpse, through a hole in the floor and down her own private stairs. By immersion in the river, she is transformed, and reenters the longhouse in the normal manner of the living. Meanwhile, her little steps are thrown in the river, just as eventually happens to the timbers of the ramp down which the corpse was carried.

Watery transitions are a common feature of Berawan myths. We have already noted one example in the story of the movement of the Berawan people out of their mountain homeland recounted in chapter two. The two brothers, Layong and Kusai, go hunting to obtain meat for their mother's *nulang*. But Layong wanders into the land of the dead, and he realizes this when he immerses in water the squirrel that he previously shot and it springs back to life. There are many incidents of the same kind, and not all of them involve reviving the dead. In one myth cycle, a hunter pursues a pig that plunges into a stream only to emerge as a beautiful woman. This instance shows that water has an association with all manner of change, and not only with life and death.

And the third level? We have the instance that I have already pointed out, the rite of *katé apok* ("throwing away dirt"). The rite occurs several times, so that in format as well as in name it implies that the widow is in a continuous state of defilement. It is consequently not a ritual of transition in the straightforward way that the "drifting steps" one is. On the other hand, it is not directly associated with contact with the corpse or places of the dead. We must conclude that the widow is in a generalized state of supernaturally induced pollution, from which ritual washing will gradually remove her. The restriction upon combing the hair inside the longhouse has the same implication.

What this analysis reveals is that the ritual use of water is not

Plate 9. Closing stages of a mud fight after the return of a "headhunting party." Some men are washing themselves clean of mud, while the women continue their forays.

synonymous with the casting off of pollution. On the one hand, it is clear that the Berawan do have a conception of pollution. It is made explicit in the rite of *katé apok*, and it is also found in other contexts, principally menstruation.[3] On the other hand, in most of the cases when water is used during the mourning rites, it is not pollution that is most forcefully implied. Instead it is something that is more germane to the specifics of Berawan eschatology, namely change of state.

Food and Hair as Codes of Separation

Two further aspects of the familial mourning observances call for comment: The presentation of food to the soul of the deceased, and the cutting of the widow's hair.

It is a commonplace of anthropology that the sharing of food generally expresses solidarity, and that failure to share indicates separation. For example, David Sapir describes restrictions on the sharing of food among the Diola-Fogny of Senegal (Sapir 1970) which serve to emphasize the distinction between generations, and to ritually detach surviving spouses from a dead husband or wife. Both rules are concerned with the separation of categories. The former is a matter of maintaining a boundary and is enforced by a taboo against parents eating from the same bowl as their children. The latter is a matter of creating a separation out of a pair who previously shared food. In particular, stocks of food that are owned jointly by a husband and wife become polluted at the death of either. Before the surviving spouse can eat from the family supply, it must be ritually cleansed.

In Berawan society, food produced by the efforts of the residential group is as much the property of the wife as it is the male head of the household. Yet there is no suggestion that it becomes polluted or uneatable at the death of either. In fact, the use of food in the funeral and at subsequent rituals hardly implies separation at all; just the opposite. In the minutes after death, the corpse is offered cigarettes, then it is taken into the kitchen and fed with cooked food taken from the family supply. During the funeral, plates of food are placed regularly atop the coffin or jar containing the corpse. All this, as we have seen, expresses the continuity of the deceased and continuing membership in the social group.

Of the rites of mourning observed by the family, the most essential, I was told, is *tepá dulīt*, which involves the giving of a share of the harvest to the lingering soul of the deceased. The offerings inside the inverted cone are the sort of things put into spirit houses (*beran, melíga*i): small glasses of rice wine, sweet things, and tobacco. But the outside of it is covered with hundreds of ears of the new rice. This rice is not cooked, or even husked, and it is proffered outside the longhouse, probably adjacent and complementary to the effigy set up during the headhunting rituals. This is in contrast to the *cooked* rice provided *within* the house at the funeral. What is expressed is decreasing intimacy, a slow separation in accordance with the eschatological ideas set out in chapter six.

Hair is also frequently manipulated ritually in accordance with ideas of pollution and separation. P. Hershman (1974), developing an argument made by Edmund Leach (1958), and utilizing data from the Punjab, suggests that the symbolism of hair frequently has two components. The first is a universal psychodynamic one, and involves the symbolic identification of hair and genitalia. The second is culturally variable, and is utilized to express all manner of sociological distinctions.

As regards Berawan men, the hair cutting that goes on after the funeral constitutes nothing more than a return to the status quo. They simply cut their hair neatly, as opposed to the disheveled appearance maintained during the preceeding week or two. This is true of a widower also. The principal ritual manipulation of hair is the widow's distinctive tonsure. It is assumed at the commencement of a period of enforced celibacy on her part, and so corresponds to the psychodynamic interpretation that Hershman points to. The prohibition upon widows combing their hair indoors is a detail that fits nicely with this aspect of Hershman's argument: The hair is polluting because the widow's sexuality at this time is dangerous to the entire community. It is also true that grooming the hair of the head, as well as plucking out facial hair, is intimate behavior usually performed by spouses. However, unlike the Punjabis, Berawan men will cut each others' hair without embarrassment, and assist in the shaving of the back and sides of the head in the distinctive male haircut of central Borneo. Moreover, the type of haircut given to the widow is not such as to focus upon her sexuality, or lack of it. Hershman shows that in the Punjab, and presumably elsewhere as well, it is the long hair at the back of the head that must be controlled in order subconsciously to control sexuality. Elaborate codes spell out just when a Punjabi woman may allow her long hair, which is never cut, to hang freely. But Berawan women wear their hair up in a knot for convenience, or down, as they see fit, and the back of the widow's hair is only trimmed a little. On the other hand, the shaving of the front of the head changes the appearance of the face in a very noticeable way. It is impossible to mistake a widow. The barbering of the widow acts more forcefully to mark a social status than to express subconscious messages about sexuality and pollution.

The Nature of the Widow's Pollution

Among the Ngaju of southern Borneo, the polluting quality of the corpse is graphically expressed. In his essay on death, Hertz, drawing on Hardeland (1858:218), says that the Ngaju believe that the corpse is surrounded by an "impure cloud" that "pollutes everything it touches; i.e., not only the people and objects that have been in physical contact with the corpse, but also everything that is intimately connected, in the mind of the survivor, with the image of the deceased" (Hertz 1960:38). Affected in this way are all personal belongings, fruit trees, and even places where the deceased liked to fish.

The Berawan have no expression akin to the Ngaju "impure cloud," and do not think that the corpse pollutes everything around it. As to fruit trees and fishing spots, there is a vague notion that it is wise to avoid the old haunts of the deceased for fear that the soul might be lurking there, but there is no insinuation that the trees or their fruit are unclean. In the Berawan view, it is only people and not objects that are put into a special status by the death, and not because of mere physical contact with the body. The people that handle the corpse when it is being washed and dressed, moved about, and arranged on the death seat are not infected by it. They may feel private qualms, but they are not afterwards socially marked or obliged to cleanse themselves in any way. While the corpse is exposed on the death seat, people touch it casually, as for instance when they light the cigarette that is put between the corpse's fingers, which needless to say goes out again immediately. Children play near the body at this time, and throughout the funeral an important visitor to the longhouse will be seated in the place of honor directly in front of the coffin or jar. Were the close proximity of the corpse a source of contagion, this would be an odd honor indeed.

Pollution, in the Berawan view, is not a matter of contact with, but relationship to, the source of contagion. The crucial relationship, as we have noted, is that of spouse. Hertz says that among the Ngaju the body of the spouse is regarded as so polluted as to be almost as dangerous as the corpse itself; a secondary source of infection.

But the Berawan widow or widower is not so much inherently unclean as made unclean. I never received the impression that bereaved spouses became the object of disgust or rejection. The sentiment is instead one of compassion for unavoidable hardships. The result of imprisonment within the "widow's wall" during the funeral is that the surviving spouse becomes corpse-like, but this is an artificially created condition. Hertz mentions a custom reported in the nineteenth century whereby a widow is obliged to rub onto her own body the products of decomposition of the corpse (Hertz 1960: 51). Why should the widow seek out the very source of pollution in this way? Clearly, in order to render herself impure, to make her condition closer to that of the deceased. One of the proscriptions visited upon Berawan widows in their confinement is that they may not stretch out their legs straight in front of them. This cramping position has no role in inhibiting the spread of contagion.[4] Instead, and explicitly, it has to do with discomfort, which in turn is to assuage the jealousy of the deceased spouse's soul.

Pollution and Transition

Throughout Indonesia, concepts of pollution are generally most in evidence in connection with death. So it is among the Ngaju, with their "impure cloud" emanating from the corpse. It would be surprising if the Berawan were so exceptional as to completely lack notions of the pollution of death, and they are not, as is shown by the rite of *katé apok,* "throwing away dirt." But those notions are overshadowed by other, perhaps simpler, symbolic valences. The pollution of the widow has a relatively nonmystical character; it is something manufactured by the community rather than an inherent quality of the corpse. It is removed by a series of rites that reiterate themes of transition.

I have not tried to explain just why dirt, water, noise, and so on present themselves to the Berawan, and other people, as suitable objective representations of transition. There is a certain common-sense logic to it, perhaps. The ability of water to flow suggests time and change, so that we speak of "water under the bridge." Dirt, especially the sticky pot black, suggests darkness, night, death, and thus changes of state, for all changes are little deaths. Percussive noise seems to punctuate and divide time ("mark time") . . . But these musings would be more suitable to a comparative study of particular modes of symbolism rather than an ethnography. What is significant here is that the emphasis upon the liminal in the rites of mourning supports and expands the analysis of eschatological notions arrived at in chapter six. In them, as in the funeral, there is always a principal actor that is hidden in the wings; the soul, itself in transit.

Notes

1. The song implies that after only a few months the soul is already settled in the land of the dead. But my informants agreed that this is poetic license. Were that really the case, there would be no point observing the mourning usage.

2. H. B. Low observed a rite in a Kenyah village in the upper Rejang which combined making people dirty with the kind of sexual license discussed in the previous chapter (Low 1882:94). He calls it a "festival of fertility," without specifying whether it was connected with mortuary rites, or the annual cycle of rice production, or something else. He was shocked by the spectacle, which involved nudity, and an "orgy" in which men and women smeared soft rice and soot on each other.

3. Berawan prohibitions on menstruating women are not severe; principally they may not cook. But there is usually some other woman to do the

kitchen work, and men are not particularly adverse to cooking if the need arises. Some Kenyah formerly banished menstruating women and women near childbirth to special huts away from the longhouse. The Berawan never had this practice, as far as I know. It is interesting to note that menstruation can be seen as a counterpart to headhunting. The former is a way that women pollute men, the latter involves men polluting women, by bringing the heads into the house. This correspondence extends themes explored in the last chapter.

4. It has been suggested to me that the prohibition on a widow straightening her legs has to do with keeping her vulva securely covered, as befits a widow, or to prevent menstrual pollution being added to that of death. But this is contradicted by two facts: First, the modest position for a woman to sit in is precisely with her legs out straight in front, knees together. Second, widowers suffer the same prohibition.

IV

---

*Celebrating
the Ancestors*

CHAPTER NINE

Lanau Comes Home

Nulang, the great festival of the dead, offers an imposing spectacle. But it is in several ways a paradoxical institution: It is sociologically crucial yet rarely held; it is the culminating expression of a doctrine of souls yet resembles a reprise of the funeral; it is the most sacred of rites yet it is associated with, and set in motion by, nothing more solemn than a child's game of tops.

Concise Statement of the Nature of Nulang

In ideological terms, the *nulang* celebrates the termination of a final and unpleasant phase in the soul's career. Now it has completed the dreary metamorphosis to pure spirit, and is consequently acceptable in the land of the dead. So the festival is also a celebration of the reunion of the deceased with his or her ancestors. Furthermore, because the dead individual is, as it were, a messenger traveling from the community of the living to the greater community of the dead, it becomes also a festival of the ancestors. They are conceived of as being present *en masse* throughout the event and more especially at certain moments in the death songs, and it is their presence, the fusion for a brief period of the living and the dead, that gives *nulang* its supremely sacred character.

Ritually what is involved is the recovery of the remains of the deceased from their place of temporary storage, bringing them to the longhouse, and, at the conclusion of the rite, placing them in permanent storage in a mausoleum. Sometimes the container used for temporary storage is opened, the bones are taken out and cleaned, and then rehoused in a new and finer container. Sometimes the mausoleum used for final storage is very splendid, representing many man-hours of labor and the cooperation of the entire village. Always the week or so that the remains are at the longhouse is spent in eating, drinking, and elaborate diversions.

Ideology and ritual intersect in the metaphor of soul and body explored in chapter six. It is because the bones are now dry and free of putrescence that the soul is converted to spirit and acceptable to the dead. Ritually, this association is most emphatically made when the bones are washed to ensure their cleanliness. When the container is not opened, it is simply assumed that the time elapsed since the funeral is sufficient to guarantee that corruption has run its course. As the bones are now hard and imperishable, so the deceased has become untarnishable spirit.

There are two further features of the rites that need to be stressed. First, the *nulang* is at once a repeat and an inversion of the funeral. In overall format it follows the pattern set by the funeral, with many days and nights of noisy socializing near the mortal remains, concluding with an especially intense final night in the longhouse, and then a journey by barge to the graveyard. It is for this reason that I speak of the "second wake." But on the other hand, everything has changed. The metaphorical connection between body and soul is identically the same as that expressed in the funeral, but its impact has been reversed. The funeral is dominated by themes of defense. As the days go by the corpse sinks further and further into ruin, and the menace can only mount. By contrast, the *nulang* looks at the process from the other end, and consequently has a sunnier air. Attention is directed towards, not the hovering soul, but the benevolent company of the ancestors.

Second, the relationship between *nulang* and the metamorphosis of the soul is indeterminate. If the *nulang* has been delayed, then the metamorphosis of the soul has surely been completed long before, just as the process of putrescence of the body has been completed. The soul-become-spirit is acceptable to the dead, and has had no further need to linger near the living. Consequently, the dead need not be feared for all the time that it takes to make preparations for the *nulang*—unless, that is, they show themselves in ghostly form *(uted)* precisely to remind the kinsmen of their duties. *Nulang* does not transmit the soul to the land of the dead, it only celebrates the fact of that arrival.

Nulang has the same relationship to spiritual maturation that a debutante ball has to puberty. Those who do not receive *nulang* are not excluded from the land of the dead, it is simply that their arrival goes unmarked by ritual. This explains why the extended ritual sequence is an honor and not a punishment. No condition is more miserable than that of the soul in the period directly after death. If those awaiting *nulang* were trapped in this condition, perhaps for years, while their kinsmen dithered around making arrangements, then their lot would be considerably worse than the souls of humbler folk who make their unassuming entry into the land of the dead much sooner. But that is not the case. Men do not control the process of release of the soul from the bonds of the flesh, nor the corresponding acceptability of the newly dead to their ancestors. Instead, *nulang* provides its subject with a formal introduction, a moment of consummate splendor.

Because the rites of secondary treatment are celebratory rather than instrumental, they need not be performed in every case. In fact, they are reserved only for a small minority. At first blush, the infrequency of *nulang* would seem to undermine the claims that Berawan make of its importance; how can something rarely seen have any real impact on peoples' day-to-day lives? In sociological terms, the answer is that the very rarity of *nulang* gives them extraordinary political impact. In terms of ideology, *nulang* exists as a logical compliment to the funeral rites.

There is, however, more to it than merely dropping the other shoe. The festival offers a mystical union with the ancestors that reinvigorates the entire community. In the following chapters, the ritual means by which this end is achieved are examined in detail. They are complex enough to require description in several phases: Chapter ten describes and analyzes the ritual format. Chapters eleven and twelve focus upon one activity of the *nulang,* the singing of special songs that form the sacred core of the rite. The former examines the difficulties involved in studying the songs because of their esoteric nature. The latter recounts the contents of the songs, and explains their dramatic impact. Because the concern of this book is with eschatology, I deal with the rituals of *nulang* in detail. However, it is not possible to proceed without at least sketching in the sociological significance of *nulang.* The remainder of this chapter is concerned with the who and why, and by way of illustration, describes the circumstances leading up to two recent *nulang*.

Selection of the Extended Rites

The infrequency of *nulang* is not a modern phenomenon. Berawan claim that they have always been performed only in a minority of cases, and a census of graveyards bears them out. The hardwoods from which the finest mausoleums are built are remarkably durable, so that they can still be seen a century and more after they were built, despite the ravages of the encroaching jungle. Each one implies a *nulang*, because the remains it houses must have been stored elsewhere while it was under construction. However, each is invariably surrounded by evidence of simpler earth tombs associated with the abridged rites. *Nulang* were certainly more frequent prior to, say, 1960. A rough estimate based on my (probably incomplete) list of mausoleums, and aggregating all four Berawan communities, suggests a rate of at least one per year since 1900, or approximately one for every fifteen to twenty adult deaths. Since 1960, the frequency of *nulang* has decreased even at Long Teru, where the traditional religion is preserved. But the change is quantitative, not qualitative.

The political impact of the rites of secondary treatment lies in the opportunity that they offer for display and maneuver. In order to successfully complete a *nulang*, the cooperation of many people is necessary. The more grand the scale on which it is celebrated, the more intense the support required, and for the very largest the energies of the entire community are absorbed for a considerable period. To be able to demonstrate this kind of control is the signal mark of leadership, so that *nulang* are important in the legitimization of authority.

The format of the extended rites has two practical advantages. First, it allows time for surpluses of rice to be accumulated. A great deal of rice is required both to feed the great crowds of guests that are invited, and also to prepare the rice wine, which is consumed in bulk. Deaths cannot be scheduled, *nulang* can. When a rising leader wished to take advantage of a death in his family in order to make a political statement, he had the year or more that the corpse of his kinsman was in storage to muster support and to make preparations. Normally, extra farms would have to be planted in order to create the necessary surplus. Second, the delay enabled the construction of a fine, carved mausoleum. There is a strict prohibition against any kind of preparation before death occurs. Consequently, if a splendid tomb is to be constructed, *nulang* is necessary. The tombs provide a permanent monument to the authority of the leader, something that longhouse residents can point to long after the hangovers of the *nulang* itself have been slept off. Jealous rivals may later denigrate the scale of consumption, but the mausoleum remains to confound them.

But it does not follow that all *nulang* were grander than all funerals. On the one hand, an important family is more likely to have on hand the stores of rice necessary to proceed directly with a funeral on a large scale, and if there is a suitable family vault already prepared, there is no need for delay. On the other hand, the ability to save up rice over an extended period is an advantage that might appeal to people of the middling sort who wish to have respectable but not ostentatious death rites for a close relative. They might use a simpler form of mausoleum for final storage of the remains. Consequently, there is no direct relationship between social status and choice of ritual sequence. Grand funerals, as opposed to *nulang,* have always occurred, and they are equally prestigious.

In recent decades, *nulang* have become more unusual than was traditionally the case. This is not primarily the result of weakened belief in the old ideas. Even at the villages that have undergone major religious innovation—conversion to Christianity or to the revivalist movement called Bungan—eschatological concepts remain remarkably stable. As an instance of this, I was once told by a young man of Long Jegan that it was a socially responsible act to become a Roman Catholic. His argument was that the unquiet souls of the Christian dead go to purgatory, where God keeps an eye on them, so that they do not bother the living. He had thus nicely incorporated his traditional ideology with his newly adopted one. He was also clear about when the dead are finally admitted to Heaven: When their bones are dry.

What has changed are economic factors, particularly the availability of credit from Chinese traders in the interior. By simply borrowing rice against future production, it is possible to proceed as if a surplus were continually on hand. This has made the abridged mortuary sequence more attractive. Moreover, the style of tomb construction has changed. No longer are the lofty wooden mausoleums built. Now dumpy concrete structures are favored, and they can be finished within the time period of a long funeral, say eight days, provided there is plenty of manpower to haul the cement upriver, make the rough boxing, and mix the concrete. Consequently, even at the one longhouse that retains the old ritual forms unchanged, *nulang* have become exceptional. One was held in 1973, and another in 1975, but before these two none had occurred for eight years. In the meantime, however, there had been several grand funerals, utilizing credit from local traders. The two *nulang* that happened in the early 1970s were the result of special circumstances, which are explained below. These cases illustrate the range of practical factors involved in selecting the extended mortuary sequence, both now and traditionally. For more details of the economics of this choice see Metcalf 1981.

Scheduling Nulang

If *nulang* is decided upon, then only a simple funeral will be held before the corpse is placed in temporary storage. The costs of such a funeral are minimal, because there are few guests to feed. Members of the community mostly eat in their own households. Only one large meal has to be provided, on the night before the corpse leaves the house, plus rounds of coffee and cookies each night of the wake. But despite the small scale of the ceremony, the ritual format remains exactly the same as for a funeral (*pata*i) in the abridged mortuary rites. The final night (i*chem mugé*) is the same, the descent to the barge and transportation to the graveyard are the same, and so are the days of silence *(liang)* and the headhunting rites *(ngachang, ngalaké, ninung ulèng)* that occur after the corpse has been temporarily stored. *Ngalăp* is not performed at small affairs. At the graveyard, a coffin is housed on a platform raised several feet above the ground, and covered with a crude roof to keep off the worst of the weather. A jar is similarly stored, unless kept within the house.

The length of time that the corpse spends in storage varies considerably. Certainly, it will await the time of relative plenty and leisure after the next harvest, that having been one reason for preferring *nulang* in the first place. But if that does not allow time for the bones to become dry (and people are explicit in using that form of expression), then it will have to wait for another harvest time. The minimum time is considered to be about eight months, and there is no possibility of *nulang* before that.

It is not easy to say how rapidly decomposition in fact proceeds. The climate is such that it must be substantially completed in a matter of weeks, but the coffin itself may interfere with the process if not equipped with a drain hole, since it is sealed with great care. A well-known story of miraculous preservation of a corpse concerns a young girl, the much-loved daughter of an important man of Long Jegan, who died while her father was off on a long journey. Returning some weeks later, the father was deranged by grief and insisted on opening the coffin. The corpse was perfectly preserved, or so it is said. Its hair had grown in the meantime, and some is preserved as a talisman. Presumably, the decomposition of the girl's corpse was impeded by the anaerobic condition in the coffin. Coffins were very carefully constructed at Long Jegan because they were stored within the longhouse while awaiting *nulang*. But this tendency to preserve corpses can only be an unintended side effect, because the explicit desire is to hasten decomposition until only sterile bones remain.

The corpse may be stored for much more than a year. The longest delay that I heard of was for Tama Tiri, the last *penghulu* (government-appointed chief) at Long Jegan, who died in 1940, not long before the arrival of the Japanese. Since a large *nulang* was called for, extra fields were planted in the traditional fashion. But no sooner had a suitable surplus been accumulated than the Japanese promptly requisitioned it for their own uses. This was repeated in each subsequent year, and there are still people at Long Jegan who grow angry remembering this. A *nulang* worthy of the great man could not be held until 1947.

During those years Tama Tiri's coffin was cared for within the longhouse, but at Long Teru and Batu Belah coffins are usually stored in the graveyard, where they are exposed to the weather. If a coffin or its temporary platform begins to rot, then rapid action is called for. If the platform falls over, or if the coffin rots through, allowing the bones to fall out, then all plans to hold a *nulang* for them must be cancelled, and the kinsmen must content themselves with the simple funeral only.

Case One: Lanau Comes Home

Of the four main Berawan communities, Long Terawan is the most distant from Long Teru. Lanau Pang went there in April 1972 to seek the help of a shaman, a man little-known outside his own village. But Lanau had already tried every other possible source of aid. He had been sick for a long time, probably with tuberculosis, the same wasting disease that later carried off Utan Nin.

In any event, the Long Terawan shaman could do nothing for Lanau. Meantime, Lanau was sinking fast, and was soon too weak to be moved. He died there early in May. Quick action was now called for from the companions who had come with him from Long Teru. Lacking the family connections that they would have needed to conduct a respectable funeral where they were, they had to move the body at once. However, they had forseen this development, and they had their plans made. A funeral barge *(magun)* was rigged by lashing two canoes together side by side, and the corpse loaded aboard. With a modicum of dignity, the party proceeded downriver, but only as far as Batu Belah, a few hours' travel away. For Batu Belah was Lanau's natal community; his residence at Long Teru was due to marriage. Already alerted to the imminence of Lanau's death, the Batu Belah folk were ready to move into action. To house the corpse, a small hut was built on the river bank in front of the longhouse.

When news of the death reached Long Teru, a hasty meeting of those most closely concerned, immediate kin and leaders of the community, was convened. It was decided that Lanau's remains should rest temporarily at Batu Belah until they could be brought back to the place where he had chosen to live most of his adult life, and where his children had been born. In other words, and assuming the cooperation of his natal village, Lanau would receive the rites of *nulang*. The following morning several canoes left Long Teru to attend the funeral. It was held on a small scale because of the secondary rites to come. After four days, the coffin was moved from its shed in front of the longhouse to the graveyard downriver, and stored in a simple *salong* consisting of a platform raised about six feet above the ground, with a tin roof and rough walls to protect it from the weather. The funeral was principally memorable for the spirited mud fight that occurred during the performance of the headhunting rites a couple of days later. There had been a certain amount of bickering between members of the two communities during the funeral, some of it over the details of the funeral, some over ancient bones of contention, and some simply so that the ambitious and contentious of temperament could display their rhetorical skills. But all was forgotten when the putative warriors, among whom were young men from Long Teru, joined boisterous battle with the young women of Batu Belah.

These events had moved rapidly. In the ensuing year, there was time to make arrangements, and mull over ritual details. This was necessary because it had been several years since the last *nulang* had been held. There was also time to reflect on why the decision had been made in favor of the extended mortuary rites. The apparent reason is that Lanau died away from home. But there were other alternatives to what in fact occurred. Though Long Teru is further away from Long Terawan than is Batu Belah, the extra traveling time is only a matter of hours, not days, even at the dignified pace appropriate to a funeral barge. Had the companions of Lanau been determined to return the body directly to Long Teru, they could have done so. Moreover, having chosen to bring the body to Batu Belah, there remained the option of laying Lanau permanently to rest at his natal village. Although I have no direct evidence of prior consultation, the decision with which Lanau's traveling companions moved after his death leads me to suspect there was some kind of tacit understanding among influential people at Long Teru and Batu Belah, where the party had stopped on their way up the Tutoh. If this was not the case, then the companions effectively committed two communities to considerable trouble and expense, because events moved too fast to allow much discussion afterwards. In either event, there are sociopolitical reasons that readily suggest themselves for why this course of action was the appropriate one. The village of Long Teru contains a large element whose forebears immigrated from Batu Belah in the 1920s, so that the former is in part a daughter community of the latter.[1] As a recent immigrant, Lanau constituted a direct link between the two, and his death afforded the opportunity to reemphasize through joint action a long-established alliance.

Early in May 1973 Lanau's remains finally came home. There had been much excitement in the days beforehand. The men were preparing the large hardwood tops that are seen only at *nulang*, and the older ones were self-importantly demonstrating techniques for carving them to younger men who had never had the chance to participate before. There was a great deal of construction activity: Several families were rebuilding their rooms in order to accomodate the many guests that they were expecting, kitchens were being expanded to handle the extra cooking, and a small extension was built onto the front of the veranda to house the coffin. Boatloads of people arrived from Batu Belah, and joined in with all this bustle. There was also many Iban men hanging about, their principal interest being gambling. Cockfighting was the favorite form of gambling, and the small open space between my little house and the longhouse veranda was the favorite spot. The patch of shade underneath my house provided a convenient place to tie up the noisy creatures between bouts, and also to sit and haggle over wagers. Cockfighting was a regular feature of major events at Long Teru, but I noticed before the *nulang* was properly begun that the continuous din was bothering me more than usual. Daily I became sicker, progressively losing interest in cockfights, sociability, ritual, and finally, fieldwork. I had chosen that moment to contract infectious hepatitis. On the fourth day of the *nulang* I left for Miri, the nearest town of any size. When I returned three weeks later, I was of course able to collect detailed accounts of the second half of the festival, since it was still fresh in peoples' memories. Nevertheless, having recovered some of my health and enthusiasm, I was disappointed to have missed the culmination of the event. Consequently, I was glad to have the opportunity of returning to Borneo to attend another *nulang* at Long Teru a couple of years later.

Case Two: Long Teru Honors Its Foremost Shaman

The circumstances prompting Lanau's *nulang* were certainly exceptional. But this is almost by definition, since the rites of secondary treatment have always been restricted to a minority of cases. The events that led up to the *nulang* that occurred in 1975 were entirely different, but equally exceptional.

Tama Ukat Sageng, the old and influential shaman, died in late March 1974 about two months after I left Long Teru. The manner of his going was in accordance with a lifetime of the extraordinary. It occurred at a moment when the longhouse was almost completely empty. In particular, there were only three men in the house, one old, one partially disabled by leprosy (of which he had been cured), and just one able-bodied young man. Such occasions are rare in a community numbering approximately three hundred souls. However, I had known them to happen during my stay; one wakes up one morning to find the great structure silent and abandoned, and there is nothing to do and no one to talk to. It is an eerie feeling, but the reason is not usually far to seek, and invariably has to do with the agricultural cycle. In this case, it was the middle of the harvest and everyone capable of helping was away at the farms, many of which are at a considerable distance from the longhouse, so that families move to their small farmhouses for days or weeks at a time. The only people left behind were a few children and old folks to look after them, mainly women.[2] As a result there was no one to do the heavy work of preparing a coffin, which would have had to be cut from a large log of hardwood since Sageng was a large man, tall for a Berawan and strongly built. Nor was there a jar *(sitong)* of sufficient proportions available. So those present were forced to adopt a unique mode of storage for the corpse. They took two of the vessels that are commonly used for storing water *(paso)*. These are large, roughly made earthenware jars, at least one of which stands in every kitchen. They can hold many gallons of water, and it is a common chore for older children once a day to go back and forth with a water carrier, usually an old kerosene can fitted with a head band, hauling water to fill the *paso*. Unlike other kinds of jars, they do not taper towards the top, but open out continuously from base to rim. Normally they are completely mundane objects with no ritual use, but in this extreme case they were pressed into service. The corpse was seated inside one, knees tucked up and head drooped forward, and the other was placed over the top. Then the two were lashed firmly together with rattan and sealed with damar gum. Later a small hole was drilled in the bottom of the lower jar, so that the products of decomposition could drain out.

These unusual circumstances in association with so special a man as Tama Ukat Sageng immediately became a source for rumor and speculation. A year later, at the *nulang*, I was able to obtain more details about Sageng's illness and death from his daughter Mini, who stayed behind to look after him when the others left for the farms. He had apparently been feverish and weak for a month or more, and near the end became senile, childish, and incontinent. He grumbled about being cold, and wanted to be nursed. His son, Tama Jok, had insisted on going to his farm on the Chet stream that very morning, even though Mini saw plainly that death was near. Sageng was not in his own room when death occurred, and Mini and the few others had had to drag him back there. A death seat was hastily prepared, and then the men rushed off to summon people from the nearby farms. Mini had been left alone with the body, and, she said, there was a moment when the color came back to its cheeks, and it appeared quite lifelike, sitting on its seat there on the veranda. Before the men got back that evening she and the other women left behind were thoroughly frightened. The very next morning they put him into the water jars. These are the pathetic details that Mini remembered. But these were not the things about Sageng's exit that became engraved on the public consciousness. A year after the event I was told by those who had been less intimately involved that there had been no men at all in the house (only a slight exaggeration after all), and there were various theories about why this was appropriate to his powers. Similarly, concerning the unique vehicle that he chose for his final journey, it was said that he had predicted long before he had become ill that he would occupy neither coffin nor jar *(sitong)*. It was a statement that had the authentic ring of prophetic paradox; Birnam Wood coming to Dunsinane.

Tama Ukat Sageng's funeral was brief, and the body was stored in the graveyard across the river and slightly upstream from the longhouse. The plain, even crude, *salong* that was built to contain it consisted of three posts about twelve feet out of the ground, and just far enough apart to allow the bulky water jars to fit between them. A floor was inserted about half way up to support the jars, and plank walls and a sheet iron roof completed the structure. As usual, red and white pennants and a large banner painted with curlicue designs were set on bamboo poles around the *salong*. There the remains were left to await *nulang*.

The extended ritual sequence was an obvious choice in Tama Ukat Sageng's case, because several factors worked in the same direction. First, the death occurred at a very inconvenient time for holding a funeral. The emptiness of the longhouse at the time may have had mystical significance, but it had very practical consequences. Slash and burn agriculture is a risky business, and if the rains come too early so that it is impossible to get a good burn, or if they come too late so that the young rice shoots wither, then there may well be nothing to harvest. When there *is* rice, it is unwise to walk away from the ripening fields, to drop everything for a week or more and leave the crops to be destroyed by monkeys, birds, deer, or violent storms. As a result it is impossible to conduct a funeral on any respectable scale. There is no other time when these constraints are so severe. The longhouse also empties in the early phase of the agricultural cycle, when families are cutting new farms and waiting for the right moment to fire them prior to planting the seed. But this phase lasts several weeks, and people could take a few days out in the middle to attend a funeral without any harm done. Thereafter, until the harvest, there are always a few people in the house and a few at the farms, with the more conscientious farmers spending more time near their fields protecting them from destructive animals and weeding them. But even they will come back to the longhouse and forsake their farms for a while, if there is a cause.[3] Not everyone begins to harvest at the same moment. Some fields ripen faster than others, and there is a variation in the time of planting because the work of sowing the seed is often done in large, convivial work parties that move from farm to farm on successive days. Cooperative work of this kind is popular because of the food and drink provided by the family receiving help, and the opportunities for horseplay between the sexes. Nevertheless, all the fields need a long stretch of dry weather in order to ripen, and when it arrives all the farms tend to become ready together. Consequently, everyone is harvesting together. Had Tama Ukat Sageng been determined to receive *nulang,* he could not have chosen a better moment.

A second factor with only slightly less force was that the close kin were too poor to undertake a proper funeral at the time. In terms of the formulae of rank outlined in chapter two, Sageng's family was not particularly distinguished. The fame of the man rested on other criteria, and indeed it is often the case that shamans are not from the noblest families. But even for folk of the middling sort, there is a minimum acceptable level of expenditure, and since that could not be achieved, delayed rites were indicated. It so happened that Tama Jok, son of the old shaman and principal organizer of his obsequies, had recently quarreled with the Chinese trader with whom he had dealt for several years. Consequently, he could not easily obtain stores on credit.

Finally, the most obvious factor of all was the personal standing of the dead man. Tama Ukat Sageng's powers made him a figure of awe, but not of fear. As we noted in chapter four, Berawan do not conceive of a shaman as being capable of maliciously doing harm, and Sageng's wisdom had made him well-loved. This meant that in conducting his death rites the community could be relied on for help. Moreover, to receive *nulang* is an honor, and there was a popular sentiment that this honor should be accorded to Sageng. But it is doubtful that this factor alone would have brought about the *nulang* had the other two not been operative. Instead, there would simply have been a grand funeral. As it was the *nulang* occurred in May 1975.[4]

These two *nulang,* the one for Lanau and the one for Sageng, provide the bulk of the material for the following description, supplemented by reminiscences of previous *nulang* and discussions of ritual niceties. Several informants talked readily about this topic at Long Teru, Batu Belah, and especially at Long Jegan. The Long Jegan rites present some interesting variations, and were vividly recalled by Sadi′ Pejong, who, as prophet of the Bungan cult there, played a large part in the demise of those rites in the late 1950s.

Notes

1. The details of how this came about are complex. Briefly, a faction from Batu Belah moved away from the parent house to Long Teru, where they settled on land provided by the original Lelak owners. Slowly the two communities became fused by intermarriage, so that they now share one longhouse.

2. These children were those of families that took education seriously. There is a small government-run primary school across the river from the longhouse, but only a few families are conscientious about sending their children on a regular basis.

3. There were a few mysterious individuals who chose hardly ever to come back to the longhouse. They were not considered to have seceded from the community because their families remained a part of longhouse life, but they were suspected of malevolent powers and tendencies.

4. The circumstances of my return visit were hectic. I was kept informed of the progress of arrangements by Michael Melai Usang, my former assistant, then working on the coast. But the link was tenuous, and I had to set out immediately upon hearing that the date for starting was definitely set. I arrived on the day before the appointed time.

CHAPTER TEN:

Games to Summon the Dead

Nulang is set in motion by a small rite called *neken*, which is performed at the graveyard. It consists basically of a formal invitation to the ancestors to attend, followed by the first playing of games that are restricted to this festival.

At Tama Ukat Sageng's *nulang*, some two dozen people went to the graveyard. They struggled up the muddy river bank from the canoes, burdened with rice wine and cups, bushknives to clear the grass around the temporary platform *(salong)* on which the remains were housed, and musical instruments, including the great funeral drum and several gongs. Several older women in turn took up a location next to the *salong*, and sent up dirges in the formal manner heard in the first few hours after a death occurs. A small fire was lit nearby. In order to inspect the condition of the jar, Tama Jok pried free a couple of planks from the wall of the chamber. The verdict came as no surprise: The jar was still intact, suitable for transportation to the longhouse as it was, and without the necessity for opening it, cleaning the bones, and inserting them in a new jar. Tama Jok had already made it known that he had no desire to conduct the latter rite, and large jars are impervious to the weather if properly sealed in the first place. Coffins, on the other hand, often rot, necessitating restorage.

Tama Jok next made a prayer. Holding up a sacrificial chicken, he summoned his father's soul and the spirits of the dead to come to the longhouse, and spelled out the arrangements for the *nulang*. He invoked the names of all the great ancestors who "reign" at Long Teru, calling them to protect their descendants. The prayer finished, the chicken's head was cut off, and its blood smeared on the posts of the *salong*. Meanwhile, rice wine was being passed around continuously among the members of the party. Occasionally someone would pour a little of the wine against the tomb while addressing a prayer to the dead man.

Finally two games were played in a little cleared area beside the chamber, one involving tops, the other rice pounders. In the graveyard they were played in only a fitful manner, since the area of play was cramped. But back at the longhouse afterwards play was much more vigorous, with many people participating. In fact, there was an excited crowd waiting on top of the riverbank, and as soon as the returning canoes touched the bank, play began in earnest.

The Games and Their Meaning

The first game is played with tops (*sunī*) specially prepared for the occasion and carved from dense hardwood. They resemble the old style of European tops: turnip-shaped with a long, tapered string that is wound around the pointed end and used to set the top spinning. A smooth area of play is chosen, and one man with a flourish sets his top spinning in the middle of it. Immediately the other players run forward excitedly and in turn shoot their tops at this target, making them spin in the air with a low moaning noise. Sometimes a single hit sends the target top flying out of the area of play, and a shout of victory goes up from the man who made the successful shot. At other times, a series of less spectacular hits is sufficient to edge the target out of play. But if it is still within the arena when it stops spinning and falls over, then its owner is the winner of that round. After the rite of *neken*, there are games on every day of the *nulang*, especially in the cool of the late afternoon. Young men are at first clumsy in handling the tops, but some older men are very skillful, and they can make a top weighing several pounds fly three or four yards and come down with a mighty crash against its target. Less-skilled persons can only manage smaller tops, thereby reducing their chances of success. The adepts have gained their proficiency by being aficionados of the sport at prior *nulang*, for it is utterly taboo to play or practice at any other time.

Throughout Southeast Asia, mystical significance is often attached to spinning tops. Among many of the neighbors of the Berawan, the association is with fertility. The Kayan play a game with tops, very much like the one described above, about the time of the rice harvest (Hose and McDougall 1912:II:163). For the Iban the connection is more specific: Ritual top spinning is thought to make the new rice ripen more rapidly (Jensen 1974:188). A more intriguing association is made by the Batek Negrito of peninsular Malaysia, who say that thunder is caused by two deities spinning stone tops and competing to see who can make the loudest noise (Endicott 1979:208). Thunder is for the Batek an important manifestation of the divine, so that we have an equation of tops, thunder, and the sacred. For the Berawan, it is also noise that provides the key. They appreciate the loud clacks produced when the tops crash into one another, and we have already drawn attention to the many ways that loud noise is constantly produced throughout the death rites. At *nulang* there is a quantum increase as compared to the funeral, and that is appropriate to the intense contact with the sacred dead that is believed to occur. Both the prescribed games played at *nulang*, the spinning of tops and the rice pounder game described below, are very noisy. But, interestingly enough, it is not the sound of the tops crashing into one another that Berawan themselves point to as connoting the sacred. It is instead the whirring noise that they make as they fly through the air. Presumably the sound is the result of the uneven, hand-carved surfaces. Some tops are louder, others softer; some emit a high-pitched whir, but the largest make a low moan. Berawan say that the sounds resemble the speech of the dead, and that is why it is safe to use them only during *nulang*.[1]

The other game played at the rite of *neken* and throughout the *nulang* uses two heavy rice pounders *(tepá)*. They are about five feet long and three inches in diameter at either end, tapering towards the handle in the middle. Normally they are used in conjunction with a wooden mortar to punch the rice free of its husk. In the game they are laid parallel across two bulks of timber, and a person squats at each side grasping one end of each of the pounders. They beat out a rhythm with them, banging them downwards first against the bulks of timber below, and then clashing them together on the second beat. A variety of different rhythms are used. The player stands beside the poles, bouncing up and down on his toes and accustoming himself to the rhythm. Suddenly he dances across the poles, placing first one foot between the gnashing jaws and then the other, and extracting them again nimbly. Back and forth he dances, using ever more elaborate steps while the speed is slowly increased. Any hesitation means a clout on the ankle. Some adepts even put their heads on the ground between the poles. It is said that this game is good for warriors because it makes them vigorous and alert *(sagem)*. But women also participate, and are often accomplished players.

When both games are in play simultaneously, as when the party returns from performing *neken,* the din can be deafening. The floor acts as a vast sounding board for the crashing rice pounders, the drums, and the gongs. The crowd on the veranda yells encouragement to the top players below, whose war whoops greet a good shot.

These games are the characteristic feature of *nulang.* They are an element in a code that uses play to make a series of statements about the death rituals, and death itself. They do so in two ways. First, by their presence or absence they demarcate ritual phases in a binary fashion. Second, by their content the games reiterate a message about the nature of the dead (see figure 3).

During both the initial and the secondary rites, there are activities that are prohibited and activities that are obligatory. From the time that a death occurs until the termination of communal mourning, no dancing is allowed within the longhouse, either of the traditional *orang ulu* upriver style, called *ngajat,* or any of the many Malay styles.[2] It is also prohibited to play the *keluné* and the *sapé.* The *sapé* is a stringed instrument carved from a single piece of wood, with a long, hollowed-out sounding box and a short fretted neck, sounding like a banjo. The *keluné* is a complex wind instrument. Its body is carved from a gourd, with the neck forming the mouthpiece and several pipes in a bundle coming vertically out of the top of it. A pipe is made to sound by covering the vent hole at its base, and the noise produced resembles a harmonica. Both the *sapé* and *keluné* are associated with dancing, parties, and entertainment generally. Most singing is prohibited, especially the praise songs and epics often sung for entertainment at parties. These proscriptions are comprehensible in terms of the eschatological ideas set out in chapter three: They express the sorrow of the bereaved and the solidarity of the community with them, and, more subtly,

	FUNERAL	*NULANG*
PROSCRIBED	upriver-style dancing: *ngajat*; Malay dancing: *joget*. Songs other than the death songs. *Keluné, sapé.*	same as for the funeral, after bones arrive back at house.
PRESCRIBED	noisiness, crowds, rubbing pot black on peoples' faces. Drums, gongs.	same as for the funeral with addition of tops, and rice pounder game.

Figure 3. Summary of proscribed and prescribed activities during funerals and *nulang*.

the danger of provoking the envy of the hovering soul. Meanwhile, as we have seen, there is a special kind of festivity enjoined upon all but the closest kin that is accentuated with special games. These often have provocative, even vindictive, overtones, as in "fishing" and rubbing pot blacking on peoples' clothes and faces. As regards the musical instruments, there is one, the great bass drum, that is reserved exclusively for death rites, and the other instruments retained all employ special rhythms. All of them are percussive and noisy—the drum, the large and small brass gongs, and the bamboo slit gongs.

At the *nulang* the same proscriptions are reimposed. But their force is lessened: On the first evening of the *nulang* for Tama Ukat Sageng I unwittingly started a debate on what precisely was prohibited, and a respected older woman stated flatly that dancing and playing the *sapé* are allowed until such time as the bones are brought back to the longhouse. Later a group of young people did indeed dance a Malay-style *joget*, but they tucked themselves away in a room at the other end of the veranda from the main event and they looked sheepish all the while. Others expressed the opinion that although it may not be strictly forbidden to do these things at a *nulang*, it is unseemly and unwise. Such ambivalence accords well with the circumstances of the soul as the Berawan conceive it. Since it is close to its apotheosis, it should be proof against the envious malice that is so much feared in the weeks immediately following death. By the same token, the soul is passing over into the powerful world of spirits, so why risk provoking it?

While the prohibitions are being cautiously relaxed, the schedule of prescribed activities is increasing and taking on a new character. The games played with tops and rice pounders are specifically and exuberantly for fun. It would be a poor show indeed if people played them in only a half-hearted manner. They lack the punitive quality of the games played during a funeral, and that is because they are designed not to assuage a malevolent soul but to entertain the benign ancestors. The playfulness of the living during *nulang* is the equivalent of the playfulness of spirits during a shamanistic performance. In the latter the spirits (usually ancestral spirits) dance and sing for the living in order to restore to them a member whose soul is wandering; in the former the living dance across the clashing rice pounders and sing the death songs for the spirits in order to transmit to them a soul that should wander no more. Moreover, the games have an unmistakable vigor about them that lifts the community out of the torpor of death. Force and coordination are needed to make a heavy top fly accurately to its target, and the lethargic player in the rice pounder game will soon pay the price of inattentiveness.

The Second Wake

After the opening of the *nulang*, the rhythm of daytime and nighttime activities is established in much the same way as during a large funeral.

But there are differences. Many people arrive even before the ritual commencement, because everyone has had plenty of advance notice. There are guests in every room, and the casual feeding of their own guests constitutes another way in which the house members subsidize the cost of the festival. There seem to be people playing cards, getting drunk, or trying to recover from a bout of drinking in every nook and cranny of the house, twenty-four hours a day. If one tries to escape for a moment in a canoe, it is surprising to find how far away one can go and still hear the noise of the house.

At a *nulang* as at a grand funeral, the chores of the kin of the dead man are endless. However, many of the tasks involving long days in the sun, such as building the mausoleum and collecting supplies, should be largely completed. People are thus able to throw themselves more vigorously into the festivities. During the day there are games of tops and *tepá*, playing the drums and gongs, cockfights, and casual socializing. At night the crowd gathers on the veranda outside the family apartment of the deceased person, and bright lamps burn throughout the hours of darkness. Drinking is heavy, and the death songs are sung each night, moving towards their climax on the final night, just as at a funeral.

At Long Teru the second wake lasts up to ten days, but shorter periods may be chosen in the same manner as for a funeral. There is some variation possible in the schedule for bringing back the remains of the deceased to the longhouse. At Lanau's *nulang* in 1973 the coffin was loaded onto the funeral barge directly after the initiating rites of *neken* in the graveyard at Batu Belah, and then brought to Long Teru, arriving the same day. At the *nulang* for Tama Ukat Sageng the *neken* was split into two parts. On the first day, tops were played in the graveyard across river, but the bones were not brought back until the fourth day, so that they spent four nights at the longhouse.

At Batu Belah and Long Terawan the timing of events was different. They kept the jar or coffin within the longhouse for only one night, or at most two. Evidently, these communities wished to cut as short as possible their contact with the powerful relics of the dead. They represent the extreme of rejection in this respect, in contrast to the acceptance of the Long Jegan Berawan who kept the relics continuously within the house.

But the Batu Belah folk had more death songs than they could sing in one night. So they began singing them when the tree was cut that was to furnish the *lijèng* (post monument), or when work began on the *kubor* (vault). The *lijèng* made by the Berawan of the Tutoh River are not as complex as the great *salong* (mausoleums) of the Long Jegan people, and the work of hauling, carving, and erecting them could often be completed in one month. During that period a little snatch of death song was sung every night. As the time drew closer to the climax, the singing grew more determined. The *nulang* was in progress for a month or more, but only on the last few days was the house filled with guests. In this fashion, the *nulang* at Batu Belah was coterminous with the work of erecting the funeral edifice, and the same was true at Long Jegan. But at Long Teru the length of *nulang* is not related to the time needed to finish the tomb.

Although the mortal remains may not return to the house until the *nulang* is well under way, the spirit of the dead person, and indeed the spirits of all the ancestors, are expected to arrive earlier. They are summoned in a special death song on the night that the *nulang* begins, and this is true of the Batu Belah practices as well as the Long Teru ones. This practice supports the conclusion that the soul of the dead man is not conceived of as attached to the corpse.

Fetching the Bones

On the day appointed for transporting the remains, a barge *(magun)* is prepared as usual, by lashing two or three canoes together side by side. Arriving at the graveyard, the women of the party keen beside the jar or coffin while the men prepare to lift it down from the temporary *salong,* which is then destroyed.

Now is the time for cleaning the bones if it is planned to perform this rite (though this has not happened for some years now). The remains of both Lanau and Sageng were left in their original containers. Ideally a close male relative should wash the bones, but if there is none brave enough someone else with more experience in these things may be asked to officiate. This man receives a large gong, a *parang* (bush knife or sword), and a small pig for his troubles. Those involved fortify themselves with stiff shots of distilled rice spirit. I was told that even in the good old days when men had stronger stomachs, it was common to bribe a Penan to do this repulsive chore, and that the officiant would often get so soused as to be barely able to complete it. The lid of the coffin was pried open, and the bones removed one at a time. They were dipped in a container of water and a cloth used to roughly wipe them clean, especially the skull. Then the bones were stacked on a fine cloth. When they were all assembled, they were wrapped in the cloth and inserted in a small jar brought for the purpose. Often it was a jar of some antiquity and value. The coffin and all of the apparatus used to clean the bones were pushed unceremoniously into some out-of-the-way place and left to rot.[3] The mouth of the jar was closed with a large plate tied on firmly with rattan bands and then sealed with damar gum.

If it is planned to use the same coffin for secondary storage of the remains, it is not opened but carried directly to the waiting canoes. At Batu Belah the practice was to loosen the bands around the coffin and open it only a crack, as if in token of cleaning the bones. Jars used for primary storage may also be opened.

Arriving at the longhouse, the canoes are met by women who wail formally to the spirit of the dead person. The coffin or jar is carried directly into a small lean-to *(ungá)* that has previously been built onto the front of the house outside the family room of the dead person. The floor of the lean-to is about twelve feet square, and a little lower than the floor of the veranda. It is walled on the three sides that do not face the house, and its roof is an extension of the longhouse roof. The coffin may not sit on the veranda itself, nor can it be brought along the veranda to its little shed. Instead, the outer wall of the lean-to is opened up to allow access by means of a ramp. In this way the prohibition against bringing corpses into the longhouse continues to operate, but is almost overcome in view of the purity achieved by the bones.

A fine cloth is put over the coffin or jar, and tobacco and candy are placed on top of it. All around it are stacked cloths and brassware and all manner of valuables, just as during a funeral. The widow or widower takes a position near the foot of the coffin and remains there for much of the time that it is in the house. However, the privations visited upon him or her during the primary rites are not repeated, and all that is required is mourning attire and a moderately sober bearing. Tama Jok, son of Tama Ukat Sageng, played this role at the latter's *nulang*.

After the arrival of the remains, the *nulang* builds to its climax, the final night of the wake.

The Final Night—Ichem Mugé

The preparations made for the *ichem mugé* of a *nulang* are more elaborate than for the final night of a funeral.

Great quantities of food are prepared, some of it in a curious fashion. Monkeys of several species are hunted, and they are gutted as usual, but their heads, paws, and fur are not removed, and in this condition, they are roasted slowly over a low fire. On the final evening they are hung up along the veranda, and to add to the bizarre effect beads are put around their necks, loincloths tied around their waists, and cigarettes placed in their mouths. Berawan considered them a great joke, but the contorted, blackened bodies have a macabre appearance. I was told that other kinds of game animals could also be used, but I only saw monkeys cooked in this way.

In the festivities of the evening these curiosities act as booby traps for the unwary. They are hung up along the center of the veranda, which, beginning shortly after sunset, is crowded with longhouse residents and visitors. People tend to sit on either side of the veranda, their legs stretched out in front of them and their backs against either the low wall at the outer edge of the veranda or the median wall that divides the veranda from the family apartments. Anyone passing down the veranda must walk between these rows of people facing each other, and since it is a grave discourtesy to step over a recumbent person, must also stick near the center. Moreover, etiquette requires that a person who is walking near others who are seated should hunch the head and shoulders forward and bring the hands down near the knees. The crouching gait that results is designed to avoid assertive or threatening body language, but it also makes it hard to see what is just in front and above. Consequently it is all too easy to stumble into one of the charred animals suspended in the path. When this occurs an immediate howl of delight goes up. The butt of this humor must now take down the bottle of rice wine that is also hanging there and drink it down. When he falters, the crowd roars encouragement until it is satisfied with the victim's effort. Next he must eat some of the roast meat, gnawing on the shrivelled body, breaking it apart and sharing it with those sitting nearby. Children or young women are seldom subjected to this teasing; if they accidentally bump into one of the objects everyone looks away. An extroverted man or older woman is the desired victim. Luckily, they are not in short supply. Early on in the evening there are invariably men well into their cups who are not only likely to collide with one of the obstacles sooner or later, but also to revel in the resulting public attention, hamming up their part and rushing up and down the veranda to answer with mock ferocity the taunts hurled at them from the crowd. When a suitably talented candidate is found, these little incidents are good for a half hour of general hilarity.

Another item prepared for the final night, the *beluvit*, is employed in a similar manner. These are elaborate structures made of bamboo, colored paper, and tinsel. Families vie with one another to produce the most elegant and elaborate ones, and five or six may be constructed, most of them three or four feet tall. Generally they have a central post and crosspieces at two levels supporting little roofs under which are hung cigarettes of native manufacture, hundreds of them, strung together with a needle and cotton and draped in long loops. In addition there are the essential bottles of rice wine, to be consumed by whoever it is that finally brushes against them during the course of the evening. The cigarettes he shares with anyone who wants them, and the *beluvit* itself he takes home as a prize. Months after a *nulang* they may be seen hanging in the rafters of farm houses, gathering dust. On the night of *ichem mugé* they are the most conspicuous objects on the veranda, and one might assume that they have some deep ritual significance. They suggest the little houses built to accomodate spirits *(beran)* or they could be seen as resembling the death edifices *(salong)* because of their little roofs. However, I was assured that they have no ritual function or meaning, and that they could be dispensed with entirely.

The chief significance of the *beluvit* and the charred monkeys is as games; further items to add to the list reviewed above. They are not prescribed as is the case with the playing of tops or the rice pounder game, but nevertheless they provide a suitable adjunct. They have a faintly vindictive quality, but mostly they are there to encourage entertainment for all. They involve excess (bottles of wine drunk down in one go, hundreds of cigarettes), and they mark the specialness of the last night of the wake.

The following day the remains are removed from the longhouse and taken to the graveyard, where they are placed in their permanent mausoleum. The details of this process are similar to those recounted in chapter five, and they will not be recapitulated here. If a previously used mausoleum is to be opened, then prayers and sacrifices are offered to ask those already inside to receive the new addition. If a new edifice of any size has been prepared, then prayers are needed calling on the ancestors to sanctify it.

The day after the trip to the graveyard is observed as the great day of silence, which severs the contact with the sacred dead.

Nulang *at Long Jegan*

An overall similarity of format enables us to describe the *nulang* rites of Long Teru, Batu Belah, and Long Terawan together. The Long Jegan sequence is sufficiently different to require separate description. This description is based on the accounts of several old people at Long Jegan, but particularly the headman Sadi″ Pejong.

The most obvious difference was that the coffin was not removed from the longhouse after the initial funeral. Instead, a kind of miniature tomb was built around it where it lay. One wall of the chamber (*diching lunggong, diching* = wall, *lunggong* = coffin) was provided by the central partition of the longhouse, which divides the veranda from the family apartments. A spot outside the family apartment of the deceased was chosen, and since the sleeping accommodation is adjacent to the same partition, the living were divided from the dead by only a few planks throughout the intermediate period. The other three walls stood about four feet high, and enclosed a space just wide enough to enclose the coffin. An inclined roof of bark was added, leaving a gap between the top of the walls and the roof so that it was possible to look in at the coffin. The walls were painted in designs similar to those used on the older *salong*, with geometric rows of dots as the major device. At one end was a curious carving projecting out of the wall. It represented the face and front legs of a tiger, and was painted in stripes of black and yellow (tigers are not found in Borneo, but nevertheless figure in Bornean folklore). Valuables, such as gongs and old jars, were stacked around the chamber, but not cloths, which are too perishable to be left for prolonged periods on the veranda. Large, decorated sun hats were hung on the wall nearby, and small models of swords and paddles were hung around the roof of the chamber, together with one or two human statuettes. A picture of one of these little structures appears in Hose and McDougall (1912:II:82) and also in Haddon (1901:34).

Haddon was told that the carved face represented the little boy whose corpse lay within, and not a tiger. I was told just the opposite, that the head *was* intended to represent a tiger, and it may be that the statement made to Haddon was figurative, meaning to imply that the dead boy was of high rank. Another mystery concerning tigers and coffins relates to the shape of the coffin itself (see note 5). One elderly and knowledgeable informant told me that coffins of high-ranking people were made in the representation of a tiger, with legs at each corner, a head at one end and a tail at the other, and painted with stripes. He even carved a little model to show me how they were made. However, I investigated many mausoleums, including some very old ones from which the coffins had fallen or in which the coffins were visible because the structure was partly rotten, and I never saw a coffin of this kind. Other peoples in Borneo do indeed carve coffins into elaborate designs, representing fantastic creatures or slaves holding the casket, but I saw no coffins of this kind among the Berawan.

During the period that the coffin is inside the house it was protected by the partition around it. No particular reverence was paid it, and utilitarian things such as fish traps and nets were dumped on or near it. If *nulang* was delayed, it might get very dusty and unkempt.

Finally, however, the time arrived when the family of the deceased were ready to begin constructing the mausoleum for the dead person. On the evening of the day that work began felling and hauling the logs that furnished the posts of the mausoleum, the roof of the little lean-to on the veranda was taken off, and the singing of death songs began. Now the *nulang* had commenced, and death songs had to be sung every night that work was still in progress on the death edifice, though a few minutes of singing sufficed if the process was a long one. Also the games with tops and with rice pounders could be played, and the funeral drum sounded.

For days, or weeks, or months the construction of the *salong* crept forward, and during all that time the *nulang* was officially in progress. Few restrictions, however, inhibited the lives of the close kin during that time. Their only mark of continued mourning was the white clothing, or at a minimum a white headband. The bereaved spouse continued to lead a sober lifestyle, avoiding flirtations with the opposite sex, and was judged respectful if he or she sat often by the coffin. One little taboo, justified by a myth, had to be observed by a widow at this time. She might not prepare *kelupé* (rice cakes), lest her husband's coffin get up and chase her. *Kelupé* is a food associated with festive occasions.

When only the finishing touches remained to be put on the mausoleum, the final stage of the *nulang* could begin, and this lasted exactly four nights. On the first of those nights, the little partition was torn down and the coffin moved to the center of the veranda. A framework *(tajuk)* of bamboos was suspended over the coffin, from which were hung fine cloths, and the usual range of valuable objects were stacked around it. Then the most important sequence of death songs was sung, climaxing in the one that sings the deceased person to the land of the dead. At that point, the singing of the death songs ceased, gongs were beaten noisily, and the women wailed for the final time.

When day broke, the death songs should have been be completed and a special meal could then be eaten, called *kanan bijei* (*kanan* = food, rice, *bijei* = crocodile). This meal was served in a peculiar fashion. Along the veranda a strand of rattan was suspended, about four feet above the floor. At the downriver end a tray was hung on which was a great pile of rice molded into a representation of a crocodile's head. Pieces of cake formed its eyes. At the upriver end, a similar pile of rice represented the tail of the crocodile. In between, all kinds of things to eat were hung along the rattan: Rice wrapped in leaves, roast fish, and chunks of pork. Also hung from the rattan were monkeys and other game animals cooked in their skins, and fish with their scales, similar to those prepared for the final night of the wake at Long Teru. When all was ready, two older men of high rank were selected from among the guests and asked to begin eating first, one at the "head" and one at the "tail." A little flag of red cloth was hung at either end of the rattan, and these the two guests took down and tied around their heads. Then the men came to eat, standing up, from the food hung in the middle, and following this they sat down to eat the rice. The women ate afterwards, and then the spare rice was taken and thrown around the veranda.

Although the spirit of the dead person had already been sung to its final home, the coffin was not immediately moved. In fact, the noisy part of the wake had only just begun. The members of the community were expected to gather on the day prior to the climax of the death song cycle, and guests were also intended to arrive on that day or before. The festivities continued for three more nights. Other kinds of songs were allowed, such as praise songs for the guests, and epic sagas of the old times, and various types of games were played. But dancing was still proscribed, and it was no longer allowed to play the games with tops or rice pounders. The funeral drum was only sounded one further time, as the coffin left the house on the morning of the fifth day, down a special ramp, and to the mausoleum.

Roast Monkeys and Rice Crocodiles

The odd feast that follows the completion of the death songs at Long Jegan calls for some commentary on animal and culinary symbolism. As in the treatment of symbols of transition in chapter eight, I take this opportunity to pull together a number of interwoven themes. To treat with these themes exhaustively would draw us into a discussion of Berawan zoological classification. Moreover, the Berawan rituals display anomalies that might best be resolved by looking at the usages of neighboring peoples from whom the Berawan have borrowed items of belief and practice. To follow that path would lead us away from the mortuary rites, toward the kind of analysis that Claude Lévi-Strauss makes of South American myth, a sort of Bornean *Mythologiques*. In the meantime, we can perhaps explain why the monkeys are roasted in their fur, why Berawan insist that they are so amusing, and why they are juxtaposed with the rice crocodile.

Though the feast has not occurred for many years at Long Jegan, Sadi′ Pejong was definite about the details of cuisine, and his account was corroborated by other senior folk. They are evidently not mere whimsical invention, although no one had any explanations to offer for them. The meal was clearly a climactic event of *nulang:* The scheduling of events shows that it was what Hertz called the "grand feast." The roast monkeys are also to be found at Long Teru, although the context is different. There is also an echo of the rice crocodile. After the Long Jegan rite called *kanan bijei*, all the uneaten rice was supposedly thrown about the veranda. A similar prodigal use of rice occurs at Long Teru at a corresponding moment in a funeral or *nulang*, just before the coffin or jar is moved out of the house. The rice is not, however, molded into the shape of a crocodile. At Long Jegan I was told that the peculiar meal was a custom borrowed from the Punan Bah, who live a day or two's travel away on the Kemena River.

Let us begin with the roast monkeys. Berawan rarely roast anything. In common with most upriver folk, almost all their food is boiled: rice and sago are cooked with water almost of necessity, what vegetables and edible grasses are available are always boiled, and even meat and fish are treated in the same way, chopped up into small pieces and served in a watery gruel. Among coastal folk familiar with longhouse life, the propensity to boil everything was a subject of jokes. Berawan shared the same observation, but they placed a different value on it. It was often asserted, with a kind of prickly pride, that "we Berawan do not care what we eat." The remark cannot be taken literally; they have their rules about what is edible and what is not. What their statement really means is that their cuisine is unelaborate compared with Chinese, Malay, and other coastal people, and by extension, that their lifestyle is simple, honest, manly, and straightforward by comparison with the latter. This piece of metonymy is strikingly reminiscent of an argument made by Claude Lévi-Strauss, to the effect that boiling is a mode of cooking that expresses a democratic ideal, in contrast to roasting: "Boiling provides a means of complete conservation of the meat and its juices, whereas roasting is accompanied by destruction and loss. Thus one denotes economy; the other prodigality; the latter is aristocratic, the former plebeian" (Lévi-Strauss 1965:23).

Sometimes small fish are toasted to a crisp consistency by laying them directly in the embers of a low fire. But the only time when I saw any amount of food prepared by roasting was at major death rituals, when quantities of fish were roasted over large fires built out of doors. This much is consistent with Lévi-Strauss' observation: such events call for prodigal, aristocratic uses of food. The only meat that I ever saw roasted was—the charred monkeys at the termination of the wake. But they are only very marginally food at all, and they hardly connote aristocratic consumption. Instead they are a joke.

There is another aspect: Given that plenty to eat and drink, including exotic dishes, is appropriate to *nulang* as a grand celebration, it is not hard to see why monkeys must be roasted and not boiled. To be boiled, they must be chopped up and so rendered anonymous, indistinguishable from pork. But why must the monkeys be recognizable as such? And why are they dressed up in skirts and beads? The answers to those questions take us away from the universal level of symbolism addressed by Lévi-Strauss toward a more localized set of associations first pointed out by Rodney Needham in an article entitled "Blood, Thunder and the Mockery of Animals" (1964). Both in the Malay peninsula and in Borneo there are peoples for whom laughing at animals is taboo; all animals, but especially monkeys. To mock these creatures, particularly by dressing them up in clothes, is considered dangerous. It causes thunder and torrential rain. The Berawan share these attitudes, yet at mortuary rituals they carefully preserve the identity of monkeys through the process of cooking, and then dress them up in skirts and necklaces. The reason must be that they do not care about the consequences.

At mortuary festivals for people of note meteorological disturbances are expected. I was told in a completely matter-of-fact way that extensive flooding throughout the lower Baram some years before was caused by the passing of an important leader of Long Teru. Needless to say, at Tama Ukat Sageng's *nulang* there was heavy rainfall on several occasions, including the final night of the wake. Thunder at such times is felt to be a manifestation of the sacred, and torrential rain that seems to make the whole world into water is appropriate to the major transition in progress. But in addition to these general associations, Berawan say that it is the *utam,* spiritual power, of the deceased that causes the disturbances. It is as if the energy formerly concentrated within the person of the deceased is now somehow discharged into the atmosphere. It is not clear whether the monkeys are there simply because the expectation of storms provides a kind of immunity to the usual sanction, or whether it is intended to actually provoke more rain. But it is clear why the Berawan insist that the macabre little objects are so funny: It is the laughter that is associated with rainstorms.

It remains puzzling, however, that the monkeys are cooked at all. It would seem that the joke would be better if live monkeys were dressed up. Moreover, the carcasses are burned to a cinder, so that they are barely edible. One solution is to view the hunting of monkeys as a parody on the hunting of heads.[4] The latter is dangerous to undertake, the former is not. But monkeys are in a real sense enemies, because of the damage they do to crops. While they are frequently hunted and eaten, monkeys principally figure in Berawan concerns as vermin, a natural scourge against which the farmer must contend. A group of macaques can do a remarkable amount of damage to a field of ripening rice, destroying months of effort in a single night. The roast monkeys are hung up in the rafters, which is where heads were kept. Moreover, the human skulls hung in the rafters are always described by Berawan as being black, because fires were kept burning underneath them. Since they were never touched, they became progressively blackened by the smoke. The carcasses of the monkey victims are similarly smoked. The blackness of the monkeys has a further symbolic significance. On the final nights of funerals and *nulang,* two cloths many yards long are passed over the rafters above the veranda, so that they make a kind of canopy over the celebrants gathered below. These cloths are kept for this purpose alone, and they make a festive show, draping slightly between rafters, because one is white and the other red.

When the charred monkey carcasses are added, all the colors are present that symbolically create a thunderstorm.

As destroyers of crops, monkeys appear in the guise of nature as enemy. The damage that violent storms can do is much the same. When men kill humans by taking heads, they mystically acquire vitality. When men kill monkeys, they seem to control natural forces. The thunder and rain that is expected on the last night of the wake is, in Berawan thinking, mainly a product of the supernatural power of the deceased. But through the medium of the charred monkeys, the living share in, or perhaps augment, that power. Though no Berawan ever expressed this to me directly, there does seem to be a sentiment that the killing and the mocking of the monkeys is a kind of revenge. Ultimately, perhaps, and this can be no more than a conjecture, the account that is balanced is nature's uncontrollable ability to kill men.

If monkeys appear as natural enemies, what about the crocodile with which they are juxtaposed in the great feast of Long Jegan?[5] Paradoxical though it may seem to us, crocodiles are regarded in many contexts as being quasi-human. It is said that the feet of crocodiles resemble those of humans, and there are several myths that recount how men were turned into crocodiles. In one, a widower marries a woman from another ethnic group. Out of jealousy, she kills the son of the first marriage and feeds him—boiled, of course—to the father. He is slowly transformed into a crocodile, but not before he has explained that henceforth men and crocodiles shall be as kinsmen. If a human is taken by a crocodile, as does occasionally happen, then crocodiles are hunted so that revenge can be taken. This is described as "war" (bawa).

The tribe of crocodiles are supposed to have their own world at the bottom of the river, where they have longhouses and farms just as men do. Moreover, they do not destroy the rice of human beings as monkeys do. We are left with the following commentary upon man and nature: At the Long Jegan feast, the roast monkey, which is actively anti-rice, is contained within the bounds of the boiled crocodile, which is by association pro-rice. Moreover, the monkey meat, which is cooked in a natural state with fur included, is eaten in an antisocial manner, standing up, while the "crocodile," which is molded out of culturally produced rice, is eaten in a social fashion, sitting down.

Notes

1. Heard over a distance, the sound of the large gong used to summon people to the longhouse when a death occurs resembles the moaning sound of the tops. This is a further association of the sounds of instruments, the use of which is restricted to contexts of death.

2. The style of Malay dancing that is best known at Long Teru is the one called *joget*. The young folk were also keen to learn about Western dancing, and there were several embarrassing times when I was forced to put on demonstrations of everything from the waltz to the twist.

3. Low (1882:63) reports that the Kajaman put vacated coffins into the lower branches of a tree near the graveyard, there to rot or be swept away in the next flood. The tree was stripped of its leaves and decorated with pieces of brightly colored fabric. The decoration of the tree as if it were a mausoleum is suggestive of tree burial, a practice reported in scattered references from several parts of central northern Borneo (Hughes-Hallett 1938).

4. I owe this suggestion to David Sapir.

5. At Long Teru, the juxtaposition of crocodile and monkey appears to be only weakly developed, and the ritual elements that make up the Long Jegan feast are dispersed or absent. Also lacking is any reference to tigers in connection with death rites. At Long Jegan, tigers appear in connection with coffins and their storage, and there is a brief myth that relates tigers and crocodiles: Two brothers attempted to leap a stream. One fell short, and got his feet wet. He became a crocodile. The other succeeded in jumping the stream, but stumbled into a rock and became a tiger. The terseness with which this story was recounted to me suggests that it also is borrowed from the Punan Bah or other non-Berawan folk to the south. Tigers are associated with military prowess, and Hose reports that tiger skin cloaks were regarded with great awe (Hose and McDougall 1912:II:72). The tiger is not native to Borneo, so that these skins and the animal's reputation for ferocity were presumably imported. Hose also reports that outstanding men liked to name their children *Lenjau* (tiger), in order to draw forth the right values in the child, and it may be that the little boy whose coffin Haddon saw on the veranda was so named, or at any rate so considered. This was perhaps the source of the linguistic confusion: Haddon's informants were insisting that the carved head was an image of the little boy because he was a true *tiger*, thus honoring the father. Tigers would appear to have ambiguous social connotations. On the one hand, tiger-like men are leaders of the community, but on the other, their ferocity may be socially destructive. The tiger is an appropriate symbol of political power. It is also interesting that the Long Jegan myth associates tigers with stone. The ultimate punishment for mockery of animals is that the longhouse of the offenders will turn to stone along with all those inside.

CHAPTER ELEVEN

The Sacred Core

The sacred, Durkheim argued, can be recognized by the interdictions that hedge it about. By this criterion, there is nothing in the death rites, and little in Berawan religion, that is so sacred as the death songs *(gu)*. They are held in awe because of the power invested in them to bless and to kill. This chapter examines that sacred character, and the problems of exposition that it entails.

Recent History of the Death Songs at Long Teru

When it became clear, in May 1972, that Lanau's death would involve the staging of a *nulang* some time in the future, it occasioned considerable discussion. No such festival had been held for several years, and there was much to organize. But the controversial issue was the death songs.

Two or three years previously, the people of Long Teru had decided to suppress the songs, to discontinue their use and to outlaw the singing of them on any occasion whatsoever. When I first arrived at Long Teru and began to understand something about the importance of the death rites, I was first disappointed and then puzzled to hear of this decision. Disappointed because I would not have a chance to record the songs, and puzzled because I could not understand why so important a cultural element should be jettisoned in this way. I took it as an instance of acculturation, something engineered by those impatient with the old ways. But I was wrong. There was no party within the longhouse that felt that the songs were useless or obsolete, and the move was initiated by some of the very people most skilled at singing the *gu*. The songs are long and complex, so that a considerable effort is required to learn them. Why would they want to throw that effort away?

This attitude toward the death songs was, I gradually learned, part of a more general phenomenon. When Tom Harrisson, long-time Curator of the Sarawak Museum, visited Long Teru in the early 1950s, he had no trouble getting his hosts to talk about songs concerning which there was considerable secrecy two decades later, even though his visit was very brief (Harrisson 1954). Mr. Harrisson was no doubt a persuasive man, but there was more to it than that. In the early 1950s religious innovation—conversion to Christianity and revivalist cults—had only just begun among most of the upriver folk on the Baram, and the Tinjar region was barely touched by these influences. By 1972, Long Teru was a last beleaguered outpost surrounded by converts of one kind and another. Just why Long Teru held fast to the old forms is a question that I cannot take up here. To answer it would require detailed analysis of the political circumstances of all four Berawan communities. But the religious changes outside the community, not to mention the growth of a Christian (Roman Catholic) minority within the house, had direct consequences on the attitudes of those responsible for the maintenance of indigenous ritual.

Very influential in shaping those attitudes was Biló Kasi, senior noblewoman of the house and widow of the most revered leader of recent decades (see plate 10). Kasi felt that it was inevitable that the traditional religion would disappear, probably in her lifetime. The young folk, she remarked, were simply not learning the prayers and songs, nor were there any new shamans to replace those growing old. Who, she asked, would defend the community against malign influences when Tama Ukat Sageng, the wise old shaman, passed on? Then the people of Long Teru, willy-nilly, would have to rely on whatever protection the priest had to offer, and so would convert.[1] She was unsure whether those who converted would go to the same place after death. But if there was to be a parting of the ways, Kasi[2] knew which way she wanted to go. Much as she loved her children and grandchildren, she would rather rejoin her husband, her parents, and those generations of Berawan who went before. She would be the last.

What Kasi did not want to see was the step-by-step debasement of the traditional religion, with rituals performed in an incorrect and halfhearted manner. There is a Malay phrase often used by Berawan that has exactly the right connotation of ineptness and incompleteness: *alang-alang*. It was the term used with manifest irritation when I repainted the inside of my large, outboard motor–driven canoe, but left the outside peeled and stained. It did no good to explain that I had run out of paint; I had committed a public nuisance by beginning what I could not finish. It was a sentiment of this kind that conditioned Kasi's views about the perpetuation of traditional ritual. But it was not merely a matter of aesthetics, for the rites are powerful, and that power must be properly channeled or it will cause more harm than good. This is especially so with the death songs. If they are correctly done, they bring many benevolences on the house, but if they are done incorrectly, then they can just as easily accelerate rather than halt the chain reaction of death. Better, in Kasi's view, that they be lost entirely than remembered imperfectly.

Not everyone shared Kasi's attitude. In particular, the single most important vocalist, Tama Usang Weng, felt none of Kasi's reticence. He customarily sang the lead part in many of the longer *gu*, including the all-important one which makes up the bulk of the singing on the last night of the wake (*ichem mugé*), and I am not sure that there was anyone else in the house who could or would take on this task. Weng is older than Kasi, who refers to him as "grandfather," although, since both are old and not closely related, this cannot be taken as other than figurative. I was never able to form a confident estimate of his date of birth, but certainly it was before the turn of the century. His age did not, however, guarantee him the universal respect of the community. Although vigorous in body, so that he continued to work his own farm, he was sometimes absentminded. When excited, he would unpredictably drop into another language, most often the isolect of Long Tutoh, a community in which he lived for several years as a young man, and so become incomprehensible to many people at Long Teru. He had also, it must be admitted, a fondness for the bottle, although he was not alone in that. Taken together, these tendencies undermined his influence in the house, and he was often treated with a certain condescension.

Between him and Biló Kasi there was sometimes tension; she could not deny his ritual expertise, but she was impatient with what she considered his improvident use of it. For example, a con-

Plate 10. Biló Kasi as a young woman. This photograph was taken in the early 1950s when Kasi was married to Penghulu (government-appointed chief) Lawai, a much respected leader of the Long Teru community.

tretemps occurred as a result of the visit of a stranger to Long Teru, a man who came alone seeking help for a condition involving a kind of palsy. What was unusual about the incident was that he was a Muslim, albeit from a community that converted only in this century and has historical affiliations with the Berawan. Tama Usang Weng welcomed the man into his own room, and became engrossed in establishing distant familial connections. By his own enthusiasm, Weng generated public interest in the man's case. He talked his sister Tapan, who had only recently begun to practice as a shaman again after a lapse of many years, into performing for him. Tama Ukat Sageng, preeminent shaman, close friend of Biló Kasi, and not lacking in generosity, also helped. But while Sageng's curing session was in his familiar low-key style, Tapan's was more elaborate. In three successive nights of well-attended performances, Tapan diagnosed her patient's illness as resulting from the abortive entry of a spirit into him, and tried to expel it, and these efforts were followed with mounting interest by the community. Failing to expel the invading spirit, Tapan decided instead to "seat" the spirit correctly, that is to induct the sufferer as a shaman in his own right. With this in mind, she ordered up a battery of new equipment, some of it bulky, designed to appeal to a range of spirit agencies. This was a rite not seen at Long Teru in recent years, and on the afternoon prior to the event there were plenty of willing hands to prepare the props.

Throughout all this Kasi had played an important role as Tapan's assistant, interpreting her statements and looking after her when she was in trance. But now she evidently began to feel uncomfortable with this exceptional activity, especially directed at a stranger. She seems to have felt that the rites were being taken too lightly. In the middle of the afternoon Kasi came purposefully down the veranda to where a small crowd was preparing for the evening session, and made a brief speech. Quietly but firmly she told them all to stop work, that it was not the right time for such things, and that the rite should be delayed until, perhaps, after the harvest.[3] Then she went back to her room. Shamefacedly, the crowd melted away. Only Weng, Tapan, and one other person worked on for a short while before they too abandoned the project. As instigator, Weng was embarrassed and wounded. He simply did not understand Kasi's scruples. He saw no reason why the old religion should not continue indefinitely, even restricted to Long Teru, and there was some sense in this, since the nature of traditional religion was that it was unique to a particular community.[4] But Weng's optimism sometimes seemed out of touch with practical realities; he once told me that when he died his knowledge of the death songs would pass spontaneously into someone else.

One of the things that had, I suspect, convinced Kasi to intervene in this case was the chance presence of two government extension officers in the longhouse, an agricultural officer and a home demonstrator, who announced their intention of staying to see Tapan's performance. Here was the proof that the event was becoming burlesque. In addition there was, as always during that period, myself. Because of the conclusions that Kasi had reached concerning its imminent demise, and her concern that its dignity not be compromised in its passing, Kasi was necessarily ambivalent about my interest in ritual. There were many occasions on which she provided much useful information. But there were one or two topics that she preferred not to discuss, and she used her considerable influence to inhibit others from discussing them. There were a number of death songs (not, as it turned out, the crucial ones) about which she was secretive. In the end it was old Tama Usang Weng, endlessly genial and slightly daffy, popping up everywhere like a mischievous elf, who forced Ḃiló Kasi's hand.

In April 1973 these events lay in the future. I had not heard the death songs, let alone tried to penetrate their meaning, and I was still trying to grasp the motives that lay behind the banning of the *gu* two or three years before. As the time for Lanau's *nulang* approached, the subject of the death songs was hotly debated. These debates reached their climax in a house meeting in late April. Several people made impassioned speeches, so that it might have appeared to an outsider that there was considerable difference of opinion, but in fact a consensus clearly emerged. Tama Bidung, a spokesman for the small Christian minority, argued that the observance of such customs had nothing to do with being Christian or pagan, but rather being Berawan or non-Berawan. His position displayed considerable sociological awareness, although I doubt his priest would have agreed. Lian, a conservative in ritual matters and usually allied with Biló Kasi, counted thirteen people capable of singing the *gu*, enough so that they could be performed adequately. Several people, including Kasi, reported that they had had dreams which they interpreted as meaning that the death songs should be reinstated.

Why this change of heart? It is possible that my presence in the longhouse, and the interest that I showed, played some part, a kind of anthropological Heisenberg effect. But I have no doubt that the principal motivation was inherent in the situation. At Long Teru the *gu* may be sung at funerals as well as at *nulang*, but they are particularly significant at the latter. So much is this the case that people felt uncomfortable about holding the rites of secondary treatment for Lanau without the *gu*. This was a possibility that had not been properly considered when the songs were previously suppressed, because there was no *nulang* envisioned at that time.

Difficulties in the Study of the Death Songs

Because of the reintroduction of the death songs in 1973, I was able to tape record a large corpus during subsequent funerals. The problem was then to transcribe and translate them, and it proved intractable. The difficulty is this: During a wake, things are far too hectic to get much done. What I needed was for one of the half-dozen or so old people who are expert in singing the songs to sit down with me and work through the recordings, stanza by stanza. But this is tedious work at any time, during a wake it is virtually unthinkable. It would have been too much of an imposition to ask dignified senior people of the house to first sit up all night singing the songs, and then work all day explaining them to me. With prayers made in the language of *piat* it was possible simply to get the recording during the proceedings and then work on it weeks or months later when the opportunity presented, for instance when the younger folk were away at the farms. But this strategy does not work with the death songs. Outside of their rightful occasion, during the course of a funeral or *nulang*, it is totally forbidden to sing even a snatch of the death songs; even humming the tunes makes people immediately very uneasy. To infringe upon the prohibition is to risk being accused of causing the next death that occurs in the longhouse. Unfortunately, the rule also applied to my tape recordings.

As if this was not difficulty enough, there is a further complication. At Long Teru, where I was at least able to record the songs as they are actually used, they are not sung in Berawan, but in Lelak. The Lelak people are the ancient inhabitants of the area of Long Teru, but they have now been integrated almost entirely into the culture of the more recently arrived Berawan. The mortuary rituals, and in particular the *gu*, are the last major survivals of Lelak culture, and this piece of ritual conservatism is not surprising when it is remembered that the songs are addressed to the ancestors: At Long Teru the ancestors are Lelak. Meanwhile, I had difficulty collecting even a basic word list in Lelak, so thoroughly has the language fallen out of use in day-to-day affairs.

At Long Jegan the problem was no less obstinate. There the *nulang* had been abolished on conversion to the Bungan cult, and the *gu* had never been allowed at mere funerals. At the same time, the fear of the songs was still considerable, so there was *no* occasion whatsoever on which they could be sung. I finally obtained some snatches in a drifting canoe several miles away from the longhouse. But hard things were said about my informants and myself. Further work could very usefully be done with Long Jegan folk, if they could be removed from the area of the longhouse to a town on the coast, for instance. There they would feel less inhibited about the songs, and it would be possible to transcribe and translate their extensive repertoire.

The Batu Belah people were not worried about singing the *gu* because they feel protected from any ill effects by their Christian faith. But unfortunately they remember nothing more than a few snatches of them.

The fragments collected at Long Jegan and Batu Belah proved only slightly less difficult to translate than the Long Teru ones. Although most of them were supposed to be in Berawan, it was a language unlike everyday speech. Occasional words are familiar, others are cognates of regular words, but many are incomprehensible. Several younger people tried to puzzle their way through them, without much success in terms of word-by-word translation, although they knew the general intention of different verses because they recognized certain key words that were in ordinary Berawan. They commented blithely that the songs are the speech of spirits anyway, and therefore not to be understood fully by men.[5] This is in accordance with the myth of the origin of the songs recounted in chapter twelve. It was also suggested that the songs represented an archaic variety of Berawan, preserved in the *gu* but changed in everyday speech.

In addition to these technical problems, there was an undertow of reluctance to share the secrets of the *gu* noted above. The person who felt this reluctance the most strongly was Biló Kasi, who identified with her Lelak cultural heritage. Because of extensive intermarriage with Berawan immigrants, there is no one at Long Teru who can claim pure Lelak descent, but Kasi came as close to it as anyone did, and moreover she was descended from the last powerful leaders of the Lelak people before their assimilation by Berawan. Her sentiment that she would be the last custodian of the old Lelak ways, and that they would perish with her, was focused principally upon the death songs.

The particular combination of factors reviewed above made the Berawan death songs a particularly hard nut to crack. But in similar, if less extreme form, the same situation is found in many cultures across Borneo. Complex traditions of sacred songs, often performed in connection with death rituals, will soon disappear forever. For example, David Prentice collected a large corpus of songs from an adept of one of the Murut subgroups of northern Borneo. She was the last of her kind, but unfortunately she died before anything but a small fraction of the material was translated (Prentice: personal communication). There are some materials available for study. Before the Second World War, J. Mallinckrodt and L. Mallinckrodt-Djata (1928) recorded and translated a long death song in priestly language *(basa sangiang)* from the Ngaju of southern Borneo. Probably the greatest corpus of all was collected by Hans Schärer, also among the Ngaju, but unfortunately he did not live to prepare much of it for publication so that most has disappeared or is inaccessible (Josselin de Jong 1963:vii). Recently, little work has been done on this topic. An important contribution is a translation by Reverend A. D. Galvin of a death song of the Sebop, upriver neighbors of the Berawan (Galvin 1972). The Sebop do not practice secondary treatment of the dead, and do not attach such sacred power to their songs. Moreover, the language of the songs is evidently relatively close to standard Sebop.

The difficulties of the Berawan case defeated my attempts at literal translation. What I obtained instead, and what provides the basis of the account offered in the next chapter, were précis. Although from the point of view of a linguist or folklorist much is lost in not having a complete text, the précis obtained are sufficiently detailed that it is possible to gain a good grasp of the significance of the songs as a component of the entire sequence of mortuary rituals. Even for those young folk who had only a nodding familiarity with the content of the *gu*, they constituted a repository of community lore, and a dramatic evocation of it. My account is designed to make clear the roots of that drama.

The précis were obtained in several ways. First, it was possible by listening to repeated performances of the major songs to grasp the structure of verse and chorus, which is often relatively simple. For example, the bulk of the song called *siroi*, which at Long Teru must be sung on the final night of the wake, consists of successive verses that are virtually identical except for a word or two—the names of places as it turned out. Such pervasive repetitiveness made it easier to penetrate the general meaning of the songs, not to mention making it easier for the adepts to commit to memory. Luckily, the most important songs are generally the simplest in terms of structure.

Second, it turned out that the songs about which there was most secrecy were not those that were the most significant. For most of the prescribed songs, I was able to piece together their substantive content from the interpolative comments of elders during the performance. I also gained information from taking the recordings of the Long Teru songs and playing them at Batu Belah and Long Jegan. At the latter house particularly, this sparked considerable discussion. There was no anxiety about listening to the tapes because the songs were not native to that community. Meanwhile, there were several older people who wanted to display their own knowledge by interpreting and criticizing what they heard on the tapes. They usually liked to preface their remarks with: "All wrong! Those people at Long Teru have it all wrong!"

Plate 11. Tama Usang Weng in festive attire. He wears valuable cloths across his shoulders, a war bonnet, and a necklace of beads connoting aristocratic rank. His upper earlobes are pierced in the manner of a warrior, and he wears simple wooden plugs in the holes. There are a variety of other ornaments that may be worn in them. Such finery was not an everyday sight in the longhouse. Weng's usual dress comprised a baggy pair of trade store shorts.

The songs that were shrouded in secrecy are not among those that must be sung every time the *gu* are employed. The ones that owe most to the Lelak heritage peculiar to Long Teru are optional. But even in their case, Tama Usang Weng had several times hinted that he would come to my aid, against Biló Kasi's known wishes. Finally, one day not a month before I left Long Teru, Weng came abruptly into my small house and without preliminaries told me to collect my pen and notebook because it was time that I was told about the *gu.* While I was overcoming my surprise, Weng went around closing the wooden shutters on the windows and barring the door. This precaution was not designed to prevent detection by members of the community. My one-room house stood not twenty feet in front of the longhouse, in full view of the veranda, and nothing could have been more conspicuous. Moreover, Weng planned to make his actions public anyway. Rather it was intended to decrease the chances of attracting the attentions of the dead. This despite the fact that a funeral (for Utan Nin, whose death is described in chapter three) was actually in progress. Moreover, he did not plan to sing the songs, only recite them. His hesitancy once again demonstrated the seriousness of the songs. So we sat inside the gloomy house through the heat of the day and into the late afternoon, talking softly to one another. What Weng provided me with was a synopsis, a key from which particular verses are constructed to make up a performance which lasts many hours. Having explained this to me, he had me read back to him what I had taken down. By the time this was done, I was tired, but my afternoon was not over. Weng insisted that we go directly to see Kasi in her room at the other end of the longhouse, where I was to read back my notes again, so that Kasi could hear them. As Weng told us both bluntly, he did not want people to say later that he had told me incorrectly. I began nervously. Weng sat back comfortably, his work done, and sipped distilled rice wine. Kasi, summoned from her nap, and taken aback at these developments, sat tightlipped at first. But slowly she began to smile more tolerantly, bowing gracefully to what was a *fait accompli.*

Weng was in part revenging himself upon Kasi for the occasions when she had scolded him for carelessness in singing the *gu.* Having profited from this rivalry, I had to ask myself whether there was any way in which I was damaging Kasi's interests by writing down the contents of the songs, and here there is an irony. A synopsis of the death songs about which Kasi had been secretive is already in print, in a short article by Tom Harrisson in the *Sarawak Museum Journal* (1954). Kasi herself had been one of the informants who had explained the myths that lay behind these songs during a brief visit that Harrisson had made to Long Teru on his way upriver more than two decades previously.

Having in these diverse ways pieced together the meaning of the death songs, the analytical problem is to understand their place in the ritual sequence. Simply stated, the function of the *gu* is to transmit the soul of the deceased to the land of the dead. But here an anomaly immediately appears.

The Use of the Death Songs in the Abridged Sequence

At both Long Jegan and Long Teru, the *gu* are associated with the rites of secondary treatment, and that association was one of the reasons why the songs were reinstated for the *nulang* for Lanau. At Long Jegan the songs were never sung at any other time. However, at Long Teru they can be, and are, utilized during funerals, and this presents us with an anomaly in terms of the analysis set out in chapter seven. When the songs are sung at a funeral, do they achieve their function of sending the soul to the land of the dead? If so, why ever bother with *nulang?* If not, what is the use of singing the *gu?*

Informants at Long Teru were disinclined to expound upon questions of this kind, but they agreed that the answer to the first question is no, and the details of ritual observance bear them out. Even after the songs have been sung at a funeral, considerable anxiety revolves around the soul of the newly deceased person. The community is still threatened, and the mourning observances described in chapters seven and eight continue to be observed. Why then are they sung? Only a measure of sophistry can reduce the practice to a logical consistency: At a funeral the soul, though still mired in corruption and unacceptable to the spirits of the dead, is shown the proper way to its final destination. Then at least it will be prepared for the journey when the time finally comes to make it, regardless of whether the living chose to celebrate the occasion or not.

Clearly this rationalization did not appeal to the people of Long Jegan, who claimed that to sing the songs at a funeral would cause the corpse to get up and walk. They preferred simply to leave the *gu* unsung in the abridged ritual sequence, and presumably the soul would find its own way as best it could. The Long Jegan custom accords better with the metaphor of body and soul. But a moment's reflection will show that the indeterminacy remains between the singing of the songs and the entry of the soul into the land of the dead. As noted above, if the *nulang* is long delayed it is not considered that the soul continues indefinitely to haunt the abodes of humans. It follows that the soul may have completed its metamorphosis and entry into the land of the dead long before, and the singing of the songs at *nulang* must then be a second journey down the same route.

It is pointless to push too far these niceties of logic, because they neither elucidate the rites for us, nor figure in the Berawan view of things. For the participants, the songs make sense at a different level, the level of performance.

Performance

My first impressions of the death songs were disappointing. Foolishly perhaps, I had expected, after all the brouhaha involved in deciding to reinstate them, that they would be immediately impressive. But the sacredness of the *gu* does not imply that the audience should sit in hushed awe throughout. Even in the past, it was probably the case that a small core of older people led the singing and that only a minority of the crowd on the veranda would be participating at any one time. However, there were modern distractions that further drew attention away from the singers, and it must be conceded that Tama Usang Weng, who did much of the singing, did not command the respect of the younger folk. Also, many of the songs are long, and repetitive. The upshot was that on many evenings Weng and a small circle of supporters would be sawing away, verse after verse, in a corner near the corpse, while the veranda was filled with people intently playing cards. The playing of cards had reached epidemic proportions at Long Teru in the early seventies, and the leaders of the community worried about controlling the gambling involved. Precisely because of this tendency to monopolize people's attention, cards were outlawed on the final night of the wake. On other nights perhaps, cards were appropriate, to help wile away the long hours of the vigil. But not on *ichem mugé*. However, they were replaced by another distraction, namely the dozens of overdressed young men who showed up from nearby lumber camps. The more people that can be gathered together on these occasions the better, and these visitors, like any others, do honor to the deceased by their presence. Yet they also dilute the impact of the rites: What does the *gu* mean to them?

But first impressions are misleading. An effort of imagination is required in order to discount the trivializing effects of modernity, and to appreciate the songs from a Berawan viewpoint.

There was a time when the Tinjar was almost exclusively a Berawan river. In those days, all of the visitors to a major death ritual would have understood the significance of the death songs, even if they were not familiar with the ones peculiar to the host longhouse. They would have been able to rapidly learn how to participate as part of the chorus, and they would have had more opportunity to learn: Berawan longhouses were, and are, spaced well apart from one another, and in the days before outboard motors a considerable effort was required to visit another house. Consequently, visitors at major events did not come for one evening, but participated throughout the event. On lesser occasions, when there were few guests, the atmosphere was more cozy, and the songs provided a focus of group activity and solidarity. B016 Kasi told me of evenings spent around a flickering wick lantern, in the days before bright pressure lamps were known upriver. An adult would sing the lead part of the *gu* and teams of boys and girls would take turns singing the chorus, seeing who could sing the fastest or the slowest or the loudest or the softest. Some of the girls with whom Kasi sang on the veranda many years ago are dead now. Those who remain are mostly grandmothers. Yet there is schoolgirlish intimacy between them still, a charming playfulness that is the heritage of those evenings.

Moreover, it must be kept in mind that the audience are aware of what in general is happening in the *gu*. There is hardly much suspense about the outcome, and consequently little motive for hanging on every word. In traditional drama all over Southeast Asia it is the norm that plots are known in advance, and that the attention of the audience is incomplete:

> . . . the over-all impression . . . is one of muted chaos as food vendors, children and adults ceaselessly move up and down the aisles. Audiences do not concentrate on each word, gesture, or nuance of meaning that comes from the stage, as Western audiences have been trained to do. If your neighbor talks, you don't try to quiet him. Plays are longer than they are in the West, and no one can be expected to sit through an eight- or nine-hour performance without talking, eating or getting up. (Brandon 1967:260)

In the Indonesian shadow play *(wayang kulit)*, which has a quasi-sacred character, the show often lasts all night, and the audience dozes during less interesting scenes. But, by the same token, they know when to expect exciting moments in the action, and will rapidly bring their attention to bear. For example, if a hero-figure makes a stirring speech, asserting vigorously important social values, then there will often be a brief hush in the crowd, followed by applause. The applause is for the sentiment, not the performer.

The *gu* operate in a similar fashion. As at the shadow play, social life goes on around them without undermining their real significance. Moments of intensity are interspersed with long, slow episodes. When those moments occur, they carry considerable power, an almost tactile awareness of the supernatural. There is a section near the beginning of the entire sequence where the dead are invited to attend the wake, and I recall one occasion when I heard this performed. It was not a large funeral, and there were not very many people attending on the first night. Consequently, there was something of the familial atmosphere that Biló Kasi had described from her youth. Kasi had told me that when the dead are invited she can feel them arriving; a slight rustling and a chilling of the air. Just as they reached that point in the opening *gu*, a faint evening breeze caused the lamp to dim.

Notes

1. Biló Kasi was scathing not only in her assessment of the power of the priests to defend her community against evil, but also in regard to the power of most of the other shamans. It was almost exclusively in Tama Ukat Sageng that she placed her trust.

2. Kasi is a personal name; Biló is a teknonym meaning widow. I usually specify people by giving their full teknonym as used while I was in the field (teknonyms change in response to events in the owner's life). But for brevity's sake I sometimes utilize simply the personal name without the teknonym.

3. In fact, there is no seasonality to this rite at all. It could be done at any time, and Kasi was simply making an excuse.

4. As of 1980, it is Weng who appears to be borne out. The traditional religion persists at Long Teru, even though Tama Ukat Sageng died in 1974. Tama Usang Weng is still alive.

5. The phrase the young men used was in Malay: *bantu cakap*, meaning the speech of evil spirits or ghosts. In using this expression they dismissed the whole topic, but it did not mean that they were contemptuous of the mystical power of the songs. On the contrary, they seemed almost as awed by them as the older folk were.

CHAPTER TWELVE

Singing the Dead

The death songs are at once sacred and intractable. On the one hand, the words and tunes are invested with awful power; on the other, most of the participants in a wake barely listen to the songs, and many have only a sketchy idea of their meaning. It is not, however, a unique situation, as S. J. Tambiah has shown (1968, 1970). He argues that anthropology has traditionally underrated the role of words in ritual, and he points to the widespread belief in their inherent mystical power. In northeast Thailand, Buddhist monks conduct lengthy rituals that consist largely of chants in the sacred language of Pali. Very few of the congregation understand the chants, yet it is strongly held that the listeners gain merit and protection simply by hearing them. There are even parables that emphasize the value of listening without understanding.

The tendency towards sacralization of texts is a universal one, Tambiah argues, found in all the world religions:

> The sacred words . . . acquire their power and efficacy not so much because they are in a sacred language which is different from the language of ordinary use, but because of a threefold character represented in most if not all religious systems. First, there is an original authority—be it God, or prophet, or first ancestors—who is the source of the sacred words, the doctrine, myth and message. Secondly, this doctrine itself becomes a heritage and a sacred object in its own right, transmitted over time in orderly succession. . . . Thirdly the words are effective because there are religious experts who recite them (and perform other ritual acts) and who have a pedigree of links with predecessors (leading back to the first source). (1970:197–8)

It is not hard to make out the same "threefold character" in Berawan use of the death songs, and it helps us to put into perspective their sacred character.

The efficacy attributed to the songs is considerable. On the debit side, they can, if incorrectly performed, alienate the ancestors instead of winning their aid. The outcome will be an acceleration of the chain reaction of death, and that is why Biló Kasi felt so strongly that it was better not to do the songs at all rather than do them badly. On the credit side, the songs have the power directly to manipulate the interactions of souls and spirits. We have already seen that the songs in particular, and the *nulang* in general, do not bring about the release of the soul of the deceased from the bonds of the flesh. *Nulang* is merely a "coming out"; the metamorphosis may have been completed long before. But during the ritual the dead and the living are brought together by the power of the songs in a mystical union with the ancestors, from whom vigor and worldly wealth largely flow.

How the contents of the songs move toward that conclusion is shown in this chapter. Those contents are not unimportant, even to a Berawan with no special skill or learning in the songs. In northeast Thailand, Tambiah explains, it is not the case that the audience is entirely out of touch with what is going on in the sacred chants, even if they do not speak Pali. Some men have probably been monks or novices in the past, and have some familiarity with the texts, and many people can recognize chants, know which are appropriate for which occasion, and can keep up generally with what is happening by recognizing key words. All have had the contents of the chants explained to them at some time or other, or could have if they chose to ask. So it is with the *gu*. There is a range of participation and of appreciation for the songs as performance. But the sacred import of the songs, their thrust, if you will, is familiar to all.

Types of Death Songs

There are two types of death songs: Those that must be sung, if any are sung at all, and those that are optional. Of the latter some are serious, some lighthearted.

The order and timing of the compulsory songs are also pre-scribed. In each Berawan longhouse, this sequence of songs is unique to that community, although there are overall similarities. On the first evening of a wake at which *gu* are to be employed, a set of short songs are sung that perform one or more of the follow-ing purposes: They inform the deceased that the wake has begun; they invite the ancestors to attend; they recount the origin of *gu;* and they provide a checklist of observances to be kept during the wake. After that, on the same and succeeding nights of the wake, any of the optional death songs may be sung, at the whim of the main singers. But the final night of singing is entirely devoted to prescribed songs, and this is when the whole sequence reaches its climax. At both Long Teru and Long Jegan, the songs of the final night are in three parts. First, the short *gu* sung on the opening night are repeated. Then two lengthy songs are sung, one of which is designed to bring the soul to the land of the dead, and the other to make sure that no souls of living members of the community have accidentally gone off with it. Beyond these general features, it is necessary to describe the sequences of the two houses separately.

Most, but not all, of the songs require a lead singer and chorus. People join the chorus for a while, and then wander off casually. Not so the lead singer, who must persevere until the song is comp-leted, which often takes several hours. He or she may stop for refreshment from time to time, and if stamina really begins to run out there are always ways that the performance can be cut short by eliminating all decoration. The chorus is usually easy to learn by rote. No musical instruments are used for accompaniment.

Playful Songs

Some of the songs are little more than games played to entertain the crowd, and they can be stopped whenever enthusiasm for them runs out. For all their innocence, however, they are nonetheless taboo at times other than a wake. A couple of examples will show their nature.

To play *pukèt anak* (*pukèt* = to look for, *anak* = child), the participants sit in a circle with one person in the middle. They sing a little verse to the effect that they have lost their baby. Meanwhile a little bundle of rags, the "baby," is passed from hand to hand around the outside of the circle. At the end of the verse, the player in the center challenges someone whom he or she believes is holding the cloth bundle, asking, "Where is my baby, . . ." and inserting the name of the subject. If the choice is a correct one, then the two players change places. If not, the reply comes, "Gone to Marudi," and the game resumes. If the baby gets all the way to Singapore in this fashion, via Miri and Kuching, then the person in the center must pay a forfeit, usually making a funny face or singing a song. At the end of each round, the baby's soul is dutifully sung back to Long Teru.

Another variant of the games sung while sitting in a circle requires that the participants huddle close together and stretch out their arms in front of them, so that they can catch the man who stands in the middle with his arms folded. A lead singer tells him that he is very drunk, and instructs him to walk like a drunken man, to stagger, to fall forward, and then to fall sideways, and so on. The people in the circle must catch the falling man, and propel him onto his feet again.

Serious but Optional Songs

On a rather more serious note, the *gu katong* (*katong* = to drift or float) sends the soul of the deceased on an errand designed to promote the wellbeing of the community. The soul is instructed to embark in a canoe and paddle downriver, following the right bank. The verses of the song mention in turn the places that he passes as he goes down. Arriving finally at the Chinese bazaar at Marudi, the soul is told to go to the shops and obtain all manner of things that modern day Berawan feel the need of: sugar, salt, cloth, kerosene, *ad infinitum*. These the soul is told to load into the canoe, and then it is sung back upriver, again following the bank on its right-hand side so that a different list of place names is recited. At the climax of the song the soul reaches the longhouse, and the goods are distributed to everyone there. This song takes several hours to complete, and it is allowable to do half on one evening and half on the following, leaving the soul in the meantime in Marudi. Alternatively, the lead singer can abbreviate the performance by leaving out place names on the return journey. On one occasion when Tama Usang Weng was leading the singing, he became too weary to continue, and perhaps a little drunk as well, so he abbreviated the homeward journey to just six stopping places. People made a joke of this, saying that the soul was a very vigorous paddler.

Another category of *gu* are the *gu lakanya* (*lakanya* from *tanya* = to ask), of which there are several, varying from community to community. The lead singer, impersonating the dead person, asks a series of questions to which the chorus sings the reply. Often the questions relate to the observances of the mortuary ritual. Most *gu lakanya* are relatively short and therefore suitable for evenings when it is desired to sing only briefly.

There are three long death songs that are peculiar to Long Teru. These were the ones concerning which Biló Kasi was so secretive. I give here a summary only:

(1) *gu vea up*i. A man goes fishing, but catches only a fruit seed. He throws it back, but the next day he catches it again. Three times he rejects it, and has no luck at fishing. Finally, he decides to keep the nut, and immediately catches more fish than he can carry in his canoe. He plants the seed. It germinates, and stage by stage grows into a mature tree. The fruit of this tree is called *vea up*i, and it has three lobes inside it. Always they are found with two lobes full of flesh and one empty, having been eaten by spirits. Should anyone find a fruit of this type with all three lobes full, then certainly his death is not far off. When the fruits were eaten, it was found that men became drunk and violent. So they chopped the tree down, and as it fell its flowers turned to beads, and its fruit to gold. This was the source of wealth of the Lelak folk before.

(2) *gu Julak anak Teluan.* A married man named Julak went on a war party, and in a longhouse far from his home he fell in love with a beautiful girl and married her. His first wife was jealous and angry when she heard of this, and went to the place where her husband was staying. She hung a knife above the sleeping place of the second wife, and told it to fall down on her husband if he came to sleep there. That night, the husband was duly stabbed to death by the magical knife. Now the second wife cried inconsolably, and begged the first wife to restore life to

Julak. So the first wife repented of what she had done, and brought the unfaithful husband back to life by sprinkling water upon him. He returned to his proper home a chastened man.

(3) *gu anak tau*. A man went one day to work on building a canoe in the forest. He laid his weapons aside, and so could not fight back when attacked by an eight-headed monster, who killed him and chopped off his head. The dead man's wife later produced a son, who is referred to in the song as *anak tau* (the orphan child). As the orphan grew up, he had many magical adventures. Once he came upon some boys playing tops, but he had no top and, moreover, the other children were rude to him. Then there appeared a spirit (perhaps the ghost of his father in a new guise?) which gave its heart to the orphan child to use as a top. With this magical top, he drove all contestants from the field of play. But then a man appeared who was so skillful that even the magical top could not defeat him. So they discovered that the man was the brother of the orphan's father. Later, when almost grown up, the orphan went to walk in the jungle near the house and found his father's weapons by a tree. So he knew that this was the place where his father had been killed. He decided to finish the work on the canoe that his father had begun, and called the omen animals to help him. When the canoe was finished, he set out to find his father's killer, over the protests of his old mother. When he finally found the house of the monster, he saw his father's head hanging up on the veranda, and had conversation with it. The eight-headed demon ran out of the house, making horrible threats against the orphan, and they fell to fighting. But neither could win. Despite all his skill, the orphan child could not kill the monster because his sword would not penetrate its hide. So then the little omen bird *sekoték* advised the orphan to hit at the monster's right kneecap, because that is where the magical stone was hidden that gave the monster its powers *(utam)*. The orphan struck off the kneecap, and slaughtered the now helpless monster. All the slaves who had been held captive in the house ran out in delight, and helped in the preparation of a *tapó* (prayer site, shrine) and in the calling of the major omen bird *(plaké)*. The orphan was now able to restore his father to life again by bathing the dried skull in water previously consecrated by *plaké*.

These three death songs are sung only at Long Teru because of their Lelak origin. In addition, songs have been borrowed from other

Berawan communities and from even farther afield. The *gu katong* is sung in Berawan, showing that it has been borrowed from Batu Belah or Long Jegan. The two playful little circle games that are described above are both Punan Bah in origin. At Long Jegan, where several fluent speakers of the Punan Bah language are to be found, the songs were sung in the original dialect (or something close to it). At Batu Belah and Long Teru, they have been adapted to a Berawan form.

Each community has a variety of death songs; a few that are heard only there, and a number that are shared with other longhouses. But Long Jegan had by far the largest repertoire, several dozen different songs. This is a result of the very prolonged *nulang* celebrated there. We noted that both at Long Jegan and at Batu Belah, the *nulang* continued throughout the time that the mortuary edifice was under construction. At the latter house, this period might last several weeks. But at the former, where very elaborate *salong* were built, it could last many months. Throughout this period death songs had to be sung every night. This situation contrasts with Long Teru, where the period during which *gu* could be sung never exceeded ten days. The opportunities to learn songs and increase the repertoire was much greater at Long Jegan than at Long Teru.

The Prescribed Songs at Long Jegan: A Cosmological Journey

Turning to the prescribed *gu*, we look first at the sequence from Long Jegan, where they had not been heard for two decades. Nevertheless, it was possible to obtain detailed synopses of the songs from Sadi″ Pejong, the headman, and other senior members of the community, just as it was possible to collect accounts of other aspects of *nulang*.

The sequence began on the first night of the *nulang* with three short *gu*. The first invited the dead to attend, and specifically summoned the soul of the individual honored at the festival to return from whatever spiritual realms it may have wandered into. The second recounted the origin of the death songs, and the third explained the mourning usages, such as the wearing of white headbands by the kinsmen of the deceased. Only about an hour was required to complete these short songs, and thereafter some of the optional *gu* could be sung until sometime after midnight, when it was necessary to begin the prescribed song called *sa'o*.

The *sa'o* had an important purpose: The recovery of any souls of the living that might have been tempted to wander off with that of the dead person. But it was sung in a playful manner. A verse, lead part and chorus, was sung for every member of the community, working steadily along the house from room to room, beginning at the downriver end. Each soul was summoned to return, and some other person of the opposite sex was delegated to "pull" the soul home. This was an opportunity for innuendo, at which no one was supposed to take offense. Teenagers were mentioned with their sweethearts; young married people were coupled with those suspected of having an illicit interest in them; and old crones paired with feeble grandfathers, who made lecherous advances to amuse the crowd. Infants were usually assisted by parents. The *sa'o* took several hours to complete, and it was timed so that it ended near dawn. Then the short *gu* inviting the spirits of the dead to attend was repeated, so completing the songs for the first night of the *nulang*.

On subsequent nights, until the last, there were no prescribed songs, and a selection could be made from the large repertoire of less important songs. If the *nulang* was prolonged, usually because an elaborate mausoleum was under construction, then there was on most evenings nothing but the briefest of performances until very close to the time when the edifice was ready. If on the other hand, a tomb was available for storage of the coffin, then the singing would go on for only eight days, and each night there would be several hours of singing.

The climax came on the final night. It began with the repetition of the three short *gu* and the *sa'o*, as on the first night. Then came the last and most important song of all, the *bulu biling*. It was sung in an unusual manner. First, the walls that had surrounded the coffin during its period of storage, and during the *nulang* up to this point, were taken down. Then the coffin was moved to the center of the veranda, and surrounded by all manner of valuable things. Next, the team of men that was to sing the *bulu biling* assembled.

Each had to be wearing a clean breechclout, and it was said that anyone who was dressed in a slovenly manner would die soon after. Traditional Berawan male dress consists of a strip of fabric that is passed between the legs and then wrapped around the waist, in such a way as to leave a flap of material hanging down both in the front and back. The lead singer took his place at the head of the line of singers, and each man tied the flap on the front of his cloth to the tail of the man in front's. The men had to remain on their feet, and tied together in this fashion, until the song was completed, which might take several hours. Should anyone need to answer a call of nature, insisted Sadi̇̕ Pejong, then he had to do so with his colleagues in tow. At the start of the song the lead singer was standing beside the coffin, facing upriver. He took up a section of bamboo *(bulu)* that had been standing beside the coffin ever since the funeral, months before. Large diameter sections of bamboo were traditionally used for carrying water, and this bamboo was the one that had brought water to wash the corpse. Firmly, the lead singer struck the top of the coffin with the bamboo, making a resonant sound. He called upon the soul of the deceased to get up and to prepare for its final journey.[1] Then, as he began to sing, he simultaneously moved off down the veranda, weaving first to the right and then to the left, so that the line of singers behind him advanced with a snake-like motion. Reaching the upriver end of the longhouse, he turned around and wove his way back to the other end of the house, and so on, back and forth until the song was finished.

To begin with, the song consists of instructions given to the soul by the lead singer, and repeated by the chorus. The soul is told to go to the river and bathe, and then to come back to the longhouse and dress in fine garments appropriate to the sex of the deceased. For a man, the soul would be told to put on a clean breechclout, and then to trim the hair. All the steps necessary to produce a neat appearance are mentioned by the lead singer, down to cleaning the fingernails. Then the soul is instructed to put on a bead necklace, which is a mark of high rank, and then the accoutrements of a warrior: the bindings that go around the calves and biceps, the tiger teeth ornaments that are worn through a hole pierced in the upper earlobe, the war bonnet, and the war cloak. Then the soul is told to go out onto the veranda of the longhouse, secure a *parang* (short sword) around its waist, take up a spear and a paddle, and descend towards the river. The soul is instructed not to look back at the longhouse, lest it loose resolution for its departure. Instead, it must go directly down to the water's edge, climb into a canoe and paddle off upstream, sticking to the same bank as that which the longhouse is on.

It must be emphasized that this *upstream* journey of the dead is unique to Long Jegan.[2] All of the other Berawan communities sing their dead downstream to a mythical river of the dead near the coast. Only at Long Jegan is the reverse direction chosen, and when I pointed this out to my informants there, they were quick to claim that this was clear proof that they were the true owners of all the land in the upper Tinjar, since they had used that route to their ancestors since time immemorial. As we shall see, the format of the main part of the *bulu biling* dramatically expresses just this point. But does that mean that their dead exist in some region removed from the ancestors of other Berawan? This question, like others of a theological nature, took them by surprise. It was something they had not asked themselves before. Sadí́ Pejong once more came to the rescue: It was a difference of route only, he opined, the destination was mystically the same. In support of this interpretation Sadí́ Pejong pointed out that there was an alternative to *bulu biling* called *patulo*. The *patulo* was borrowed from the Sebop people, and could be substituted for *bulu biling* at the desire of the close relatives; yet *patulo* sings the dead downriver in the more common fashion.

As the soul begins its journey upriver, the format of the death song changes. Now the lead part consists of questions posed by the traveling soul, through his voice, which are answered by the chorus, representing the entire community. The lead singer asks:

> *Long iniu, lasan?* "What place is this, you live ones?" and receives the reply from the chorus:
> *Long inoun, ladiern.* "The place of the longhouse, you dead one" and then the chorus repeats a little formula that says that this is the song that sends the soul upriver. Now the soul asks again:
> *Long iniu, lasan?* and is answered:
> *Long bek, ladiern.* This refers to a place a short way upriver from the longhouse.

The word *long,* which is common to virtually every language of central northern Borneo, means a river mouth, usually a place where one stream joins another. Standardly, place names are formed by putting the word *long* together with the name of the sidestream that joins the main watercourse at that location. Long Teru, for instance, is the place where the Teru sidestream joins the river Tinjar. The formula Long Inoun is used only in the *gu,* and signifies the place where the longhouse is. The word *bek* is an everyday Berawan word meaning a tiny stream, one too small to have a name of its own. The next time that the soul asks its whereabouts it is told: Long Marude, the Marude being a small watercourse that flows into the Tinjar a few hundred yards above the longhouse.

So the soul's journey continues, verse by verse, rivermouth by rivermouth. Since the terrain is broken, and there is high rainfall, there are many sidestreams, some named and others not. For the Berawan, the river provides their principal highway. They use it to get to their farms, and to travel to other villages. Consequently, they know all its twists and turns and sidestreams intimately. This journey was one that everyone present could readily imagine, since it was one that everyone had taken at some time or another, at least part of the way. Occasionally a verse is inserted telling the soul to paddle vigorously, making the spray fly up behind its canoe.

But this is not merely a journey in space, it is also a journey in time. Every time the site of a previous longhouse is passed that place is referred to as Long Inoun, just as when it meant Long Jegan at the outset. Consequently the song reiterates the migration route of the ancestors of the community. For as long as their traditions have to tell, the Long Jegan folk have lived in the middle and upper Tinjar. For much of that time, they were virtually the only inhabitants in an area of perhaps a thousand square miles. This has given them plenty of room to move around, and when they moved their longhouse sites every couple of decades they sometimes decamped dozens of miles in one step. Generally, the movement has tended to be downriver, but not invariably so. Especially in the days when they had the watershed to themselves, they would move to sites almost as far down as present-day Long Jegan, only to head back into the upper reaches a generation later. Since the arrival of other settlers in the headwaters, beginning in the middle of the last century, it has become increasingly difficult to move back upriver again, and the tendency has been to move steadily toward the coastal plain. But the upper reaches of the river are more attractive, with a clear running river and vistas of the mountains, and the Berawan of Long Jegan proudly assert their ancient patrimony over it.

In the song, the skilled singers remembered dozens of sites where the people of Long Jegan had their longhouses before, and each site has its special associations. Long Miri, only a few miles above the present house was a place where the community was united and vigorous under the leadership of a great man, Tama Tiri. It is now difficult to make out where the longhouse stood. Many of the great posts that supported the structure were drifted down to the new site, along with all the planks that were not rotten. The jungle has obliterated the rest. But the works of men are still in evidence there. They can be made out from the river, by eyes that know where to look for them. Walking up from the river bank through the tangled underbrush, they suddenly appear, towering up into the dappled light of the forest canopy: the tall mausoleums built by Tama Tiri and his followers. Some have great chambers supported on five posts, others are smaller and loftier, with only one or two posts. All are intricately carved. The hardwoods from which they were constructed, in particular the straightgrained *bilian*, are impervious to rot and to termites. Even when the jungle creepers envelop the vaults, and finally tear them apart, the great posts remain standing. Far upriver ancient graveyards can be found. They are, in the most literal sense, the places of the ancestors.

Further upriver, at Long Tisam (see map 3), there is another collection of tombs, if anything more impressive, though sunk deeper into decay. They are a monument to the leadership of Tama Lire, who reunited the Tinjar Berawan at the turn of the century after a period of fragmentation and factionalism. But there is also a more ancient association with this location. Just a short distance away, only a bend or two downstream, is a site that reputedly was occupied many generations before Tama Lire. It represents an early migration far downriver, one that was reversed subsequently. The significance of this site is that it was here that the culture hero Tot Manyim lived as a child. Tot Manyim is the focus of a long cycle of myths that tell of his miraculous deeds. It was he who originated the use of omen creatures *(aman)*, particularly the omen birds that played such an important part in traditional practices (Metcalf 1976a). He defeated a race of cruel giants, who lived only on charcoal, and in his travels he dug out lakes and raised mountains. It is said that his canoe, turned to stone, is still to be seen on top of Bukit (Mount) Selikan, which is close to Long Tisam, and which is the most commanding topographical feature in the region. From there Tot Manyim exercises a protective influence to this day. The same hero figures prominently in the mythology of Long Teru, but, naturally, there are differences in the way the story is told there.

The soul's journey continues. At Long Batan was the massive longhouse built by Aban Jau, self-styled "Rajah of the Interior," who defied the European administration that was, at the turn of the century, extending its control inland. Upriver from here are occupation sites associated with ever more distant times. At Long Dunin is a location that was apparently occupied many times because it stands in the middle of the only flat land for many miles. Nor is this any accident, according to Berawan legend. The little plain was created by two brothers, Lai Liou and Polok Lejau, who dreamed that they should sacrifice a certain number of pigs there and make a shrine to the Creator. As they did so, the hills drew back to make room for their new longhouse and its gardens.

It was at Long Dunin that the death songs were revealed for the first time to men. A man had been working with his companions, it is said, roughing out a coffin deep in the forest before bringing it back to the longhouse for final finishing. On the way home at sunset, he suddenly remembered that he had left a tool behind, and went back to fetch it. Approaching the workplace, he heard whistling voices coming from high up in a massive *tapang* tree. They were the voices of spirits, and the man stopped to eavesdrop on them. The chief of the spirits was lecturing the others on the proper way to conduct mortuary rituals. It went over all the details of proper timing for a funeral and a *nulang*, which were already familiar to the listener below, and then it said that there was one thing that was proper that men did not yet know about. At that juncture the man understood that he was supposed to be there listening, and he paid close attention while the spirits above sang for him all the death songs. He was able magically to learn them immediately, and when he returned to the longhouse, he taught them to everyone else. Long Dunin is well upriver from Long Jegan, much closer to the destination of the song, so that presumably the *bulu biling* took less time to sing in those days.

Nevertheless, there are further house sites above Long Dunin, and the phrase Long Inoun is heard again. At Long Kapa is another site viewed with special affection. It was here that Sadí Sudan lived, and he had the distinction of ascending directly to the sky. He was a shaman, and one of his familiars took such a liking to him that it took him to its place permanently. But Sadí Sudan was lonely without his kin, so he asked if he could bring them too. Consequently, after a week during which no one had been able to find hide nor hair of Sadí Sudan, he suddenly reappeared and told them of the beautiful land in the sky that they might go to if they wished. But first the house had to be carefully scrubbed and cleaned, because nothing dirty could go there. Came the day of departure and Sadí Sudan went into a trance. His spirit friends descended from the sky and marched up and down the veranda. The whole longhouse began to shake and quiver and lift up from its supports. But just then a spirit let out a scream and struck a hole in the wall. Hidden in a partition was a puppy dog, the pet of an old woman who could not bear to part with it. At the sight of the dog all the spirits disappeared, taking Sadí Sudan with them, and the house settled back on its mundane foundations.

There are other stories associated with this upriver section, stories of houses that turned into stone, of vast magical fish that fed entire villages, of coffins that chased kin who failed to observe the mourning usages, and heros that became spirits.

But finally, in the verses of the *bulu biling*, the soul arrives at Long Lamat. Instead of passing by, as in every preceeding verse, the soul is instructed to enter the Lamat stream and to paddle vigorously up its rapidly-flowing waters. Some distance up the Lamat, the soul is told to enter the Meta, a yet smaller watercourse. This it follows to the source. There it is instructed to beach the canoe, and to go to look for *sirih*, the leaves that are used in chewing betel nut. With that instruction the *bulu biling*, and the entire death song sequence, abruptly terminates. The line of singers untie their

MAP 3. The route to the land of the dead as followed in the death song *bulu biling* at Long Jegan. Route to the land of the dead shown by the heavy black line, to the Usun Apau by the dotted line.

breechclouts, and relax before the special meal described in chapter ten.

The anticlimactic ending of the *bulu biling* leaves us wondering about the significance of this particular spot at the head of a tiny stream, and what is supposed to become of the soul after it is abandoned there. As usual it was only with some difficulty that exegesis could be obtained from senior people at Long Jegan, but it is better to begin with topography. As map 3 shows, the upper Tinjar is dominated by the Dulit range. Not only are the Dulits high by comparison with other mountains in the area, but also they comprise an extended crest in a terrain that is broken, with only isolated peaks. They rise dramatically from the left bank of the Tinjar, which runs in an unusually straight course because it is confined in a narrow valley. The death song brings the soul to a point that is near the highest summit in the range. Actually the highest point of all is slightly to the south of the headwaters of the Meta stream, but it is notoriously difficult to judge which peak in a range is the highest, because from different vantage points different summits look more impressive. The problem is complicated when the dense rain forest limits the view. From the Tinjar, the spot selected in the song can easily be taken as the highest in the entire region.

From this point, an observer would be afforded a view into the headwaters of the Tinjar and beyond to the edge of the eroded tableland that comprises the Usan Apau (see map 2). In fact, with a little gerrymandering, the Dulits can be conceived of as a barrier between the valley of the Tinjar and the ancient homeland of Berawan mythology. In reality, the center of the Usun Apau lies more to the east, but the migration stories of the ancestors of the Long Jegan folk bring them down the Dapoi and Nibong streams, which hook away to the south. Far up into the Dapoi there are groves of fruit trees that Berawan claim were planted by those first migrants. They are associated with the most distant mythological epoch, when the living and the dead maintained traffic with one another. In the Long Jegan version of the migration stories described in chapter two, it was down those streams that Kusai led the faction that decided not to go directly to the land of the dead.

As for what happens to the soul when it reaches the summit of the Dulits, the answer is contained in Sadí˝ Pejong's dream, recounted in chapter four. As the soul is hunting around for *sirih* leaves it is encountered by the radiant spirits of the dead. Being itself perfect spirit, it may join them without inhibitions, and proceed down the other side of the mountain towards the place where Layong stayed with the ancestors who never died.

In the course of the singing of the *bulu biling* the audience is carried imaginatively upriver and backwards in time. In parade before them are summoned first the great men of the past, men like Tama Tiri, who were certainly larger than life, yet still remained mortal men. Further back are heros who performed prodigious feats, pushed mountains aside and climbed the sky, and others who originated whole departments of Berawan religion, and themselves became minor deities. Lying at the end, both very near and impossibly distant: the ancestors, the sacred dead.

For an audience attuned to the references of the song, the *bulu biling* constituted a drama that drew upon the wellsprings of Berawan culture. Its power depended upon the simple device of having the dead travel upstream instead of down. At Long Teru the impact of the songs is achieved in a different way.

The Prescribed Songs at Long Teru: An Inverted Rite de Passage

At Long Teru the singing of the death songs is initiated with a short *gu* consisting of twenty-four verses. The first twenty verses explain the usages of mourning, such as the faces blackened in play and the plain clothes worn by the close kin. These verses serve as a checklist of these items for the living, but more importantly they serve to point out to the soul of the deceased the care that the living are taking to observe them. At Long Teru the *gu* are sung during funerals, as well as *nulang,* and it is as well to ward off the evil of the lingering soul by emphasizing the concern shown by the living. The last four verses consist of a summons to the spirits of the ancestors to attend. Each verse is sung several times: the first twenty, in blocks of four, are repeated four times; the final four are repeated in sequence eight times. These songs are called the *gu umī*

(*umī* = small, little),[3] and they take about an hour to complete. After that songs may be sung for the rest of the evening and subsequent nights, chosen from the repertoire of optional *gu*.

As at Long Jegan, the final night of the wake is entirely taken up with prescribed songs. It begins with the repetition of the *gu umī*, then the *siroi* is sung. The *siroi* is the counterpart of the *bulu biling* at Long Jegan, while the final song at Long Teru, the *tijun*, is the equivalent of the Long Jegan *sa'o*.

At Long Teru there is no special manner of singing the *siroi*. The lead singer takes his place near the coffin or jar, surrounded by those adepts who will persevere with him throughout the night. The format of the song, aside from its destination, is similar to the *bulu biling*. The soul is instructed to arise, to bathe, and to put on clothes appropriate to the sex of the deceased. Then it is instructed to go down to its canoe. Reaching the top of the river bank, the soul looks back, but the longhouse is invisible to it and everything behind is dark. So it sets its face toward its destination, and looks back no more. However, it does not travel alone. The souls of seven bachelors are sent along as an escort, although the song does not specify them by name. The soul is instructed to begin paddling, this time downriver, and following the right-hand bank regardless of which bank the present longhouse is on. The journey of the soul is toward the sea, and it bears no relationship to any migration route of the ancestors of the Lelak or the Berawan of Long Teru.

Nevertheless, the verses proceed in a fashion similar to the Long Jegan songs, naming in order the watercourses large and small that join the main stream from the right, and occasionally inserting a verse that urges the soul and its escort to paddle with vigor. Slowly the soul makes its way down to where the Tinjar debouches into the Baram. Then on down the Baram, until the small town of Marudi is reached. Marudi consists of a government post with an airstrip, a few Chinese shops, and a Malay village. There the soul and its escort is told to stop for coffee and a short rest. Often the singers do the same, and the opportunity is taken to make a break in the song while cookies and coffee are served to the company assembled for *ichem mugé*. When the song recommences, the soul is sent off once more downstream, for a still considerable distance, involving many verses.

Finally it arrives at the mouth of the Apek River, which supposedly leads away from the right bank of the Baram towards the north, not far inland from where the Baram finally flows into the sea. For many of the peoples of the lower Baram area the Apek is the route to the land of the dead. It cannot be seen by the living. Having entered the Apek, the party is instructed to stop in order to cook a meal by the side of the river. In unloading its possessions from the canoe, the soul finds the cooking pots cracked, and all the utensils chipped. This is the case because, as we have had cause to notice above, things that are to be transmitted to other worlds must be spoiled in this one. Confronted with these reminders of the irreversibility of its journey, the soul sings a lament, through the medium of the lead vocalist, telling of its pity for the spouse and child left grieving behind. For those paying attention to the performance, this is a poignant moment, and one in which the tension begins to build toward the culmination of the song.

Speedily now, since the living do not know the names of places inside the Apek River, the soul and its party approach the habitations of the dead. They hear the noises characteristic of longhouse life; first the barking of dogs and the crowing of cocks, then the rhythmic pounding of women preparing rice, and finally voices. As the canoe touches the shore, the relatives of the dead person who have died before stream out of the house to greet the new arrival. The vast and splendid longhouse of the ancestors comes alive with the music of gongs and drums. The soul, or rather the spirit that was until now a soul, ascends with the souls of the seven bachelors to the veranda of the ancestral longhouse, and the spirits press drink after drink of rice wine upon them.

At this climactic moment in the *siroi* a mystical union is supposed to occur between the entire community of the living and that of the dead. Precisely how this occurs is not clear. The old folk were unanimous in saying that this is a moment of joy, and Biló Kasi added that it was as if they all lived together again in the olden days. Perhaps it is that the "seven bachelors" are a metonymic representation of the entire community, so that throughout the laborious naming of places the singers have been transporting themselves and everyone else steadily toward the land of the dead. Viewed in this manner, the journey provided the vehicle for a slow building of tension towards the highly dangerous direct contact with the spirits of the dead.

There is an alternative interpretation. Biló Kasi told me that at the crucial moment in the *siroi* the dead come flooding onto the veranda and mingle freely with the living. The entire wake has been a sacred season because the dead have been invited to attend. But this moment is something more. It is as if, instead of the occasional visitor sitting politely on the edge of the group, there were suddenly a veritable host of spirits present in every part of the house. But what of the journey recounted in the *siroi?* Perhaps it is best taken as a metaphor of the great distance between the living and the ancestors. Biló Kasi remarked to me that, of course, no one goes anywhere in the song, we all stay here, and there is a logic to this that fits nicely into a Durkheimian conception of religion. The longhouse is explicitly a ritual community; both its solidarity and its uniqueness is expressed in terms of corporate rites. A large part of that ritual is focused upon the ancestors, and the rites that add to that company are the most compelling of all. The cosmic significance of the ancestors persists because, and as long as, the community exists, so that the longhouse is de facto their temple. In that sense they have been there all the time. In the *siroi* the sacred center of the religion is directly confronted. There is no need to choose between these interpretations. Like a piece of poetry, the power of the performance to move the audience is only enhanced by this indeterminateness.

But whatever the nature of the fusion of the living and the dead, it cannot long be tolerated. Such a radical confusion is intolerable. After the singers have downed a glass of rice wine, the song continues. Now the spirits of the dead become alarmed, it says. They realize that if the souls of the "seven bachelors" linger, they too must soon be dead. Technically, of course, by the definition set out in chapter four, they are already dead, but this special mission provides them with an immunity. But only a limited immunity. The souls of the "seven bachelors" are hustled unceremoniously out of the longhouse of the ancestors, and they flee down the Apek, making the spray fly up behind their canoe. Regaining the Baram, they turn back upriver, once again following the bank that is on their right hand, so that a different set of place names are recounted.

Now that the climax of the *siroi* is passed, the travelers are often made to paddle at great speed on the way home. At Marudi, the small bazaar some seventy miles upriver from the coast, the party is instructed to stop and to visit the stores there. In a manner reminiscent of the *gu katong* described above, the "seven bachelors" are instructed to fill their canoe with cloth and kerosene, and sugar, and flashlight batteries, and all the things that come from the bazaar. Rapidly, if the singer is growing tired, they ascend the Baram, enter the Tinjar, and finally arrive home. Joyfully they enter the long-house, distributing candy to the children, and greeting their friends. So ends the *siroi*.

Only the *tijun* remains to be sung. Its purpose is to make sure that the souls of every member of the community, plus those of all the guests, are properly back where they should be after the confusion momentarily generated in the *siroi*. Its purpose is serious, but by this stage in the evening no one is in a mood to behave solemnly. Many are drunk and rowdy, others are looking drained, and the progress of the *tijun* is accordingly erratic. Because the *siroi* is long, it is not usually possible to begin with the *tijun* until well after midnight, sometimes as late as four A.M. and it consequently drags on into the morning, delaying the departure of the coffin or jar from the longhouse. Every now and then an attempt is made to speed up the process by singing faster, but this often generates more raucousness than accuracy and verses have to be repeated, producing the opposite effect to that desired. The *tijun* is very easy to sing because every verse is identical except for the name of the individual for whom it is sung.

A core of participants, changing personnel from time to time as the night goes by, sit around a large metal tray (*duling*). As they sing each verse calling back a soul, they beat upon the tray rhythmically with sticks of firewood. After each verse a divination is made to check that the soul in question is indeed back with its owner. This is done with three narrow lengths of polished hardwood, each about four inches long, and with one flat and one half round face. They are held between the first fingers and thumb of the diviner, round side uppermost, and dropped carefully onto the tray from a height of about eight inches. For a favorable outcome, all three should land flat side down.[4] Should one turn over in falling, this would indicate an insecure connection of the soul of the subject, with consequent threat of illness. If two or three were to invert themselves, the omen would be progressively more threatening. In the case of a less-than-perfect reading, the verse is repeated, inserting an appeal to the Creator Spirit to retrieve the soul. The test is repeated, the diviner taking even more care in dropping the sticks. On one occasion in 1973 a proper outcome could not be obtained for a particular old man after three tries, and he did indeed die some weeks later.

But usually the outcome is favorable, and the singers may proceed to the next person. The practice is to begin with the most downriver apartment, and to sing a verse for everyone who lives there, plus any guests who are staying there. Great care is taken to leave no one out, especially children. Then the singers move to the next apartment, and so on along the length of the house. In their desire to be thorough, the group of singers, weary and inebriated as they are, often fall to quarreling about whether so-and-so has a third child, or is merely pregnant, and whether the child, if there is one, has a name. All this slows down what is already a slow process, but it has an interesting sociological side effect. The *tijun* acts as a kind of census, a public tally of the strength and membership of the community. At Long Teru there were upwards of three hundred names that needed to be rehearsed, not counting the guests.

As,the party of *ichem mugé* breaks up in the hazy early morning light, and people for the most part wander off to bathe or nap, the singers of the *tijun* are still there hammering away at the tin tray with their sticks. Occasionally they receive reinforcements, people who have suddenly revived and now reappear bringing fresh supplies of rice wine and bonhomie. When the job is finally done, anytime between sunup and noon, the tin tray is unrecognizable: beaten entirely out of shape and with no scrap of enamel left adhering to it. The triumphant singers nail it to the wall as evidence of their labors.

As a dramatic performance, the death songs of Long Teru utilize some of the same themes as those of Long Jegan, such as the journey of the soul by canoe.[5] But their impact is entirely different. As we saw, the *bulu biling* terminates just short of the encounter with the spirits of the ancestors. The moment of fusion achieved at

Long Teru is absent, and there is no mention of the metonymic "seven bachelors." By the same token the *sa'o,* counterpart of the *tijun* at Long Teru, is sung *before* the *bulu biling,* which expresses the same sense of dissociation from the lonely journey of the deceased: The living are pulled back from a contact with the ancestors even before the soul has left the longhouse on its journey. In this way the Long Jegan performance lacks a sublimity that is richly expressed at Long Teru.

In the *gu umī, siroi,* and *tijun,* we are presented with an encapsulation of the entire mortuary season, and a striking reversal of the usual phases of a *rite de passage.* A funeral or *nulang* is special because of the propinquity of the dead; at the former it is the lingering soul of the recently deceased that is the principal focus of attention, at the latter there is more concern with the fellowship of the long dead. But in each case, the closeness must only be temporary. In the death songs of the final evening the pattern is reproduced and emphasized. First the invitation to the dead to attend is reissued. Then there is a long, slow approach of the living and the dead, and, as we saw, it is ambiguous who is approaching whom. This is, in Van Gennep's classic terminology, a phase of integration. Then there comes the liminal moment (we can hardly call it a phase), when categories are abandoned and spirits and humans are the same, initiands of some great mystery. The third phase is one of separation, which is carried out with great thoroughness. Not only are the "seven bachelors" sung back home, but another song is used to ensure that each and every living person has properly been extracted from the liminal chaos.

Integration, liminality, separation; the process of the rite of passage is reversed. The only way to put them in their normal order is to place the end of the festival season at the beginning of the liminal period, and surely there is a certain sense in that.

Notes

1. In telling the soul to "get up" from the coffin, the implication is made that the soul is homomorphous with the corpse. But this is a poetic figure only, as is shown by the short *gu* that summons the soul of the deceased back to the longhouse before the death songs of the final night begin. There is

no need, of course, to summon back the mortal remains, which have been there all the time.

2. Rodney Needham points out to me that the word *sa'o*, which is the name of one of the required songs at Long Jegan, means in Penan down-river, or to go downriver. This is consistent with the ritual purpose of the song called *sa'o*, which tries to ensure that all the souls of living members of the community are back where they should be. Since the soul of the deceased goes upriver, the souls of the living need to be brought downriver.

3. The phrase *gu umī* is confusing. *Umī* is most obviously glossed as "small," and at Long Teru, as applied to the short prescribed *gu*, small means "short." But at Long Jegan the same phrase is used to designate the optional *gu*, and in that context small means "unimportant." The contras-tive pair *gu kijī* (*kijī* = great, large) is sometimes heard, but is equally confusing. I have avoided it here.

4. This method of divination is likely to owe something to Chinese models. In Chinese temples there are often found kidney-shaped blocks of wood that are rounded on one side and flat on the other, as in the Long Teru version. They are clapped together to attract the attention of the deities, and then thrown into the air. According to whether they fall in a similar or contrasting fashion, the answer to a question posed to the deities will be received as affirmative or negative.

5. I have few details of the death songs at Batu Belah or Long Terawan, but they evidently followed the same pattern of a journey by river. At both these houses the journey was downriver to the mythical river Apek, just as at Long Teru, but the song in which the journey was accomplished was called by the Berawan term *bulu biling*, as at Long Jegan.

V

*Cosmology
of the Ancestral Spirits*

CHAPTER THIRTEEN

The Geography of Heaven

When *nulang* is completed, and the last guest has unsteadily made his way home, the rituals of death are finally over. The long metamorphosis is certifiably completed. But the ritual significance of the dead does not end there, because the collectivity of the dead figures prominently in attempts to intercede in the world of spirits. The description of Berawan eschatology is not complete without consideration of the cosmological place of the ancestors.

Most Berawan agree that the land of the dead is reached via a river, invisible to the mortal eye, that runs southward into the Baram. This geographical specificity may strike the reader as naive. But further questioning showed that it was more apparent than real. To the north of the lower reaches of the Baram lies the small, autonomous state of Brunei. Is that where the land of the dead is? Or does the mystical river rise up somehow into the sky? These questions produced giggles, or shrugs, or irritation, but no answers. The reaction was different to that elicited by my persistent probing concerning the changes that the soul undergoes at death.

The specificity is a byproduct of the death songs, which recount a physical journey. Yet at Long Teru the songs were abolished for a period of years, without there being any suggestion of either a loss of faith in the traditional forms or a failure of souls of the recently dead to join their ancestors. At Long Jegan the songs were never sung for the majority of people. Moreover, there was a choice of songs with different routes to the land of the dead in each. The *bulu biling* might be sung for a man and the *patulo* for his wife, without the implication that the pair would be put asunder in the afterlife. In chapter twelve, I dealt with these contradictions by emphasizing the aspect of performance, making the various journeys figurative ones. That interpretation is consistent with the manner in which Berawan refused to entertain my literal questions about the river of the dead.

The death songs provide the most detailed itineraries, but there are journeys to the afterworld that occur in other contexts, notably in mythology. We have already noted an example in chapter two: In the story of the brothers Layong and Kusai, the former first arrives in the land of the dead by falling down a great hole into the bowels of the earth. There are others with this same motif:

> A man died while away from home on a hunting trip. His wife dreamed that if she looked for a certain kind of fruit tree, then these trees would provide a trail that would lead her to her husband. She followed the path set out by the trees and came to a hole in the ground. She entered it, and walked down a long gloomy cavern. Emerging into a bright place, she discovered the longhouse of the dead, and found her husband there. He agreed that she could stay with him, but insisted that they first go back to his old abode in order to fetch various belongings. The husband waited at the mouth of the cave while the wife went to their farmhouse, but she was delayed there because she could not find the small woodworking chisel (sulat) that the husband had particularly requested. It was tucked away inconspicuously in the thatch of the house. Meanwhile, the husband was being bitten by mosquitos, and, growing impatient, he headed back into the tunnel alone. When the wife finally arrived back, she found the cave mouth closed up. After that time there has been no passage back and forth to the land of the dead.

Upriver, downriver, below the ground; this is hardly very specific. All that these locations have in common is that they lie beyond the everyday world.

Moreover, there is a further confusion. The spirits of the dead are also thought of as inhabiting the graveyards. The reason that cemeteries are left totally uncared for, unless there is a new addition to be made, is that to cut back the encroaching jungle at any other time would, they say, alert the dead there to expect a new companion. If that expectation were frustrated they might take matters into their own hands. Again, if game runs into a graveyard the chase is abandoned, even if the animal runs out the other side again. The feeling seems to be that the wild animal may be some kind of incarnation of an ancestral spirit. Partly the avoidance of cemeteries has to do with the corpses that are stored there awaiting secondary treatment, or those that will never receive it. They present two risks: the lingering presence both of corruption and the malicious souls that go with it. But even long disused graveyards, even ones so old that no one remembers who is entombed there, are avoided. This taboo has the character of what Durkheim referred to as a "negative ritual," indicating that the tombs are manifestations of the sacred. In fact, they are explicitly likened to villages of the dead. The great vaults are raised on tall pilings well above the ground just as houses are, and the names used to refer to the parts of the structure are the same as those used for ordinary houses.[1] Usually they are sited across the major watercourse from the longhouse, so as to place a water barrier between dead and living. If not, they are well away upriver or down, requiring a waterborne journey to reach them.

The temptation is to conclude simply that Berawan notions of the afterworld are vague. But that would be an error. If instead we distinguish two types of ambiguity, a clearer picture emerges. The first has to do with the inherent bilocality of the dead, both in their tombs and in their "land." The second relates to the contingent issue of which direction to send your dead in songs, or your heroes in myths. The first is the more substantive, because it is a necessary consequence of the schema that underlies the entire mortuary sequence, and because it is reflected in prayers and cosmology. Of this duality I shall have more to say below. Meanwhile, it must be emphasized that there is a coherent concept of a society of the dead that resembles that of the living. The most common phrase used to refer to it is *lia dé lo letá,* literally "the community of those who are dead." But *lia* is a word of wide reference; it can mean a larger group than we would normally think of under the term "community," something like "nation," but it can also refer to the territory pertaining to those groups. In addition, Berawan do speak explicitly of a "place" *(atak)* of the dead, so that the gloss "land of the dead" is justified. The usual term *lia* neatly preserves the locational reference, while emphasizing the collectivity of the dead.

The second type of ambiguity tells us more about ethnology than ideology. At the turn of the century Charles Hose, Resident of Baram District, noted that: "The beliefs and traditions of the various tribes in regard to the other world seem to have been confused through the intercourse between them, so that it is not possible to mark off clearly what features belong to each of the tribes" (Hose and McDougall 1912:II:43). A nice example of this is the following incident in the journey to the afterworld, collected at Long Teru:

> After traveling for a long time (evidently by land), the soul arrives at a deep ravine. The only way across is by a perilous bridge, the *bitang sekipa* (*bitang* = log, *sekipa* = shaking), consisting of a tree trunk suspended at both ends by a rattan. It is guarded by a spirit that constantly keeps the log in motion by swinging it about with its foot. The only hope of crossing safely lies in distracting the guardian spirit for long enough that the jerky motion of the bridge ceases, allowing the errant soul to run quickly across. It is for this reason that the two beads are put into the mouth of the corpse when it is displayed on the death seat *(tèlorèn)*. The spirit is passionately interested in beads, and sits on a huge treasure of them. While the new acquisitions are being examined, the soul may cross. At Batu Belah, a small bell was substituted for the beads. With this the soul could summon its relatives from the other side to hold the bridge still. Should the soul arrive unprepared, it will most likely fall into the gorge below, where it will be consumed by ghastly worms *(ulan temitèk)*.

The tale provides a rationale for the practice of putting beads or bells in the mouths of corpses. But it is, of course, inconsistent with the journey to the land of the dead recounted in the death songs sung at Long Teru. They are entirely by water, and they bring the soul all the way to the longhouse of the ancestors. When I pointed this out to my informants, they merely looked peevish, as if they thought my cross-questioning a poor reward for a perfectly good story. The failure to integrate the incident into any wider framework hints at a borrowing, and sure enough Hose recounts an almost identical episode in the Kayan account of the journey to the afterworld, where it fits in naturally (Hose and McDougall 1912:II:41, the bridge is called *bitang sekopa*). The stories differ in one detail: only men suffer the ordeal, evidently, and they cross the bridge with ease if they bear on their hands the tattoos indicating participation in a successful headhunting party. Consequently the story does not explain why beads are put in the mouths of corpses, assuming that the practice predates the borrowing, or if it does not, why beads were substituted for tattoos. The historical circumstances of the borrowing are, of course, something we are never likely to know.

The Kayan account of the journey to the afterworld has the soul wandering on foot through uninhabited jungle until it reaches the crest of a mountain ridge, from where it looks down upon the basin of a great river that is the home of the dead. Having descended the ridge on the far side, it reaches the gorge where the spirit guards the wobbly bridge, and having crossed, is met by its kin. Hose remarks that the Kenyah version is much the same, though the names of the places are different, and they usually conceive of the first part of the journey as being made by water (Hose and McDougall 1912:II:43). Given the close links that the Long Jegan folk had in the last century with immigrant Kenyah groups, it is not hard to see here a model for their itinerary. In chapter twelve I emphasized how powerfully and distinctively the *bulu biling* integrated the migration stories and cosmology of Long Jegan. On the other hand, it is easy to see how the Long Jegan account is parallel with the Kenyah and Kayan ones. Like the Kenyah, it begins by going upstream in a canoe. Like the Kayan, it takes the soul to the top of a prominent ridge. But that ridge is still some distance away from the Usun Apau, the region associated with the most ancient ancestors. There the song stops; no shaking log, no meeting with the dead. The geographical specificity of the Long Jegan songs gives them power, but cheats them of their climax.

As for the other three Berawan communities, they share the seaward route. An association between the open sea and spirits of the long dead recurs across the entire Malayo-Polynesian world. The Berawan journey (except that of Long Jegan) is toward the sea, but, consonant with a riverine people, stops just short, at the invisible Apek River. Berawan claim that the Apek route was employed traditionally by all the peoples of the lower Baram; the same ethnic groups, many now Muslim, that originally practiced *nulang*. If this is true, then we may see in the downriver journey a distant echo of the ancient maritime heritage of the diverse and scattered Malayo-

Polynesian stock. And, of course, secondary treatment of the dead is presumably another such ancient element.

The subterranean routes that appear in myths may be related to the notion of an underworld, which is important in the cosmology of the Ngaju of southern Borneo (Schärer 1963).

But in Berawan ideology it is not essential where the land of the dead is located. Berawan are also uninterested in its internal geography, in contrast to some of their immediate neighbors. The Kayan specify five regions abutting the great river (Long Malan) that runs through the homes of the dead. Apo Leggan is the largest, and it is the dwelling place of those who die of old age or disease. Those who die violent death, whether in battle or by accident, live near a lake of blood (Bawang Daha), where they live in comfort and grow rich without having to work. Their wives are provided by women who have died in childbirth. Those that die by drowning live under the water, and possess all the property that mortals lose when their canoes tip over in rapids. Stillborn children dwell in Tenyu Lalu, and are very brave because of not having experienced any pain while alive. Finally, there is a dismal region, Tan Tekkan, assigned to suicides, who only have roots and berries to eat. The Kenyah version was not greatly different, and one informant went so far as to draw for Hose a rough sketch map of the river of the dead and its tributaries (see map 4). In some accounts, a place is made for Malays and other coastal folk. Generally the right bank going upriver is reserved for upriver folk, and the soul is sometimes warned to avoid the left bank (Hose and McDougall 1912: II:40–43).

A few Berawan, individuals who had spent time in Kayan houses, could reproduce this description, or something similar. But they always pointed out its origin. Berawan generally only distinguish one special region within the land of the dead, and that is for children who die in childbirth or very young. It is a sad, cold place, and the children cry pitifully for their mothers. It is said that the journeying soul passes through this region, and that the soul comforts the children and gives them rice to eat. Supposedly the rice is that which is poured into the gong at the corpse's feet when it is on the death seat, and that is the purpose of the custom. But the same inconsistency appears here as with the shaking log story: At Long Teru at least there is no opportunity for this incident to occur in

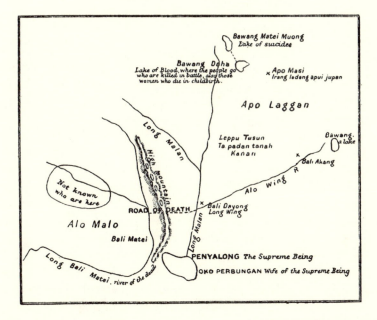

MAP 4. Map of the land of the dead. Drawn by a Kenyah informant for Charles Hose (from Hose and McDougall 1912:II:43).

the soul's voyage as sung in the *siro*i. This hints at a further borrowing from Kayan eschatology. However, the borrowings must have occurred long ago since Hose reported the same practices and rationalization given him by a Berawan in the 1890s (Hose 1896:364). Whatever their ultimate origin, the stories have coexisted for several generations at a minimum with the *siro*i, and the obvious inconsistencies have been tolerated.

Notes

1. This applies most forcefully to the large multiuse vaults built at Long Teru and Long Jegan. At Batu Belah and Long Terawan single post edifices (*lijèng*), designed for only one use, were more common (See Metcalf 1977).

CHAPTER FOURTEEN

The Cosmological Importance
of the Dead

There are inconsistencies in the details that Berawan offer of the location, internal arrangements, and route to the land of the dead that reflect borrowings between several neighboring groups, and teach us little about Berawan eschatology. But there is, nonetheless, a conception of the land of the dead that is perfectly clear in certain essential points: The land of the dead is a pleasant place, and the generations are reunited there. These are group-held values, not personal opinions. They have the force of collective representations.

When Sadi' Pejong of Long Jegan described his encounter with spirits of the dead (see chapter four), he appeared deeply moved. As he recounted it, he had been in a high fever, and dreamed that he traveled up the Tinjar and into the Meta stream. Reaching the crest, he saw on the other side the most beautiful vision. People there were harvesting rice that shone like gold. Each of them was richly dressed in the manner of olden times, and each was perfectly proportioned, graceful, and radiant. Sadi' Pejong constantly referred to them as "golden" and I questioned him to see what he meant by it. It was not that the spirits, as he afterwards realized they were, were made of the metal. Their skin resembled that of living mortals, but they were like gold in that they seemed to shine in the sunlight, that they were without any blemish, and that they bore no sign of age. Sadi' Pejong did not say that he recognized any of these spirits, but he felt a sense of delight in going with them, until he realized the consequences of his act and with difficulty turned away.

When the contents of the *siroi* song were explained to me at Long Teru, there were several episodes that people dwelt upon.[1]

One was the moment, just after entering the Apek, when the soul discovers the broken vessels in the canoe and realizes that it cannot return to its living kin. Another is the stop at Marudi on the way home, when the "seven bachelors" fill their canoe with every conceivable luxury. But the episode that caused the most animated description was the brief entry of the "seven bachelors" into the longhouse of the dead. It was stupendous; vast, unimaginably lofty, made of the hardest of hardwoods, and carved and decorated elaborately. It was full of rich things, and all about it neat gardens produced fruit and vegetables in profusion.

It was only on a couple of occasions that I provoked descriptions as vivid as these. But in the course of ordinary conversation reference would be made to the happy and communal nature of the dead. These fundamental values about the land of the dead are necessary underpinnings to the place accorded the ancestors in ritual. The ancestors are seen as active agents in the affairs of men: As the land of the dead is pleasant, so the long dead are benign toward the living. As the dead are reunited there, so they are seen as an aggregate, and individual ancestors are fused into an anonymous whole. It is in this guise that they frequently appear in prayer. As a rough test of the cosmological importance of the ancestors, I counted the references to them in six lengthy prayers. I have already mentioned in chapter two the formalized language of prayer *(piat)*. It is heard on a great variety of occasions, and there is variation in which particular spirit agency is principally addressed. These six prayers were selected for the relatively general appeal that is made in them. Four occurred in front of prayer sites *(tapó)* during the annual festival celebrated for the welfare of the house; one was made to offer thanks for the recovery of a sick child; and the final one was made at a graveyard near the conclusion of a funeral. The parallel language characteristic of *piat* means that any reference is multiple, and such formulae were counted only once. In the six prayers, the dead in general (usually employing the formula *bilí vi, bilí sadí, bilí ukun, bilí dupun*) were invoked twenty times. By comparison the Creator Spirit (*Bilí Puwong, Bilí Ngaputong*, but other names occurred) was mentioned twenty-seven times. Reference to particular named ancestors occurred eight times.

Named and Anonymous, Near and Far

In the section of prayer quoted in chapter two, we saw the ancestors situated in the immediate environs of the longhouse. Tama Langet, Tama Julan Tinggang, Lawai, and Orang Kaya Luwak, were said to "prop up this land," to "rule the region around this lake," and to "rule this river Bunok." (The lake referred to is shown in map 5.) But at other times, the ancestors appear more removed and anonymous. A section in another prayer calls upon the ancestors of the ancestors:

ka ni kanai kamé ngaran	we here do not know (your) names
tapi kamé tu ni tawa tupan kam	but we people still call all of you
tupan kam bilí ví bilí sadí	all of you old ones, grandfathers,
bilí ukun bilí dupun kamé uni	ancestors, forebears of ours long ago
lo mukong liek	that have for so long received
aki sema dirk sema bikui	blood of the chicken, blood of the pig
uvi sadí kame uni atak tu	from our ancestors long ago in this place.

In addition, prayers often call upon a generalized category of "spirits of the place" *(bilí atak tu),* or spirits of particular places (*bilí lum luvak, lum* = in, *luvak* = the lake near Long Teru). These phrases are a catch-all, designed to make sure that there is no supernatural agency that is being left out. If the makers of prayers are asked who they are thinking of in this category, they mention spirits of natural features like marshes, hills, even trees. This does not imply an all-embracing animism, but merely that the Berawan acknowledge that the spirit world is unbounded, and that their knowledge of it is limited. But the spirits most often mentioned as spirits of the place are, once again, ancestral spirits.

This dual reference to the ancestors, sometimes named, sometimes anonymous, is something that we noted at the outset, in chapter two, when the dead were introduced as spirit agencies. The named ancestors are those who were leaders of the community in the past. They are associated with the grand mausoleums that are so prominent in old graveyards.[2] Those baroquely carved vaults, impressive in their very decay, filled with venerable bones, are the reliquaries of the cult of the ancestors. The great dead with whom they are associated, and whose names are constantly invoked in prayer, are its saints. The bones of humbler folk are also there, scattered on the jungle floor, or buried in underground vaults, long collapsed and leaving only a slight depression to mark where they were. They are as anonymous as their tombs.

In addition to being named and nameless, the dead are also near and far, as we saw in the last chapter. They are long distances away, in a land that can only be reached by arduous journeys. They exercise a benign influence from remote spirit worlds, in a manner analogous to the Creator. But they are also closely associated with the land which they "rule." Nor is it possible to simply subsume one distinction under the other; to divide the dead into those near and named and those far and anonymous. That division is untenable because of the nature of the bilocality of the dead, which is a further result of the relationship between body and soul that underlies the mortuary rituals. When an individual is alive, there is a close but problematic relationship between the two. The soul may be absent from the body, and travel far into spirit worlds, but it must return before too long or life is threatened. When death occurs, the physical association only becomes looser. The soul cannot reenter the body, but it must share its fate, and it hovers between the world of the living and the dead. Slowly, as the bones dry, soul moves toward spirit. The physical association loosens again, but it is never completely broken. In Berawan eschatology the metaphorical link between the material and immaterial existence of the individual is too strongly made ever to be quite extinguished, and that is why the dead, *all* the dead, are both near and far.

There is no division in the community of the dead. It is just that some are more visible than others. That host of spirits is all the generations, and for any given person its most personalized members are loved kin who died not so long before, mothers and fathers, siblings, children, and favorite aunts. Their graves are well known, and cared for whenever an opportunity presents itself. It is they that the living expect to meet in the afterlife. For the community as a whole, it is the leaders who stand out, and they too are loved kinsmen of somebody. As the generations recede, only the great remain visible, in their personalities and deeds as in their tombs. But those leaders are also leaders in that fabulous longhouse in the land of the dead; they are not separated from it.[3] At the same time the humble dead continue to be associated with the land that contains their bones. They are, when they are near, spirits of the place.

On the edge of the lake that lies inland behind Long Teru there is an old tomb post jutting out of the water. There is no sign of the vault that it once supported, and the column is decayed. But its height is still impressive, and traces of carved designs can still be made out. It must have belonged to some great chief of the Lelak, for the region around this lake has been their home and their preserve since time immemorial. But no one now remembers his name. As they paddle by on the way to their farms, people look up at it wonderingly. He is, they conclude, a great spirit of the place, that forgotten magnate. But he is also no doubt a person to be reckoned with in the land of the dead. The mystery of the dead, here and not here, strangers and loved ones, fabulous and forgotten, is essential to their awesome sacredness.

The Role of the Ancestors

The spirits of the dead occupy a position in prayers almost as prominent as the Creator Spirit. Both agencies are appealed to for the same boons, listed in a formalized manner as in the segment quoted in chapter six: a life that is safe and "slow," reputation and influence for the community, and plenty of rice, fish, and money. A prayer that I recorded at a funeral expressed very plainly the continuity of the generation of the living and the dead, and the protective role of the latter:

jiu ko ka sadi' orang kaya luwak	I say to you grandfather Orang Kaya Luwak

ka sadï tama julan tinggang	to you grandfather Tama Julan Tinggang
ka sadï lawai	to you grandfather Lawai
tu tama alang mang letá	our father Alang is dead now
kiku keló mulei ngan keló	he follows you, he returns to you
tutok pí keló	he is together with all of you
lo tina lo tama	his mothers, his fathers,
kam lo sadï	you his grandparents
tu añam tu anak keló	these your grandchildren, your children
lo la'a	left behind
tubor lameng long teru	to look after the longhouse of Long Teru
kam bilï sadï	you spirits of our grandfathers
pion lia tu	protect this community
tubor lia tu	look after this community

The benign aspect of the ancestral spirits is not clouded by any judgemental quality. Only in exceptional circumstances is misfortune attributed to particular ancestor spirits (as opposed, of course, to the souls of the recently dead), and in no case that I knew of to the action of the spirits of the dead collectively. As we saw in chapter four, supernatural affliction is the result of either infraction of a taboo *(ñilèng)* established by the Creator Spirit, or soul ensnarement by an evil spirit. By the same token, there is little or no suggestion anywhere in Berawan eschatology that the dead are judged for their actions on earth. In the incident of the "shaking log" it was sometimes hinted that those who had committed antisocial acts were the ones who would fall into the chasm below with its noisome worms, but these were most likely the result of borrowing from Christian doctrine. The usual emphasis was not on good works, but on respectability. Those with proper standing in this world, with kinsmen who took the trouble to put rich beads in their mouths as they sat upon the death seat, they were the ones who crossed safely. The social order of this world is reproduced in the afterworld, without any suggestion of reward for the lowly but good of heart. I cross questioned people on this: What happens in the land of the dead to those of conspicuous evil temperament (*jat unyin*, or more strongly *jat telanak*)? The answer was noncommittal. But what incentive is there to be virtuous? There was no incentive; good people are simply good because it is their nature to be, because they like being liked. Only on one occasion did I hear a suggestion of retribution beyond the tomb, and then in a very esoteric fashion. There was at Long Teru many years ago a man who commanded respect but who was given to fits of violence verging on the psychopathic. In one such fit he murdered his own sister. Decades later, after he had himself died a natural death and received a fine funeral, and his remains had lain for years in a tall mausoleum, it happened that the probing fingers of the jungle began to break open the chamber of the tomb. One tendril inserted itself into the skull of the long-dead man, and slowly lifted it out of the chamber, as if holding it up for passersby to see. That was his punishment, finally, for the unnatural murder.

Hardly fire and brimstone; yet it reminds us of the connection between the powerful remains of the dead and their refined spirits. In all the Berawan communities, the mausoleums constructed by and for important leaders of the past are prominently located on hillsides overlooking the river. Especially while the graveyard is still in use and the brush around them is periodically cleared, the tombs have a commanding presence. But the most striking site belongs to the people of Long Teru. It is located on a small island in the middle of the lake behind the present day longhouse (Loagan Bunut, called in Berawan *luvak*, see map 5). It has been in use for much more than a century, back into a time when the longhouse of the Lelak folk was located on the southern side of the lake. That area has rising ground, free of the flooding that is so destructive of farms, and to this day it is the major rice-growing area of the community. Meanwhile the lake is rich in fish. The Lelak folk moved down to the main river in the early part of this century for totally contingent reasons; because the English Resident at Marudi wanted them where they could provide paddlers for his upriver expeditions. But the old folk still regret their move away from the self-contained Eden of the lake.

I visited the island several times, as I visited all the old graveyards that I could find. But this one is unlike the others. They are gloomy under the dense forest canopy, the mausoleums all hung about with creepers. But the island has no large trees, and from its summit there is a fine view of the lake. In central Borneo long vistas are rare; usually a view along some stretch of the river for a few hundred yards at best. But up here one can see for many miles, across the open lake to the hills in the distance. In the last century an observer would certainly have been able to make out the longhouse a mile or so away across the water, and the farms and groves of fruit trees behind it. On one of my visits, there had been a funeral a few weeks earlier, and the long bamboo poles with their triangular flags in red and white fabric were still standing. Snapping in a brisk afternoon breeze from across the lake, they evoked the standards of the captains of some unseen army. It was easy to imagine the Lelak leaders of the past watching out from this vantage point over the lands of their descendents.

Ancestral Spirits and Other Spirits

From the same hill in the middle of the lake, one can see off in the distance the conical peak of Bukit (Mount) Selikan, from which greater height the hero Tot Manyim also watches over the Berawan people. Tot Manyim, who we met in chapter twelve, was born of human parents and is consequently in some sense an ancestor spirit. But he is clearly something more. His mythical acts are stupendous. He created Loagan Bunut merely by turning his canoe around in the narrow Bunut stream. His apotheosis to spirit did not occur through the death rituals, and he has no tomb. The same is true of Sadi′ Sudan, who ascended directly to the sky with his spirit friends. Another hero, about whom there is an epic song *(suket)*, went to the sky seeking his wife who had been abducted by *bili′ gau*, the spirit of thunder. He got there by climbing up the blowpipe darts that he shot into the sky, and in his travels he visited the houses of other spirits such as *bilí̵ plaké*, the spirit of the major omen bird. Other heros became stars.

The ancestors are spirit: *bilí̵*. But the Berawan spirit world is unbounded and seamless. Sadí̵ Pejong of Long Jegan once boasted to me, after telling about the heros that became stars, that in the olden days many Berawan were skilled at becoming spirits. When I objected that the dead become spirits anyway, he corrected himself by saying that he had meant that they became "real" spirits (*bilí̵ tu'o, tu'o* = correct, right-hand side), spirits of the sky, or in the sky (*bilí̵ malau, malau* = sky, weather). In saying this Sadí̵ Pejong implied two things: First, that these heros did not rejoin the community of the dead, but instead became separate spirit agencies in their own right. Second, that there is a category of more important spirits that are generally associated with the sky. By far the most important of these is *Bilí̵ Ngaputong*, the Creator. But there are a number of others, such as the spirits of thunder, and of the omen bird *plaké*. Both are taken seriously, so that they achieve a departmental status inferior only to the Creator Spirit. *Bilí̵ gau*'s lightning is supposed to propel to earth stones that are treasured and have great magical power attributed to them. *Bilí̵ plaké* is an important intermediary between men and the Creator. The temptation is to call them deities, but there is no word in Berawan that would justify such a usage. In the Berawan view they are simply part, an important part to be sure, of the world of spirits. Concerning that world, the Berawan do not bother with taxonomy. There are multitudes of what we might call nature spirits (but there is no such term in Berawan), hosts of shaman's familiars, spirits used in divination, and so on. The point that concerns us here is that there are two agencies that are constantly invoked in prayer; the Creator and the ancestors. The former is associated with the sky, the latter is not. Wherever the land of the dead is, it is felt to be separate from the celestial realm.

This conception presents interesting points of comparison with other Bornean religions. The map of the afterworld drawn for Hose by a Kenyah chief shows the land of the dead approached by a large river called *Alo Malo* (see map 4). *Alo* is a Kenyah word, usually heard in poetic speech, meaning the region drained by a

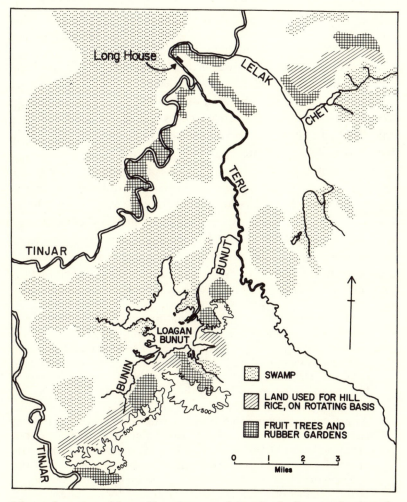

MAP 5. Location of Long Teru house and farmlands. In a predominantly marshy area, the hills in the Chet stream and near the lake provide the only useful land. The graveyard island is a speck in the middle of the eastern shore of the lake.

249

river. *Malo* is a cognate of the Berawan *malau*. So this land of the dead is approached by a river that somehow mystically has its source in the sky but flows into this world. Having used it to arrive in the sky, the souls of the dead cross a mountain range and go to their appointed place on one of the tributaries of Long Malan. That river, the river of the dead, flows into a lake, and on the edge of that lake the map shows the dwellings of Bali Penyalong, the Supreme Being, and his consort. Some older Berawan had a nodding familiarity with this Kenyah cosmology, and readily incorporated a Berawan version of the Sky River, Alo Malau, near which lived the Creator Spirit, perhaps, *bili˝ gau, bili˝ plaké*, and others. But they resisted the notion that the land of the dead is anywhere nearby. Wherever it is, they were sure that it is not in the sky. I conclude that for the Berawan the separateness of the Creator and the ancestors is ritually important.

We cannot leave the topic without some comparison with the richest Bornean cosmology of which we have a full account, that of the Ngaju of southern Borneo, described by the missionary Schärer (1963). The Ngaju distinguish two supreme deities: Mahatala who rules in the Upperworld, and Jata who is in the Underworld or primeval waters. But the two are also mystically one, representing a good male aspect and an evil female aspect. The Upperworld is elaborately structured:

> Mahatala lives on the primeval mountain in the Upperworld, which is raised above the world inhabited by men. Its entrance, in the shape of a wide river, is reached by ascending through forty-two layers of cloud. The Upperworld is a faithful image of this world, but everything there is richer and more beautiful. On the many rivers and lakes there live the *singiang*, descendants of two of the three brothers of the first human couple. These *singiang* come to the aid of the third brother who was left below on earth, on the occasion of all important religious ceremonies, partly as servants, partly as delegates of Mahatala or of Mahatala and Jata. At the headwaters of the river of the Upperworld live the higher spirits, and on the primeval mountain . . . Mahatala is enthroned, surrounded by his sister . . . and the supreme spirits. (Schärer 1963:16)

Though there are echoes of some of this in Kenyah and Berawan cosmology, most of it is unfamiliar: the forty-two named layers, the complex families of subdeities, the dual godhead, and so on. Schärer's account is illustrated with remarkably intricate represen- tations that were drawn for him, each rich in symbolism, of the spirit worlds and the village of the dead. The latter:

> . . . differs from those on the "river of the world" only in that it is bigger, richer, and more splendid. The houses are magnifi- cently built, the thoroughfares are set with gold and jewels, the trees bear perpetual fruit. Neither is life there very different from that on earth, except that it is less toilsome, offers more pleasures, and lasts for ever . . . The world of the dead exhibits the same social structure as that of the living. (Schärer 1963:142)

This description is similar to the Berawan image. But there is an inconsistency in the Ngaju account concerning the location of this village, an inconsistency that Schärer makes no attempt to resolve. On several occasions he refers to the dead as living unambiguously in the Upperworld, a region that they only abandon briefly to sojourn in the "river of the world" (Schärer 1963:61, 94). But else- where he distinguishes between two types of dead, as evidenced in the use of two types of coffins, one shaped to represent a hornbill, the other a watersnake. These two creatures are associated with the Upperworld and Underworld respectively. People of one category employ the hornbill coffin, and change into mythical hawks that inhabit the fringes of the Upperworld. The others become water- snakes and live in a deep pool in the bottom of the river, which is the entrance to Jata's watery Underworld (Schärer 1963:92, 146). Nowhere is it spelled out on what basis individuals are assigned to the two categories.

We need not resolve these difficulties here. What is of interest to us is that the dead, at a minimum some of the dead, are associated with the Upperworld. Schärer is insistent that although they partic- ipate in all the rituals that living people perform on earth, they have no power to act independently of the godhead: "The sacred dead cannot act independently. Their appearances and actions are de- cided by the total godhead" (Schärer 1963:153). The context in which Schärer makes these firm statements is an attack upon the theories of the origin of religion developed by E. B. Tylor, who argued that worship of the dead preceded worship of gods, and is characteristic of primitive ideologies. In his rebuttal, we may agree with Schärer.

But it is apparent that the absolute dependency of the spirits of the dead upon the Supreme Deity that is characteristic of the Ngaju is not so marked in the case of the Berawan. Just as the Berawan separate the Creator Spirit and the land of the dead spatially, so they seem to attribute separate powers of protection to each. Without involving ourselves in the definitional problem of whether this constitutes a full-blown case of "ancestor worship," we may note that the prominence of spirits of the dead is potentially significant for the understanding of Berawan politics. Several authors have discussed this issue in the context of Southeast Asian societies (Boon 1974, Kirsch 1973).

The Ultimate Fate of the Dead

In many Malayo-Polynesian religions there is a notion that the dead eventually disappear, or that they die again and are reborn into higher heavens. For instance, the Iban, who live to the south of the Berawan, say that the spirits of the dead eventually dissolve into dew (Jensen 1974:108). The Berawan have no such ideas, but they do have traces of a conception of reincarnation. At Long Jegan I was told the story of a young man named Lajim, who died when he was only about twenty years old. His sister was very sad and prayed for him to return. For a year or more she continued to pine, and had several prophetic dreams. Presently she conceived, and when the boy child was born he already had holes in his upper earlobes. The making of these holes is a mark of manhood, and Lajim had undergone the operation shortly before his death. As the child grew, he displayed a remarkable prescience about all the affairs of the family, such as where they owned fruit trees. When I heard this story the woman was still alive, but the brother/son had died again.

Procedures for the choosing of names for children also involve notions of reincarnation. Unlike the Kenyah, who postpone the giving of names and make an elaborate ritual out of it, especially if the child is of high class, the Berawan name children when they are only a few weeks old.[4] One system that may be used, if the parents have a number of names in mind and have not selected one in particular, is to balance a piece of down on the child's lips. Then the parents ask: Is your name X? Is your name Y? until the child sneezes or otherwise blows the feather away. It is said that the child in this way selects his or her own name, sometimes with the added implication that the child is indicating who is returning to the world of the living. This suggestion is more clearly expressed when a shaman is called in to make the selection. On one such occasion that I witnessed, Tama Ukat Sageng used a number of divination techniques, and then conferred at length in language incomprehensible to those of us sitting there with his spirit familiars and other adepts who joined him in the seance. At length it was announced that the child's name was Ballang. Ballang was the name of the mother's father's brother, and everybody expressed happiness at the "return" of this popular figure. Ballang was remembered as a sociable fellow, and it was predicted that the child would be a hard-drinking man when he grew up. I was told that the shamans sometimes conclude that the soul in the child whose name they are searching for does not come from a Berawan ancestral spirit, but from some other ethnic group. Then the new soul will be greeted in a short speech. Sadi͏̈ Pejong once told me that the spirits of the dead visit earth as we go to the bazaar.

Hose reports that the Kayan also had vague notions of reincarnation. It was generally believed that the souls of a grandfather might pass into one of his grandchildren, and an old man would try to secure the passage of his soul to a favorite grandson by holding him above his head from time to time (Hose and McDougall 1912:II:47). This practice has the interesting implication that small children have no souls, and this echoes Berawan conceptions that we saw in chapter four.

It was sometimes suggested to me that, in the recycling of spirits into souls, they would occasionally be "lost" by some accident or perhaps snared by malign influences, and that these lost souls would become spirits of the jungle that were helpful to humans. Some shamanistic spirits are supposed to have this origin. But no one was willing to volunteer any description of how this occurred, and it was not suggested that all such spirits were of human origin. What the idea indicated is, first, that the passage of souls back and forth is an inherently risky business, and second, that the boundaries of the community of the dead are not fixed and impermeable. Just as there is no precise taxonomy of spirits, so the boundary lines between types of spirits are blurred. We have already seen ancestral spirits becoming stars and minor deities, and turning back into human beings, and being lost, or turning into benign nature spirits. They can also become ugly and dangerous to humans, and the principal way in which that occurs is bad death *(letá jat).*

The Bad Dead

The notion of bad death is another cultural item that is widely distributed in Indonesia. The general notion is that certain ways of dying are so inauspicious as to make their victims virtually demonic. The Berawan list is typical:

(1) The most feared variety is the death of a woman in childbirth. I never saw it occur, but I was treated to graphic accounts of what would happen. A great howl of consternation would go up, and the men would leap up into the rafters of the longhouse where they would hide until the corpse was removed from the longhouse. The soul of the dead woman is supposed to transform itself into a vengeful spirit that longs to vent its anger on men by emasculating them. It is called *kuk lir*, literally "ball biter."

(2) Death caused by wild animals is also much feared. The most common and loathed killers of men are crocodiles.[5] Wild boar are frequently hunted, and formerly honey bear, whose skins were prized for war cloaks. They are dangerous prey. The repulsion that Berawan feel for death in this way seems mainly to have to do with the maiming that is likely to occur to the corpse.

(3) Deaths that come about through some accident may also be considered bad, particularly if the corpse is badly mutilated. A recent case of this kind involved a woman who was accidentally shot while collecting edible grasses in the forest. The wounds inflicted by the shot gun blast at close range ensured that the death would be classified as a bad one.

(4) Finally any fatal self-inflicted injury is bad, whether accidental or not, or whether death occurs immediately or later. Occasionally people hurt themselves badly when working with heavy

axes clearing new farms, and gangrene is then a threat. Some years ago a deranged woman evidently attempted suicide by burning herself. She survived the fire itself but died of secondary infections later, and her death was classified as bad.

The principle ritual consequence of a bad death is that no funeral occurs, or at least only a very simple one. The most extreme case is that of the woman dying in childbirth. The husband is obliged, if necessary forced, to remove the corpse immediately and without any help. He does so by opening up the floorboards and bundling the body through without ceremony. Then he must drag it off far into the deep jungle, and bury it as best he can. No ritual of any kind is observed for the woman's soul, which is seen as irredeemably hostile. For less horrific deaths some truncated rites are allowable; a brief wake perhaps, and a few prayers. But the corpse may not enter or approach the longhouse under any circumstances, no death songs may be sung, and the corpse should not be buried in the graveyard with the other dead. A tragedy of Biló Kasi's early life was the death of her favorite brother, who was caught under a massive hardwood tree that he and his companions had been felling. Apparently she was never reconciled to the decision that her elder brothers made to dispose of the body at once because it was so badly crushed.

Aside from death in childbirth there is some room for interpretation as to what constitutes a bad death. There were instances at Long Teru where a demise was considered sufficiently ugly as to make only brief funerary rites appropriate, although it was not technically counted as a bad death. Cases of this kind usually involved diseases that cause serious disfigurement or wasting away of the body before death occurred. Death by violence does not constitute bad death, I was assured, even for the victim of a headhunter's knife.

Schärer offers two separate explanations for the Ngaju conception of bad death, which resembles that of the Berawan. The first is that the bad dead are those who have committed criminal offences against the community and have consequently been expelled from it (Schärer 1963:142). This idea is lacking among the Berawan. I never heard it suggested that those suffering bad deaths were somehow being judged for previous crimes.[6] The second is that the bad dead are "unripe" (Schärer 1963:62). This is the conception that underlies the Berawan category, and it is explicit. Those who die bad deaths have not lived out the time allotted to them by the Creator. Consequently their souls are not permitted to enter the land of the dead. Instead they retain an evil and vindictive character indefinitely, like the newly dead except that they do not gradually improve; instead they fade into the jungle beyond the longhouse where they pose a permanent menace. That is why there is little point in honoring them with any elaborate funerary observances, and singing the death songs would be downright provocative. All that can be hoped is that they will stay away from the longhouse.

This account of the meaning of bad death was clearly expressed, but beyond that there were points upon which I could get no consensus. Are the bad dead bad for ever, or do they finally become spirits of the dead when their allotted time is finally up? Sadi͞ Pejong thought they did, and his elderly neighbor, whose mother had died in labor, offered that although they lived in a separate house in the land of the dead, they were allowed to visit back and forth. Others said that the souls of the bad dead change into spirits, but unutterably evil ones that linger forever in the jungle. That was why it was best to avoid old longhouse sites. Some even went so far as to suggest that most evil-natured spirits have their origin in the bad dead, but this view was not general and has no ritual expression.

Notes

1. It will be remembered that the *siroi* was not one of the songs about which there was great secrecy. Consequently I heard it discussed several times.

2. There is a certain sleight of hand here. When Berawan point out an old *salong* and connect it with the name of a certain leader, they do not say whether he built it or is in it. If the tomb was designed for multiple use, he may have built it *and* be in it. As the decades go by it becomes irrelevant, and it is tacitly assumed that the leader's local connections are with that tomb.

3. It was once suggested to me that the tombs that we see in this world are like the small farmhouses *(sulăp)* that Berawan build. Usually farmhouses are flimsy, small structures. Just as Berawan have two places to live, so do the spirits of the dead. The implication was: Look how grand even their farmhouses are, imagine how splendid their longhouse is!

4. Although names are usually decided upon when a child is young, they may not be used for a few years if the child is frequently ill. This is to avoid attracting the attentions of malign spirits. Instead they are given unattractive names. One boy at Long Teru was referred to into young manhood by a name that, politely rendered, meant "latrine."

5. This despite the kinship that is supposed to exist between men and crocodiles. When crocodiles do kill humans it is usually attributed to a state of spiritual danger *(sijang)* brought on by an infraction of a taboo. Nevertheless, such a death may bring about a state of "war" and a "revenge" killing of a crocodile.

6. However, there is an indirect route by which this verdict can be reached in some cases. Some bad deaths may be thought to be the result of states of ritual danger such as *sijang*. These in turn are brought about by infractions of taboo.

Conclusion

If Berawan religion had theologians—and it does not—they might devote many a learned discussion to the Problem of Layong. He has the makings of a divine mystery, like the Trinity or the Virgin Birth. Layong was the brother who walked out of Berawan history before it had fairly begun, absenting himself from the first recorded *nulang*. The problem is: How did he join the spirits of the dead directly, at will, without first freeing himself of the cloying bonds of the flesh? Perhaps he was subject to some kind of special dispensation. But why was it provided? Perhaps the Berawan of old were already spirit, even when they dwelt on the earth. But then we do not know how the fall came about, how humans acquired souls instead. Or perhaps, more subtly, Layong is an icon of the soul's nature as spirit-to-be. Aquinas notwithstanding, Berawan souls become pure spirit. On one side of that process stands the dynamics of life, on the other, the world of the supernatural. But what is most clearly etched in ritual and collective thought is the process itself.

Ritual and Dogma: A Summary

Part of the criticism recently made of symbolic studies in anthropology has been to question the orderliness that those studies have found in nontheological religions (for example in Brunton 1980). How orderly is Berawan eschatology? Is it elaborated or not, well or poorly integrated, stable over time and between individuals, or changing and variable? The answer cannot, of course, be definitively one way or the other. The question is an empirical one, and cannot be made the basis of a theoretical attack.

259

The Berawan conception of the career of the soul begins hazily and acquires definition by stages. Concerning the origin of souls, there is an almost total indeterminacy. There are hints of a theory of reincarnation, but it is not organized into any systematic dogma. No one volunteered anything but personal opinions, phrased as guesses, about precisely how and when souls enter children. In connection with dreams and illness, a clearer image emerges, but it is not possible to say just what soul is. It is in death that the concept of soul takes on firm, universally expressed form, so much so that the soul in life is best seen as a retroactive extension of the soul in death. At "loss of breath," the soul's presence is suddenly very real. It is alienated irrevocably from its former body, but bound to it by a common fate. As corruption ebbs, the soul imperceptibly eva-nesces towards that pure spirit of which the long dead are com-posed. Simultaneously it slips gently out of focus again, joining the largely anonymous company of the ancestors, about whom little is specified in Berawan dogma. The nature of their world in unelabo-rated, and there is an essential ambiguity about whether they are near or far. What is clear about them is that they are united, benign, and active in the affairs of men.

These are just the features that are important to the ritual use of the ancestors, or phrasing it the other way around, those features of the dead that are generally agreed upon are just those that achieve ritual expression. And so it is with each phase of the soul's develop-ment: There are no rituals that mark or acknowledge the passage of a soul into a child. Occasionally, in selecting a name, some weak notion of reincarnation is suggested, but that is all. Dreaming, that most personally variable of symbolic experiences, occasionally re-sults in the performance of a small ritual, as when a person seeks to "own" a dream with pleasant connotations. In connection with illness, there is a great deal of group behavior designed to manipu-late the supernatural. But the character of that activity is only partly ritual. Sometimes illness is diagnosed as the result of the infraction of a taboo, and calls for formal supplication to the Creator Spirit in front of a shrine. But more frequently it takes the form of shamanis-tic intervention. The shamans' skills are from personal inspiration, not the exercise of prescribed forms. Fundamentally they work alone, and all that the audience and supporters can do is to refrain from interfering. What the shaman has to teach of alien spirit worlds must be gleaned from a flow of only partially comprehensible talk and song; it accumulates into a chaotic body of lore that is highly variable from one shaman to another and one longhouse to another. It is not dogma.

Ritually, the unmistakable climax comes at death. The most obvious feature of Berawan mortuary rites is that they allow for a two stage processing of the corpse. From each stage we may learn something about Berawan eschatology. The first stage—the funeral —is, by the nature of things, conducted for almost every individual, with the rare exception of a case of bad death. Not surprisingly, what we learn from it has mainly to do with the recently dead. Later, another set of rites may be performed. As it happens, they are rare, but they are ideologically essential. In contrast to the funeral, the *nulang* focuses on the long dead, the ancestors.

In the rapid series of rites that occur immediately after death, there is a powerful expression of continuity. Somehow the deceased is thought of as still sentient and socially responsive. In the wake that follows the nature of the soul is made plain. For the close kin, the funeral is an ordeal, especially for the widow or widower, who suffers terrible privations. For the rest there is a kind of nervous festivity. Explicitly, the soul is near at hand and of very uncertain temper, constantly threatening further death. Without this conception, the ordeal of the spouse makes no sense. With it we may grasp the essential communal nature of the rites. Meanwhile, because the soul is an intermediary between the living and the dead, some of the themes of the *nulang* are prefigured, as in the association of all manner of valuable and beautiful things with the body.

The *nulang* resembles a second wake, but it is also, in many ways, the reverse of the funeral. The punitive elements are less in evidence; now the widow or widower is no longer in confinement, instead it is the remains of the deceased that occupy a little cubicle on the veranda. Specifically, the festive season is associated with the playing of games, sacred games to be sure, but nevertheless games. This change is because the *nulang* celebrates the end of a troublesome time as opposed to its beginning, a triumph over death. When the coffin or jar is picked up to be carried out of the house, the beating of gongs and the formalized wailing of the women reproduces that heard at the moment of death. The latter marks the opening of the extended liminal period, the former its conclusion. The death songs, meantime, tell of the land of the dead as destination, and the spirits of the dead as protectors. Nothing in Berawan religion is more sacred than the songs. The language of prayer (*piat*) is not subject to any avoidance, but the songs are thickly hedged about by taboos, and this reflects the power and relevance of the spirits of the dead.

Berawan ideology is orderly in parts, and vague in parts. Furthermore, it is orderly in just those domains that are ritually elaborated. This finding allows us to recast Robertson Smith's assertion of the priority of ritual over dogma. It is not true, as Smith seems to suggest, that ideology in "primitive" religion is invariably vague or individually variable; there really is a Berawan eschatology. Rather we should say that where dogma is clearly formulated and consensual, it exists in association with ritual. Nor is the reason far to seek. In such religions, meanings stand largely implicit behind prescriptions for doing things, and ritual provides the portable philosophy.

Things Unsaid

However implicit, the meanings are there. A second line of criticism that has been made of symbolic analyses in anthropology is that they have no basis in the experiential world of the members of the culture, and are thus at best false to the ethnographic purpose, and at worst, a tissue of lies (for example in Lewis 1980). But the metaphorical relationship of corpse and soul during the long process of dying is made manifest in the rituals, not once, not just in the overall two-part format of the rites, but over and over again in gross features and details alike. It is verbalized, in an indirect way. Any adult will promptly respond to a question as to when the soul of a deceased person rejoins its ancestors with the same stereotyped reply: "When the bones are dry." At the same time, it was remarkably difficult for them to express these implicit notions in terms of a systematic account of what happens to the soul in death.

Once these features of the case are accepted, it becomes clear that it is an instance of a general proposition: That there are some truths that are not expressed in words, and perhaps cannot be expressed in words. Those truths are unexpressed not because they are unimportant, but because they are fundamental. The axioms are seldom stated that underlie such issues as what constitutes a proper life, what death means, what kinds of power people may have over one another, or how kinship is to be evaluated in contrast to other kinds of relationships. To discover them is a large part of the project of social anthropology, and one that draws heavily upon the symbolism of ritual.

Envoi

The prescriptive nature of ritual, and the implicitness of its deepest meanings, does not mean that they restrict Berawan consciousness. On the contrary, they provide a field of expression. To illustrate that, let me close with a vignette, a moment in a mortuary rite when rules were broken.

The moment came near the end of the *nulang* for Tama Ukat Sageng, the old shaman. It was about eleven o'clock in the morning, and they were preparing to remove the body for the last time. The singing of the final death song, the *tijun*, had dragged on into the morning, and then the preparation of the final meal, and all the other details, had been carried out in a desultory manner. The day was getting hot, people were tired, and tempers short. Then, as the moment for moving the container (Sageng's idiosyncratic double water jars) came close, tension once again began to mount. People began to swirl around on the veranda near the jar and at the foot of the ramp that gave access to the ground, jostling one another and giving advice on how to pick up the heavy jars. The confusion was increased with the sound of gongs and drums, and the wailing of women, sending up the familiar dirge.

In the midst of this Biló Kasi suddenly appeared. She had been very much present the evening before, singing the short death songs and assisting in the all-important *siroi*. But she had disappeared for several hours, during the tedium of the completion of the *tijun* and all the lackadaisical preparations. Presumably she had been in her room. She appeared calm and rested by comparison with most people there. She motioned to the men to put down their load for the moment, and for the crowd to become quiet, and she sat down beside the jars to address her old friend, the man in whom she had placed so much trust, for the last time. What was expected of her was a dirge in the formal fashion, or possibly a prayer in the rapid-fire style of *piat*. Instead she produced a bottle of rice wine and a glass, deliberately poured out the wine, and held the glass up toward the jars. This was unexpected behavior, and the attention of the crowd was riveted upon her. Kasi hummed a low note for a few seconds, a sound that indicated to all what was to come, and then launched into a praise song. No dirge this, but the kind of song one sings on festive occasions to flatter a guest or honor a friend, and strictly prohibited at funerals and *nulang*. Now, old friend, she sang, the time has come to say farewell. How many times have we sat together quietly you and I, as we do now, to drink a little rice wine? How many times have you come to cure our children? Now you must journey far away, and I must wait here. It will be lonely. . . . Through this performance, Kasi remained perfectly composed, but hers were the only dry eyes in the house. Exhausted by their sleepless night, and the nights that had gone before it, everyone cried helplessly. When Kasi's song was finished, she lifted the glass once more in salute, then poured some of the contents down the side of the jars, and quaffed down the remainder. There was a long pause, until slowly the men who were to pick up the container began to shuffle into position. Someone fired a shotgun, and the crowd came alive again as the jars began to move down the ramp. Kasi sat motionless in the midst of the confusion, until the crowd moved away from her toward the river bank. Then she got up and walked quietly back to her room. She had no further part to play in these rites. It was finished.

Bibliography

N. B.   Where a reprinted or revised edition of a work is cited in the bibliography, page references in the text refer to that edition.

Beidelman, Thomas O.
1974 *W. Robertson Smith and the Sociological Study of Religion.* Chicago: University of Chicago Press.

Boon, James A.
1974 "The Progress of the Ancestors in a Balinese Temple-Group (pre-1906–1972)." *Journal of Asian Studies* 34:7–27.

Brandon, James R.
1967 *Theatre in Southeast Asia.* Cambridge: Harvard University Press.

Brunton, Robert
1980 "Misconstrued Order in Melanesian Religion." *Man* 15:112–28.

Burrow, John W.
1966 *Evolution and Society: A Study in Victorian Social Theory.* Cambridge: Cambridge University Press.

Cooley, Frank L.
1962 *Ambonese Adat: A General Description.* Series in Southeast Asian Studies. New Haven: Yale University Press.

Dentan, Robert
1968 *The Semai: A Nonviolent People of Malaya.* New York: Holt, Rinehart and Winston.

Durkheim, Emile
1965 *The Elementary Forms of the Religious Life.* Translated from the 1912 French edition by Joseph Swain. New York: Free Press.

Dworakowska, Maria
1938 "The Origin of Bell and Drum." *Prace Etnologiezne* 5. Warsaw: Nakladem Towarzystwa Naukowego Woszawkiego.

Eliade, Mircea
1964 *Shamanism: Archaic Techniques of Ecstasy.* New York: Pantheon Books.

Elshout, J. M.
1926 *De Kěnja-Dajaks uit het Apo-Kajangebied.* The Hague: Martinus Nijhoff.

Endicott, Kirk

1979 *Batek Negrito Religion: The World View of a Hunting and Gathering People of Peninsular Malaysia.* Oxford: Clarendon Press.

Evans, I. H. N.

1953 *The Religion of the Tempasuk Dusuns of North Borneo.* Cambridge: Cambridge University Press.

Evans-Pritchard, E. E.

1956 *Nuer Religion.* Oxford: Oxford University Press.

1967 "Introduction." in *The Gift: Forms and Functions of Exchange in Archaic Societies* by Marcel Mauss. New York: Norton.

Fortune, Reo F.

1932 *Sorcerers of Dobu: The Social Anthropology of the Dobu Islanders of the Western Pacific.* London: Routledge.

1935 *Manus Religion: An Ethnological Study of the Manus Natives of the Admiralty Islands.* Philadelphia: Memoirs of the American Philosophical Society, Vol. 3.

Fox, James J.

1971a "Semantic Parallelism in Rotinese Ritual Language." *Bijdragen tot de Taal-, Land-, en Volkenkunde* 127:215–55.

1971b "Sister's Child as Plant: Metaphors in an Idiom of Consanguinity." In *Rethinking Kinship and Marriage.* Edited by Rodney Needham. ASA Monograph 11: 219–52. London: Tavistock.

1973 "On Bad Death and the Left Hand." In *Right and Left: Essays on Dual Symbolic Classification.* Edited by Rodney Needham. Chicago: University of Chicago Press.

Frazer, James G.

1890 *The Golden Bough.* Revised and abridged. New York: Macmillan, 1963.

Furness, William Henry

1899 *Folklore in Borneo: A Sketch.* Pennsylvania: privately published.

Galvin, A. D.

1966 "Mamat: Leppo Tau-Long Moh." *Sarawak Museum Journal,* Special Monograph 1: 296–304.

1972 "A Sebob Dirge (Sung on the Occasion of the Death of Tama Jangen Jau by Belawing Lupa)." *Brunei Museum Journal* 2:1–75.

Gell, Alfred

1975 *Metamorphosis of the Cassowaries: Umeda Society, Language and Ritual.* London: Athlone Press.

Haddon, Alfred Cort

1901 *Headhunters Black, White, and Brown.* London: Methuen.

Hardeland, August

1858 *Versuch einer Grammatik der Dajakschen Sprache.* Amsterdam: F. Muller.

Harrisson, Tom

1954 "Berawan Death Chants (Secondary Burial)." *Sarawak Museum Journal* 6:563–66.

Hershman, P.
1974 "Hair, Sex and Dirt." *Man* 9:274–98.

Hertz, Robert
1907 "Contribution à une Étude sur la Représentation Collective de la Mort." *Année Sociologique* 10:48–137.
1960 *Death and the Right Hand.* Translation of the 1907 essay, by Rodney and Claudia Needham. Introduction by E. E. Evans-Pritchard. New York: Free Press.

Hocart, Arthur Maurice
1936 *Kings and Councillors: A Essay in the Comparative Anatomy of Human Society.* Reprint edited and with an introduction by Rodney Needham. Chicago: University of Chicago Press, 1970.

Hose, Charles
1893 "The Natives of Borneo." *Journal of the Anthropological Institute.* 23: 156–72.
1896 "A Visit to Celebes." *Sarawak Gazette* 16–364:99–100.
1926 *Natural Man: A Record from Borneo.* London: Macmillan.

Hose, Charles and McDougall, William
1912 *The Pagan Tribes of Borneo.* Two Volumes. London: Macmillan.

Hubert, Henri and Mauss, Marcel
1964 *Sacrifice: Its Nature and Function.* Translated from the 1899 French edition by W. D. Halls. Chicago: University of Chicago Press.

Hudson, Alfred B.
1966 "Death Ceremonies of the Padju Epat Ma'anyan Dayaks." *Sarawak Museum Journal* 13:341–416.

Hughes-Hallett, H.
1938 "A Mysterious Find in Brunei." *Journal of the Royal Asiatic Society (Malayan Branch)* 16:100–101.

Huntington, Richard and Metcalf, Peter
1979 *Celebrations of Death: The Anthropology of Mortuary Ritual.* New York: Cambridge University Press.

Jamuh, George
1949 "Jerunai." *Sarawak Museum Journal* 5:62–68.

Jensen, Eric
1974 *The Iban and Their Religion.* Oxford: Clarendon Press.

Josselin de Jong, P. E. de
1963 "Preface." In *Ngaju Religion: The Concept of God Among a South Borneo People,* by Hans Schärer. The Hague: Martinus Nijhoff.

Kirsch, A. Thomas
1973 *Feasting and Social Oscillation: Religion and Society in Upland Southeast Asia.* Data Paper No. 92. Ithaca: Southeast Asia Program, Cornell University.

Koentjaraningrat.
1975 *Anthropology in Indonesia: A Bibliographical Review.* The Hague: Martinus Nijhoff.

Leach, Edmund

1958 "Magical Hair." *Journal of the Royal Anthropological Institute* 77:147–64.

Lévi-Strauss, Claude

1965 "Le triangle culinaire." *L'Arc* (Aix-en-Provence) 26:19–29.

1966 *The Savage Mind*. Chicago: University of Chicago Press.

1969 *The Raw and the Cooked: Introduction to a Science of Mythology*. Translated from the 1964 French edition by John and Doreen Weightman. New York: Harper.

Lewis, Gilbert

1980 *Day of the Shining Red: An Essay on Understanding Ritual*. Cambridge: Cambridge University Press.

Low, Hugh Brooke

1882 "A Journey up the Rejang." *Sarawak Gazette* 12–190:60–64,12–202: 93–96.

MacDonald, Malcolm

1958 *Borneo People*. New York: Alfred P. Knopf.

Madang, Maping and Galvin, A. D.

1966 "Adat Suen (Sebob Graded Rites)." *Sarawak Museum Journal*, Special Monograph 1: 305–20.

Mallinckrodt, J. and Mallinckrodt-Djata, L.

1928 "Het *magah liau*, een Dajaksche priesterzang." *Tijdschrift voor Indische Taal-, Land- en Volkenkunde* 68:292–346.

Mauss, Marcel

1967 *The Gift: Forms and Functions of Exchange in Archaic Societies*. Translated from the 1925 French edition by Ian Cunnison. Forword by E. E. Evans-Pritchard. New York: Norton.

McKinley, Robert

1976 "Human and Proud of It! A Structural Treatment of Headhunting Rites and the Social Definition of Enemies." In *Studies in Borneo Societies: Social Process and Anthropological Explanation*. Edited by George Appell. DeKalb, Ill: Center for Southeast Asian Studies, Northern Illinois University.

Metcalf, Peter

1976a "Birds and Deities in Borneo." *Bijdragen tot de Taal-, Land-, en Volkenkunde* 132:96–123.

1976b "Who Are the Berawan? Ethnic Classification and the Distribution of Secondary Treatment of the Dead in Central North Borneo." *Oceania* 47: 85–105.

1977 "Berawan Mausoleums." *Sarawak Museum Journal* 24:121–138.

1981 "Meaning and Materialism: The Ritual Economy of Death." *Man* 16:563–78.

Metcalf, Peter and Huntington, Richard

1976 *Celebrations of Death: The Anthropology of Mortuary Ritual*. New York: Cambridge University Press.

Morris, H. S.
1953 *Report on a Melanau Sago-Producing Community.* Colonial Research Studies 9. London: British Colonial Office.
Moulton, J. C.
1912 "The Trings." *Sarawak Museum Journal* 1:91–95.
Needham, Rodney
1954a "Reference to the Dead among the Penan." *Man* 54:10, Article 6.
1954b "The System of Teknonyms and Death Names among the Penan." *Southwestern Journal of Anthropology* 10:416–31.
1959 "Mourning Terms." *Bijdragen tot de Taal-, Land-, en Volkenkunde.* 115:58–89.
1964 "Blood, Thunder, and the Mockery of Animals." *Sociologus* 14:136–47.
1965 "Death Names and Solidarity in Penan Society." *Bijdragen tot de Taal-, Land-, en Volkenkunde* 121:58–76.
1967 "Percussion and Transition." *Man* 2:606–14.
1970 "Editor's Introduction." In *Kings and Councillors: An Essay on the Comparative Anatomy of Society.* By Arthur Maurice Hocart. Revised edition of 1936 original. Chicago: University of Chicago Press.
1971 "Penan Friendship Names." In *The Translation of Culture.* Edited by T. Beidelman. New York: Tavistock.
1976 "Skulls and Causality." *Man* 11:71–88.
Newington, P. C. B.
1961 "Melanau Memories." *Sarawak Museum Journal* 10:103–7.
Rivers, W. H. R.
1926 *Psychology and Ethnology.* London: Kegan Paul.
Rosaldo, Michelle
1977 "Skulls and Causality." *Man* 12:168–69.
1980 *Knowledge and Passion: Ilongot Notions of Self and Social Life.* Cambridge: Cambridge University Press.
Rosaldo, Renato
1980 *Ilongot Headhunting 1883–1974: A Study in History and Society.* Stanford, Ca.: Stanford University Press.
Rousseau, Jérôme
"The Kayan." In *Essays on Borneo Societies.* Edited by Victor King. Hull Monographs on South-East Asia. Oxford: Oxford University Press.
Rutter, Owen
1929 *The Pagans of North Borneo.* London: Hutchinson.
Sapir, David
1970 "*Kujaama*: Symbolic Separation among the Diola-Fogny." *American Anthropologist* 72:1330–48.
Schärer, Hans
1963 *Ngaju Religion: The Conception of God among a South Borneo People.* Translated by Rodney Needham from the 1946 German edition. The Hague: Martinus Nijhoff.

Smith, W. Robertson
1885 *Kinship and Marriage in Early Arabia.* Reprint. London: Charles and Black, 1903.

1889 *Lectures on the Religion of the Semites: First Series, the Fundamental Institutions.* Edinburgh: A. and C. Black.
Stöhr, Waldemar
1959 *Das Totenritual der Dajak.* Ethnologica New Series, No 1. Cologne: E. J. Brill.
Tambiah, S. J.
1968 "The Magical Power of Words." *Man* 3:175–208.

1970 *Buddhism and the Spirit Cults in North-East Thailand.* Cambridge: Cambridge University Press.
Turner, Victor
1958 *The Forest of Symbols: Aspects of Ndembu Ritual.* Ithaca: Cornell University Press.

1966 *The Ritual Process: Structure and Anti-Structure.* Ithaca: Cornell University Press.

1968 *The Drums of Affliction.* Oxford: Oxford University Press.
Tylor, Edward Burnett
1871 *Primitive Culture.* Two Volumes. Reprint. New York: Harper Torchbooks, 1958.

1878 *Researches into the Early History of Mankind.* Reprint. Chicago: University of Chicago Press, 1964.
Van Gennep, Arnold
1960 *The Rites of Passage.* Translated from the 1909 French edition by M. Vizedom and G. Caffee. Chicago: University of Chicago Press.
Whittier, Herbert L.
1978 "The Kenyah." In *Essays on Borneo Societies.* Edited by Victor King. Hull Monographs on South-East Asia. Oxford: Oxford University Press.
Williams, Thomas Rhys
1965 *The Dusun: A North Borneo Society.* New York: Holt, Rinehart and Winston.
Wilson, Monica
1957 *Rituals of Kinship among the Nyakyusa.* Oxford: Oxford University Press.
Yap Yoon Keong
1963 "The Punan Corpse That Smells of Durian." *Sarawak Museum Journal* 11:94–98.

Index

afterlife. *See* land of the dead; spirits of the dead

ancestors and ancestral spirits, 175, 233, 245, 247–48, 253, 254, 260, 262; addressed in prayer, 23–25, 87, 170, 197, 241; at *nulang*, 155–57, 177, 208, 228, 261; location of, 216, 218, 223, 237, 243; longhouse of, 225, 236, 241, 251. *See also* land of the dead; spirits of the dead

Aquinas, St. Thomas, 3, 259

augury. *See* omens and divination

bad death, 92, 100, 254–56, 261

Baram River and watershed, 12, 25, 67n, 113–15, 130, 186, 191, 224–27, 233, 236–37, map 1

beads, 40, 42, 81, 125, 182, 215, 236–37, 245, pl. 11

Beidelman, Thomas, 10

Berawan: economy, 13–16, 167–68, 246, map 5; location, 12, map 1; social organization, 16–18

Biló Kasi, xvi, 40, 72, 191–202, 204–5, 206n, 208, 211, 225–26, 255, 263–64, pl. 10

Brooke Rajahs, 115

Brunei, 40, 129, 233

Bungan. *See* revivalist cults

cemetery. *See* graveyards

chang leaves, 117–18, 121, 124, 128, pl. 8

childbirth and infant mortality, 50, 57, 101, 127, 238, 254

coffins, 19, 39, 43, 100, 102, 178, 215, 227, 261, pl. 7; animal-shaped coffins, 182, 251; construction of, 73, 80–84, 101, 165, 219; storage of, 160–61, 164, 181, 184, 214; supernatural behavior of, 111, 220. *See also* corpse

commensality. *See* food

conversion to Christianity and Bungan, 18, 61, 113, 159, 191, 197. *See also* missionaries

Cooley, Frank, 5

corpse, 71, 72, 75, 77, 78, 112; and bad death, 254–55; cleaning of bones, 20, 155, 170, 177; decomposition of, 83–84, 95, 98, 100, 102, 107, 109, 133, 156, 161; exit from house, 85–88, 143, 145, 227, 261, pl. 5; fear of, 95, 101; polluting nature of, 149–51; preparation of, 38, 39, 42; prohibition on entering longhouse, 101–2, 178; smell of, 83–84, 93n, 104; and soul connection, 94–99, 110, 243, 262

Creator Spirit, 47, 50, 57, 66n, 98, 108, 119, 135n, 219, 228, 240, 243–45, 248, 250, 252, 256, 260

Crocker, J. Christopher, 92n

dance, 75, 121, 132, 137–38, 173–75, 184

death, 132, 173, 243, 261–62; chain reaction quality of, 127, 132, 192, 208; definition of, 46, 55, 63–66, 68n, 97; feast, 86; foretold, 135, 211; "losing breath," 35, 64, 65, 71,

271

SYMBOL AND CULTURE